Massachusetts
CURIOSITIES

Help Us Keep This Guide Up to Date

Every effort has been made by the authors and editors to make this guide as accurate and useful as possible. However, many things can change after a guide is published—establishments close, phone numbers change, and facilities come under new management.

We would love to hear from you concerning your experiences with this guide and how you feel it could be improved and kept up to date. While we may not be able to respond to all comments and suggestions, we'll take them to heart and we'll also make certain to share them with the authors. Please send your comments and suggestions to the following address:

The Globe Pequot Press
Reader Response/Editorial Department
P.O. Box 480
Guilford, CT 06437

Or you may e-mail us at:
editorial@GlobePequot.com

Thanks for your input, and happy travels!

Curiosities Series

Massachusetts
CURIOSITIES

Quirky characters,
roadside oddities &
other offbeat stuff

2nd Edition

Bruce Gellerman
and Erik Sherman

Guilford, Connecticut

Copyright © 2005, 2008 Morris Book Publishing, LLC

Interior photos by the author; vintage toys © Shutterstock.
Text design by Bret Kerr
Layout by Mary Ballachino
Maps by XNR Productions © Morris Book Publishing, LLC

ISSN 1555-4007
ISBN 978-0-7627-4680-4

Printed in the United States of America

10 9 8 7 6 5 4 3 2

For Yulia, Andre, and Anna,
who make life infinitely curious.

—B.G.

To my parents, who taught me to question
the wisdom of convention.

—E.S.

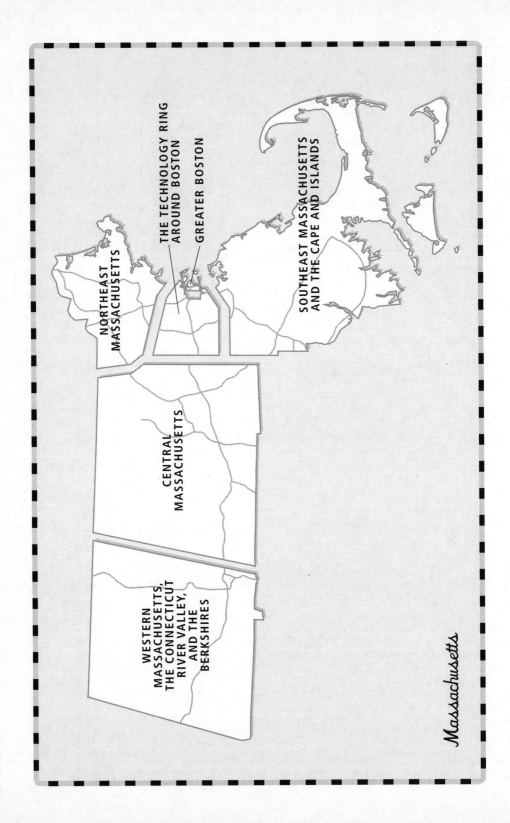

THE TECHNOLOGY RING AROUND BOSTON

GREATER BOSTON

NORTHEAST MASSACHUSETTS

SOUTHEAST MASSACHUSETTS AND THE CAPE AND ISLANDS

CENTRAL MASSACHUSETTS

WESTERN MASSACHUSETTS, THE CONNECTICUT RIVER VALLEY, AND THE BERKSHIRES

Massachusetts

contents

★ ★

acknowledgments

★ ★

As powerful as the Internet is in collecting the flotsam and jetsam of life, curious people are still the best sources for Massachusetts minutiae, and we are indebted to many for sharing their knowledge and digging deep when we set them to task.

To Deborah Douglas, curator of science and technology at the MIT Museum, many thanks for introducing us to Kismet, the world's most emotive robot. Craig Le Moult and Siobhan Houton of Tufts University helped show us which way was up regarding the antigravity monument and the tale and tail of Jumbo, the elephant. Professor Gordon Prichett from Babson College can actually tell you what an apple from Newton's tree tastes like, and we were blessed to make the acquaintance of Diane Shephard, archivist at the Lynn Museum, who introduced us to the God Machine.

Thanks, too, to Stephan Nonack, head of Reader Services at the Boston Athenaeum, who gave us the lowdown on the "skin book," and to Jennifer Spencer for opening up her skinny house. Roberta Zonghi, the keeper of rare books and manuscripts at the Boston Public Library, was a font of information about things curious about Boston, as was the entire staff at the Boston Historical Society. And the Worcester Historical Society is second to none when it comes to being friendly and helpful.

Heidi Wellman, former owner of the former Chandler's General Store in Colrain, helped by providing information on Old Glory and getting us the inside scoop on the Arthur B. Smith covered bridge. Kate Wellspring, collections manager at Amherst College's Pratt Museum, offered a firm footing on dinosaur tracks, as did Kornell Nash.

Jarvis Rockwell was unfailingly generous with his time as we asked about his toy collection. And a Global Positioning System enthusiast, with the handle Khao Mun Gai when he indulges in the sport of geocaching, led us to the Forty-Second Parallel marker.

David Olson and Susan Abele at the Newton History Museum at the Jackson Homestead always took our requests for information with a straight face, whether we were inquiring about Fig Newtons or worm farms. Chet Kennedy, founder of the Public Health Museum, is a man

acknowledgments

with a mission and a missionary zeal; and Rev. Steven Ayers, vicar of the Old North Church, was always ready with a quip and a quote about colonial Boston.

Ellen Berlin of the Boston Medical Center set us straight on the fate of Jack the Duck. Charles Ball, the president of World Smile Day, was a delight to work with. And we'll always remember Tom Smith from Woburn City Hall for remembering the *Maine* cowl and telling us about it.

If you want to know about the smallest church in the world, the Hudson Public Library and Vic Petkauskos are the place to go. Bert Cohen knows more about marbles than any person in the universe, and if you are really into bad art, the person to see is Louise Sacco, curator of the Museum of Bad Art. Deborah Henson-Conant has a taste for burnt food and curates her crispy critters and tofu dogs with aplomb. Dr. Stephen Gould is one of those rare people who actually stops and reads roadside monuments. Thanks to him for pointing out where "Jingle Bells" was written.

And many thanks to Marc Abrahams, editor and founder of the *Annals of Improbable Research,* for thinking we were curious enough, or just crazy enough, to write this book. We hope we've proven you correct on both counts.

introduction

After working on a book like this for a while, you no longer get embarrassed by asking such questions as, "Excuse me, do you know where Mary's little lamb is?" or "Are Jumbo the elephant's ashes kept in a jar of plain or crunchy peanut butter?" or "Where can I find the world's largest thermometer collection?" Yes, those around you still look at you cross-eyed, but you no longer mind: It just goes with the territory of being curious about Massachusetts, as curious a place as ever there was. After all, it got its start in part by Puritans who couldn't stand intolerance and European persecution, and who thus fled to a new land where they could have the freedom to persecute and be intolerant of everyone else. Upon reaching Cape Cod, one of the first acts of the morally upright Pilgrims was to steal corn that Indians had stored for the winter. After finally coming to their last stop—which they still thought was somewhere in Virginia—the Pilgrims set up the first public utility, a grain mill. (You can thank them for hundreds of years of misbillings and poor customer service.) And you thought they survived that first winter on turkey? We're lucky we're not munching on a giant loaf of corn bread for Thanksgiving.

You might think it easy to distill Massachusetts into a combination of Puritanism, rocky soil, and history—an image set in native granite: predictable, solid, inflexible. We thought the same when each of us moved here decades ago. And, like us, you are in for a surprise. Massachusetts is a contradictory land, full of unusual people, places, objects, ideas, and cranky misfits. Talk about ornery: The settlers couldn't even form a state, and instead chose to create a commonwealth.

Perhaps political unrest and opposing the usual order of things was a healthy release for the residents, because all you have to do is look at what happened when there wasn't some government to overthrow, action to protest, or election to contest. A colonial daredevil decided to challenge puritanical Bostonians by flying from atop the Old North Church—more than 150 years before the Wright brothers. The city leaders' reaction? You'd think that they'd be thrilled at the technical marvel. Nope. They got annoyed and banned flying. And what can you say of a place where people build giant sea horses and large granite towers, for the sole purpose of marketing? Or where a golf course includes an eighteenth-century grave or a monument to modern rocketry? Speaking of graves, you don't have to dig far to find some very curious final resting places. Massachusetts is the last stop for Jumbo, Mother Goose, and Mary Baker Eddy (founder of the Christian Science Church). It's also the birthplace of Mary's little lamb, one of the Peter Rabbits (ah, the cotton tales of literary controversy), the Cat in the Hat, and the ubiquitous Kilroy. Here you will find what might be the country's oldest example of graffiti; an ancient bowling ball found in a privy; a place that always remembers the *Maine;* and museums dedicated to collections of dirt, shovels, and burnt food.

So, come meet the pirates and the healers, the artists and the ward heelers. See the house made of rolled-up newspapers, and the giant neon flag. Visit museums of plastic and of sanitary plumbing. Catch magic shows, ax murders, and lighthouse hauntings. Experience brightly painted gingerbread cottages on an island and entire towns smothered by a manmade lake. Just stifle your laughter, as the folks here can get touchy.

Massachusetts: You've got to love it. Or else.

1

Greater Boston

You wouldn't get *an argument from anyone in love with Boston politics: The Boston State House is, as Oliver Wendell Holmes wrote, "the hub of the solar system." And what an ornate hub it is, topped with a gilded pine cone—the symbol of Maine, once a part of the Commonwealth—and decorated with the Sacred Cod and the Holy Mackerel, giving a particular decorative air to its legislative chambers.*

Interested in outsized—and outside—curiosities? How about the narrowest house in Boston, 10 feet, 5 inches wide, in Boston's North End? Or the 40-foot-tall Hood Milk Bottle near the Boston Childrens Museum? Or a giant tea kettle (this is the city that hosted the country's most famous tea party, after all)? And don't forget to Make Way for Ducklings and duck on over to Boston's Public Garden to view the sculpture celebrating that well-known children's book.

Most fabulous of all might be the Isabella Stewart Gardner Museum, housed in a Venetian palace with courtyard. Mrs. Gardner's collection includes paintings, sculptures, tapestries, and rare books, more an art attic than a museum. See those empty frames on the wall? They once contained some of the thirteen priceless works stolen in a daring St. Patrick's Day robbery in 1990.

Boston is home to the Old North Church and the Church of Baseball, Fenway Park, Major League Baseball's crown jewel. Come on Patriot's Day in April for morning baseball. Feel free to admire the Pesky Pole, the Green Monster, and Manny Being Manny . . . but leave that Yankees jersey at home.

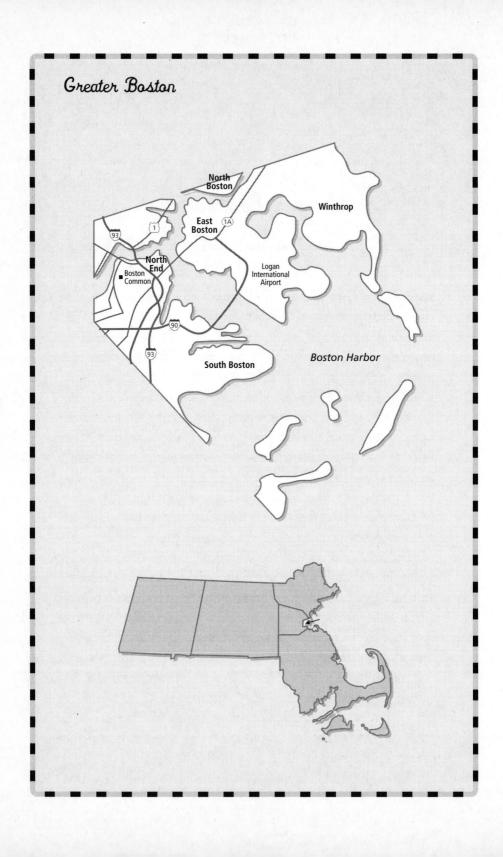

Greater Boston

North Boston

East Boston

Winthrop

North End

Boston Common

Logan International Airport

South Boston

Boston Harbor

The Hub of the Universe

Boston

Bostonians are a self-centered lot, and why not? After all, the city's immodest nickname is The Hub, as in "the hub of the universe." The phrase is actually derived from something Oliver Wendell Holmes wrote in The *Autocrat of the Breakfast-Table* about the capitol building:

> Boston State-house is the hub of the solar system. You coud n't [*sic*] pry that out of a Boston man if you had the tire of all creation straightened out for a crow-bar.

Photo by Bruce Gellerman

The hub of the universe is in the center of a fruit market on Washington Street.

3

★ ★

Since Holmes wrote this whimsical essay in 1858, the so-called center of the universe has moved a bit. You'll now find it near Filene's Basement on a spot marked with a bronze plaque about 15 feet from the store's Washington Street entrance. Perhaps fitting for its top banana status, in order to see the center of the universe, you might have to move a bunch of bananas or two . . . and perhaps some onions and a crate of oranges. The plaque, marking the hub of the universe, is now in the center of a fruit market at 426 Washington Street.

Fighting Joe Hooker

Boston

A statue of Maj. Gen. Joseph "Fighting Joe" Hooker, on his mighty steed, stands in front of the entrance to the Massachusetts State

Trivia

Can You Top This?

You would expect a statehouse to be crowned by a symbol of the state, but in the case of Massachusetts, you'd be wrong. Atop the magnificent gold dome, atop Massachusetts's magnificent statehouse, atop posh Beacon Hill, is a gilded pine cone. The white pine cone and tassel is the state flower of Maine. When this section of the statehouse was completed in 1798, Maine was a district of the Commonwealth of Massachusetts. Maine didn't gain its independence from Massachusetts until 1820, as part of the Missouri Compromise. So Maine may be gone but the pine cone remains.

Top that.

House. One shudders to think what the statue might have looked like, considering what Hooker is best known for: lending his last name to the oldest profession.

Joe Hooker was a favorite son of Massachusetts. He commanded the Army of the Potomac during the Civil War, but Fighting Joe's men were a rowdy bunch, and Hooker's headquarters was a den of iniquity. The encampment was said to be a combi-

Photo by Bruce Gellerman

Maj. Gen. Joseph Hooker lost his major battle at Chancellorsville even though he had twice as many troops as General Lee. We remember him for his activities off the battlefield.

nation barroom and brothel. Hooker allowed women who followed his troops to set up their tents nearby. Hence, the phrase "Hooker's Division" became the popular equivalent for prostitutes.

There is some evidence that the term "hooker" was used before the Civil War, but the story of Fighting Joe clearly was responsible for its common use today.

The Sacred Cod and Holy Mackerel
Boston

Suspended over the entrance to the Massachusetts House of Representatives chamber is something you won't find hanging over any

★ ★

other deliberative body in the world: a codfish. And it's not just any codfish. It's the Sacred Cod Fish. Measuring 4 feet 11 inches, the pine carved fish is a constant reminder of the importance of the fishing industry to the state's early history. The Pilgrims and Indians feasted on cod along with turkey that first Thanksgiving, and it was the state's first export. We even named the Cape after the cod.

The fish that currently holds the place of honor above the legislative body's entry is actually the third-generation cod. The first was destroyed in a fire in 1747; the second, during the Revolutionary War. The current one has been hanging around since 1787, moved from the old statehouse to the new House chamber in 1895. It has hung there ever since, with one notable exception. In 1933 pranksters from the *Harvard Lampoon* "cod-napped" the state's seafood symbol by cutting the line holding it aloft, and they made off with their prize catch. Lawmakers were outraged. The state police were called in to investigate. The Charles River was dredged. Days later an anonymous tip led to the revered fish's recovery, and it was hung 6 inches higher to prevent it from being stolen again.

Those who say something very fishy is going on in the Massachusetts State House have a basis for their claim. In 1974 the cod was

Photo by Bruce Gellerman

The Sacred Cod.

✦ ✦

elevated to the status of official state fish. Not to be outdone by the lower house, the Senate has in its chamber a wrought-iron chandelier with a fish in its design. It's called the Holy Mackerel.

Over in the House chamber, check out the second painting on the left behind the speaker's chair. It shows one of the judges from the Salem witch trials repenting for sentencing accused witches to death. The gesture is a bit late but still appreciated; after all, it's the thought that counts.

The Massachusetts State House is on Beacon Hill overlooking Boston Common on Beacon Street. Self-taught architect Charles Bulfinch designed the building, which was constructed between 1795 and 1797 on a pasture owned by John Hancock. Although it may look high now, the hill is 50 feet lower than its original height, as land from the hills was used to fill in Boston's Back Bay. The gilded dome, first made of wood shingles, is topped by a lantern and a pinecone (the latter is a symbol of the forests of Massachusetts). The fish are indoors.

Photo by Bruce Gellerman

The Holy Mackerel.

Ben Franklin: Founding Farter

Boston

The statue of Benjamin Franklin on School Street is 1 block from Milk Street where Franklin was born in 1706. It was the first portrait

★ ★

statue erected in Boston and marks the site were Franklin attended the first public school in the United States.

The four sides of the statue feature images of Franklin the patriot, the printer, the inventor, and the diplomat; and if you look closely you might detect a sly smile on Franklin's face. Old Ben, well known for his keen, irreverent wit, once wrote a satirical piece flaunting the benefits of flatulence. In his essay *Fart Proudly, Franklin the Founding Farter,* he proposed eating a food additive, "that shall render the natural Discharges of Wind from our Bodies, not only inoffensive, but agreeable as Perfumes."

Perhaps the base of Franklin's statue should have had five sides. But we shudder to think what it would have looked like.

Photo by Bruce Gellerman

A sly Ben Franklin has a mischievous air about him.

The Parker House Hotel: Revolutionary Rolls

Boston

Hotels make for strange bedfellows. John Wilkes Booth, Malcolm X, Ho Chi Minh, John Crawford, Ralph Waldo Emerson, and John F. Kennedy have all spent time at Boston's Parker House.

The hotel, now known as the Omni Parker, is the oldest continuously operated hotel in the continental United States. When it opened for business in 1855, it was the first hotel in Boston to have hot and cold running water and an elevator.

John Wilkes Booth stayed here the week before he shot Abraham Lincoln. Ralph Waldo Emerson, Nathaniel Hawthorne, and Henry Wadsworth Longfellow were members of the famous literary Saturday Club, which regularly met in the hotel's restaurant. Had the wordsmiths assembled some eight decades later, Malcolm X might have cleared their table; he worked as a busboy in the hotel restaurant in 1940.

The Parker House is famous for its rolls. Legend has it that this gastronomic delight is the happy result of an angry chef. The Parker House prided itself on meeting the needs of the pickiest patron, but in 1856, when one particularly demanding guest made one too many requests for a certain roll, it is said that a hotheaded German chef began throwing small balls of dough into an oven. Surprisingly, the rolls were delicious, and the talk of delighted guests gave rise to the famed Parker House Roll. The hotel kept the recipe a secret until President Franklin Roosevelt requested it in 1933.

Trivia

What a Grape Catch

In 1988 Paul Tavilla of Arlington, Massachusetts, earned a place in the *Guinness Book of Records* by catching in his mouth a grape dropped from the top of the John Hancock building, sixty stories high.

When it comes to grape catching, what goes down obviously also goes up. The longest distance a grape has been caught after being thrown into the air from ground level is 99.82 meters—precisely 327 feet and 6 inches. That great grape catch was accomplished on May 27, 1991, by, who else, Paul Tavilla. Check him out at http://thegrape catcher.com/index.html.

★ ★

The Boston cream pie (which is actually a cake) was also concocted here. The origin of the pie/cake is not entirely certain. Some say it was created by a French chef named Sanzian. There is no truth to the story that the misnamed dessert was part of a Communist plot to confuse American diners, although revolutionary Ho Chi Minh did work as a baker at the Parker House from 1911 to 1913.

For a taste of Old World charm, and to imagine what it must have been like way back when chefs were tossing dough and bakers were plotting coups, check out or check into the hotel at 60 School Street, (617) 227-8600. You never know whom you'll meet there.

Boston Is Planet Hollywood
Boston

Boston University is home to the largest collection of Hollywood memorabilia on the planet. The University's Department of Special Collections includes the personal papers and effects of some 2,000 luminaries of the stage and silver screen. Included in the twentieth-century archive are materials from Mary Astor, Douglas Fairbanks Jr., Marilyn Monroe, Rex Harrison, Robert Redford, and Edward G. Robinson. The Oscar that Gene Kelly won for *An American in Paris* is on view, as are Fred Astaire's dancing shoes and Elizabeth Taylor's gloves.

Howard Gottlieb, curator of B.U.'s Department of Special Collections, began going through the attics and shoe boxes of the stars in 1963. His most prized catch is 119,000 pages of material from Bette Davis. Gottlieb called Davis twice a week for thirty years before she agreed to donate her scripts, scrapbooks, and 5,000-volume library specializing in theater history.

In all, the archives take up 7 miles of shelves in two underground vaults. The Department of Special Collections is at 771 Commonwealth Avenue, fifth floor. Call ahead at (617) 353-3916 if you want to see something special.

★ ★

Tortoise and Hare Sculpture
Boston

This statue of the fabled hare and the tortoise commemorates the 100th anniversary of the Boston Marathon. The finish line is right near here and the fable fits the place—after all, the origin of the marathon is Greek and so is Aesop's timeless parable.

Photo by Bruce Gellerman

Like the fable says: slow but steady wins the race.

But ironically, the site and statue are a mismatch. The sculptures weren't supposed to be in Copley Square and the route they took to get here was long and tortuous. Local sculptor Nancy Schon felt that Boston was getting all the attention so she wanted to honor Hopkington, the town 26 miles away where the race begins. Soon, Schon ran into the hand of political correctness. The town wouldn't let her make a statue of a man, a woman, or someone in a wheelchair so Schon sculptured the two 400-pound parable critters. But she couldn't find a corporation to finance a piece of public art that was to be installed in a small town so the statues sat in her garage for seven years.

Finally, a member of the Friends of Copley Square got involved. They found funding to make this patch of the square the tortoise and hare's home, and here they are.

★ ★

Tea for Two . . . Thousand
Boston

It is only right and proper that the city where the most famous tea party in history took place would have the world's largest tea kettle. The Oriental Teashop had the giant pot cast in 1873 and hung in September 1874. To promote the tea shop the company held a contest on New Year's Day 1875. The public was invited to guess the capacity of the giant kettle. Twelve thousand people cast ballots. As officials began to pour cups into the kettle, a boy popped out, then another, and another. Finally, eight boys emerged, followed by a six-

Tea for two . . . two thousand, that is. The giant teapot in Boston's City Hall Plaza has been spouting steam since 1873.

Photo by Bruce Gellerman

Trivia

Oy, You Should Only Live So Long and Prosper

Mr. Spock from the TV series *Star Trek* comes from Vulcan via Boston. Leonard Nimoy, aka Spock, grew up in an Orthodox Jewish household in Boston. His religious background played a pivotal role in developing his Vulcan character.

According to Nimoy, the idea for the Vulcan salute, where four fingers of each hand are split, comes from a boyhood lesson he learned at temple. The gesture creates the Hebrew letter shin, representing the first letter of the Almighty and the word peace. Nimoy proposed the hand signal when the producers of the show were trying to come up with a salute for his character.

foot man—the designer of the kettle. The winner got a forty-pound chest of tea.

You'll find the exact capacity engraved on the side of the kettle: precisely 227 gallons, 2 quarts, 1 pint, and 3 gills.

The giant kettle was moved from its original location, not far from here, in 1967. Ironically, the kettle now hangs above a Starbucks store at 63 Court Street near the Government Center metro station. Perhaps if the java chain had been around in 1773, we might be calling it "The Boston Coffee Klatch" today.

Let Them Eat Sandwiches!

Boston's first public playground was a sandbox. The sand garden, as it was called in those days, was built in 1886 by the philanthropic women of the North End Union. It was created to serve the needs of immigrant Italian, Irish, and Jewish children in the area.

At the time, Kate Gannet Wells of the philanthropic committee said, "Playing in the dirt is the royalty of childhood."

The site at 20 Parmenter Street is across the street from the North End branch of the Boston Public Library, where you will find a diorama of the Ducal Palace of Venice made by local artist Louise Stimson in 1949.

JFK Ate Here
Boston

Obviously, John F. Kennedy ate at a lot of places in his hometown. One of his favorites was the Union Oyster House, where the Kennedy clan dined regularly on the restaurant's namesake mollusk. In the private upstairs dining room, you will find a plaque on Kennedy's favorite booth, number 18, dedicated to his memory in 1977.

Kennedy was just one of many Harvard students to frequent the restaurant. Supposedly, some were paid to eat there. Oyster House lore has it that an importer of toothpicks from South America hired Harvard students to dine at the restaurant and request the picks as a way to boost sales.

The Union Oyster House is located at 41 Union Street. To request a table or JFK's favorite booth, call (617) 227-2750.

★ ★

Got Milk?

Boston

The Hood Milk Bottle, near the Children's Museum at 300 Congress Street, is a pint-sized display—400,000 pints, that is, or 50,000 gallons, in case your math has gone sour. Either way, it would give you a giant milk mustache. The wooden bottle is 40 feet high and was built in 1938. During the summer it also serves as an ice cream stand and snack bar.

Photo by Bruce Gellerman

Milk with your tea? The giant Hood Milk Bottle stands near the site of the Boston Tea Party.

Trivia

The Boston University Bridge

Bostonians will tell you that the Boston University Bridge crossing the Charles River is the only bridge in the United States where an airplane can fly over a person riding a bicycle, next to a car, going over a train, that's traveling over a boat. It's true—that is, if you don't count the Brooklyn Bridge, where the train (a subway in a tunnel) goes under the boat.

★ ★

With Your Clothes On I See the Resemblance
Boston

It's only fitting that in a town known for its quirky characters, the first Englishman to call Boston home was an eccentric, hermit bookworm who enjoyed romping on Beacon Hill astride his white Brahmin bull while in the buff. William Blackstone (aka Blaxston), an Anglican minister, set up home and library on Beacon Hill in 1625. Five years later, in an act of Christian charity, the reclusive Blackstone invited John Winthrop and his band of Puritan settlers to join him and share his freshwater spring. The Puritans had originally settled in nearby Charleston but lacked clean water and were dying of disease.

Founders Monument is located in Boston Common across from Spruce and Beacon Streets.

Photo by Bruce Gellerman

The Founders Monument, in Boston Common, commemorates the 300th anniversary of Blackstone welcoming Winthrop and the Puritans. Native Indians who called the place Shawmut can also be seen in sculptor John Paramino's bas relief. In the foreground is Blackstone's spring. The monument was dedicated during James Michael Curley's second term as Boston mayor. Curley, known as the Rascal King, served four terms as mayor, once as governor and once in federal prison for mail fraud.

You'll notice that Blackstone, who liked to go bare butt on Beacon

★ ★

Hill, is fully clothed in the monument. But look close. You'll notice
Blackstone bears a striking resemblance to Mayor Curley. Sculptor
Paramino used a contemporary painting of John Winthrop to guide
him in creating the Puritan's likeness but no such image existed for
Blackstone. In a politically astute move Paramino cast Curley as the
model.

You'll find two statues of Hizzona the mayor in tiny Union Park
near Faneuil Hall. In one Curley is standing, in one he's sitting. In
both, he's wearing clothes.

The Christmas Tree *Is* the Present
Boston

If you want to see the most magnificent Christmas tree in the nation,
forget about the ones at the White House and New York's Rocke-
feller Center. They dim in comparison to the one in Boston. For more
than thirty years, Boston's official Christmas tree in Boston Common
has run rings around any and all competitors. But don't take our
word for it. The seasonal symbol comes from Nova Scotia, Canada,
the self-proclaimed "Balsam Fir Christmas Tree Capital of the World,"
as an annual gift selected after a six-month search. By tradition, the
tree has to be at least fifty years old and 50 feet tall.

The tree is a present from Halifax, the provincial capital, for the
help Boston sent to the city during its time of greatest need. In early
December 1917 a ship filled with munitions exploded in Halifax harbor. It was the largest artificially created explosion in history until the
detonation of the atomic bomb. Halifax was flattened; thousands
were killed and injured. Boston citizens braved a blizzard to deliver
food, medical aid, and supplies to the city, and Halifax has never
forgotten.

In 2005 the Hub's tree caused quite a hubbub. When the city's
Web site referred to the evergreen as the "holiday" tree, evangelist
Jerry Falwell saw red. Reverend Falwell, who died in 2007, mobi-
lized his flock. Falwell's fundamentalist faithful bombarded Boston

A Clean Getaway, Except for the Smell

On January 17, 1950, robbers broke into the Brinks offices at 169 Prince Street in Boston's North End. They made off with $1,218,211.29 in cash and $1,557,183.83 in securities and checks. The Great Brinks Robbery was the biggest heist in U.S. history. It took six years and $29 million for the government to find and prosecute the crooks.

Only $51,906 of the Brinks cash was ever recovered. A big breakthrough in the case came when one of the robbers tried to pass off money that he had hidden in the dirt. The buried loot became smelly and moldy and led to the case being cracked.

The building where thieves pulled off the Great Brinks Robbery still stands and is now known as the North Terminal Garage. It is on the National Register of Historic Places. The address is 600 Commercial Avenue.

Photo by Bruce Gellerman

The building where the famous Brinks job was pulled off made for a speedy getaway: All four floors have direct access to ground level.

city hall with half a million e-mails. Boston's mayor, not wanting to appear like the grinch who stole Christmas, quickly had the reference removed, and soon all were merry.

The traditional lighting of Boston's official Christmas tree takes place in early December in Boston Common.

Dental Plaque

Boston

At the corner of Tremont Street and Hamilton Place you'll find a plaque honoring Dr. W.H. Stowe's contribution to the world of dentistry. Dr. Stowe had a thriving private practice in Boston but was even better at making false teeth. Like a grin, his reputation spread

Photo by Bruce Gellerman

Location: the corner of Tremont Street and Hamilton Place, Boston

★ ★

far and wide, and in 1887 the good doctor, later joined by his cousin Frank Eddy, opened the nation's first commercial dental laboratory.

The dental plaque is mounted on the wall at the corner of the FedEx building diagonally across from Brimstone Corner where colonists once hid gunpowder in the crypt of the Congregationalist church that is located there. The church is also where the hymn "America" was first sung (July 4, 1831); the country's oldest musical organization, the Handel & Hyden Society was founded; and William Lloyd Garrison began his long career as an abolitionist.

What's Up, Duck?

Boston

Robert McCloskey's *Make Way for Ducklings* is Massachusetts's official children's book. The children's classic features Mr. and Mrs. Mallard's darling little ducklings: Jack, Kack, Lack, Mack, Nack, Ouack, Quack, and Pack.

A 38-foot-long bronze sculpture of the jaywalking ducklings and their mom can be found in the northeast corner of Boston's Public Garden. The statue, sculpted by Nancy Schon,

Photo by Bruce Gellerman

The ducklings celebrated their twentieth birthday in 2007.

was installed in 1987 and quickly became a favorite of residents and visitors alike. Then in 1999 someone "duck-napped" Jack. Bostonians, usually unflappable about such matters, were incensed. Thankfully, a month later the statue was found under a desk at a Boston college. But the duck-napper had sawed Jack's legs off just above his webbed feet, so a new Jack had to be made. The one in Boston Public Garden is the new Jack. The old Jack, with his legs repaired, now has a new home at the rooftop playground outside Boston Medical Center's pediatric department at 84 Harrison Avenue.

Four Star Jail

Boston

Liberty Hotel on Boston's posh Beacon Hill is the city's newest four star hotel and one of the nation's oldest jails. It's listed on the state and national Registers of Historic Places.

Originally called The Charles Street Jail, the granite structure was built in 1851 and designed to house hardened criminals in 220 cells. Among its long term guests were Boston Strangler Albert De Salvo, anarchists Sacco and Vanzetti, Malcolm X, and Boston Mayor James Michael Curley, who served time for cheating on a civil service test.

The jail closed under court order in 1990 and reopened after a $150 million dollar make over in 2007. There are 280 luxury rooms including one-bedroom "Escape" suites. You can still see vestiges of jail cells in the lobby bar and the restaurant is named "Clink."

Reportedly, an inmate once escaped to the roof of the jail and held hostages at bay, refusing to release them until they correctly named the members of TV's *Brady Bunch*. Talk about a criminal act. They should have thrown the television, not just the book, at him.

You can check into (or out) the hotel at 215 Charles Street, Beacon Hill (617-224-4000; www.libertyhotel.com/).

A Death-Defying Colonial Daredevil

Boston

One if by land, two if by sea. Three if by air? Boston's Old North Church, perhaps best known as the place where Paul Revere got the signal that set him off on his midnight ride, also happens to be where colonial stuntman John Childs took the first flight in Boston history.

Once Upon a Midnight Frogpondium

Although Edgar Allan Poe pondered weak and weary and died in Baltimore, the master of the macabre was born in Boston in 1809. Orphaned as a child, Poe lived in Boston only a short time, returning briefly in 1827 when he enlisted in the U.S. Army under the name Edgar A. Perry. While Poe was in Boston his first book of poems, *Tamerlane and other Poems,* was published, written anonymously "by a Bostonian." Poe had a love-hate relationship with Boston and may have been reluctant to have his name attached to the city of his birth; he often referred to Boston as "Frogpondium" after the frog pond on the Common.

Perhaps appropriately, Poe's exact birthplace is in dispute. Some put it at 33 Hollis Street; others say it was on Carver Street, which is now called Charles Street South. To avoid the dispute, the plaque honoring Poe is near 176 Boylston Street.

In 1757, eighteen years before Revere got his signal, John Childs used the church steeple as a launching pad. A plaque on a wall outside the Old North Church describes how Childs flew from the 190-foot steeple "to the satisfaction of a great number of spectators."

There are two versions of the event. One has Childs strapping on a leather umbrella-like contraption, putting a grooved wooden board on his chest, and sliding headfirst down a 700-foot-long guyline. The other version has him wearing canvas wings and gliding down. Either way, the colonial daredevil drew such a large crowd that he did it again the next day while shooting off pistols. The performance proved too much for Boston's Puritan prudes. They banned all future flights of fantasy, a prohibition on aviation that stands on the city's books to this day.

The plaque commemorating Childs's flight is the third from the left on the brick Washington Garden wall near the main entrance to the Old North Church, 193 Salem Street.

Red Sox, Red Seat

Boston

Boston's crown jewel, Fenway Park, is the oldest stadium in Major League Baseball. The first season was in 1912 and since then, the ballpark has steeped in history and tradition. In left field is the Green Monster: Built in 1937, the 37-foot high wall was painted green in 1947 to cover ads that graced the outfield fence.

Photo by Emily Taylor

Good luck getting any seat, let alone the red one.

Fenway has the lowest seating capacity in the Majors. Depending on who's doing the counting, the seating capacity is 34,898. All of them are painted green except for one. Seat 21 in Row 37 of Section 42 in the right field bleachers is painted red. It's where, on June 9, 1946, Sox slugger Ted Williams hit the longest homer in Fenway history, a 502-foot blast that bonked a snoozing fan, Joseph Boucher on the bean. Serves him right, turns out Boucher was a Yankee fan.

Fenway Park is located off of Kenmore Square at 4 Yawkey Way.

Hey Norton, Check This Out

Boston

You can never tell what you'll find when you spend $14.5 billion and dig through 16 million cubic yards of dirt.

Archaeologists working alongside excavators on Boston's Big Dig, the largest public works project in history, unearthed usual arrowheads, some clay tobacco pipes, and the oldest bowling ball in North America. If that doesn't bowl you over, perhaps this will: They found the ball under the floorboards in a "house of office," the seventeenth-century term for a privy.

The oak ball is flattened on two sides and is about the size of a grapefruit. It has a perforated middle to hold a lead weight to give the ball more play when rolled. Not that play was what the Puritans had in mind when they founded Boston: A statute was passed in 1646 forbidding bowling because it caused "much waste of wine and beer."

Perhaps a bowler taking a nip too much might explain why the ball was found in the toilet.

Today the oldest bowling ball in North America is on display at the Commonwealth Museum, 220 Morissey Boulevard. Admission is free, but you'll have to pay for shoes.

For more information call (617) 727-9268 or visit www.state.ma .us/sec/mus.

The Sacco and Vanzetti Death Masks

Boston

There are many proud moments in Massachusetts's history, but August 23, 1927, is not one of them. That was the day when Italian immigrants Nicola Sacco, a shoemaker from Stoughton, and Bartolomeo Vanzetti, a fisherman from North Plymouth, were executed on the site that is now part of Bunker Hill Community College in Boston.

The men, followers of Italy's most radical anarchist, were found guilty of armed robbery and murder. Both men denied the charges up to their deaths. The evidence against them was weak and circumstantial, and their executions ignited protests around the world. The case became a landmark in the judicial history of the state and nation. Fifty years to the day of their execution, then governor Michael Dukakis issued a proclamation apologizing to the men and their families.

Copies of Sacco's and Vanzetti's death certificates are housed in the rare books department of the Boston Public Library, along with a canister of their ashes, their death masks, a box of bullets, and other personal items. Boston Public Library is at Copley Square.

Visitors are asked to e-mail ahead of time so that the materials can be accessed. Write to rzonghi@bpl.org.

The Boston Public Library's special collections also contain more than 700 anarchist newspapers and periodicals from around the world.

Trivia

An Airport Named for a Very Infrequent Flier

Boston's Logan International Airport, one of the busiest in the nation, is named in honor of Lt. Gen. Edward Lawrence Logan. Logan was born in Boston in 1875 and led a distinguished career as an elected official, judge, and war hero. He died in 1929.

The question is: Why did they name an airport after him? For all of his many accomplishments, Lieutenant General Logan never flew in an airplane.

The Running of the Brides

Filene's Basement's notorious bridal gown event has been likened to the running of the bulls at Pamplona. But according to the store's PR person, Pat Boudrot, some years it's more like a prize fight, as brides-to-be go head to head in an attempt to grab a designer wedding gown at a bargain-basement $249.

Some of the women arrive with retinues that include their moms and matrons of honor, ready to do battle. Boudrot says they come wearing boxing gloves and chomping on mouth guards. It's a knock-down, no-holds- or clothes-barred fight to the finish as the gals make a mad dash for the dresses, stripping themselves and the racks bare in just seconds. The record, witnessed by a CBS news camera team, is just 36 seconds. It's a scene that makes the floor of the New York Stock Exchange look like, well, a walk down the aisle.

Filene's Basement first emptied its warehouse of designer gowns for the one-day sale in 1947. Since then, on at least five occasions, starry-eyed women, with their sights set on a "baaaahhh-gain," have broken down the doors to the store before they were opened.

The objects of their affections are dresses that come from manufacturers' overstocks, canceled store orders, and, of course, canceled weddings. The gowns may retail for up to $10,000 and sell for as low as $199 on this one lucky day. One memorable gown featured a peacock hand-painted in pastels; another had a map of the world laid out in Mercator projection on the skirt.

Marketing professors Ellen Foxman and Susan Dobscha have made a cottage industry of writing scholarly papers about the sale. Their latest, "Women and Wedding Gowns: Exploring a Discount Shopping Experience," is in the proceedings of the 1998 Conference on Gender, Marketing, and Consumer Behavior.

The bargain basement will be closed for remodeling until sometime in 2009. Then, stand back and watch the stampede.

Brides strip the racks and themselves bare at Filene's Basement Bridal Gown Sale.

★ ★

Tanks Vermilion, Ho Ho Ho Chi Minh
Boston

The world's largest copyrighted work of art is on permanent display just south of downtown Boston in Dorchester on Route 93. It's the so-called Rainbow Tank, a 140-foot-tall liquid natural gas tank featuring five huge stripes of color: vermilion, orange, yellow, blue, and purple.

In 1971 Boston Gas commissioned artist Corita Kent to paint the tank. Kent, a former nun best known for designing the famous LOVE postage stamp, said the Rainbow Tank was an expression of peace.

Photo by Erik Sherman

The gas tank along Interstate 93 is a roadside Rorschach test. Some people say they see Ho Chi Minh's profile painted on the tank.

How Sweet It Isn't

About half past noon on January 15, 1919, a disaster like no other struck Boston's North End. A giant concrete-and-cast-iron tank, 52 feet high and 90 feet in diameter and holding 2.3 million gallons of molasses, exploded. The powerful blast propelled a gooey, 2-story tidal wave down Commercial Avenue at thirty-five miles an hour. Steel supports for a nearby elevated train line were severed, and a fire station was crushed. Twenty-one people were killed, 150 were injured, and an untold number of horses drowned in the steaming, sweet lava. Left in its wake was a 2-foot layer of molasses that had spread for blocks. Cleanup crews and sightseers brought it on their shoes and clothes all over Boston and as far away as Worcester. While the sickly, sweet smell allegedly lingered for decades, there's not a trace of the molasses today. Not even a plaque marks the spot where the doomed tank once stood, but if you look down from Copp's Hill onto Commercial Avenue, you'll see a park next to an enclosed recreation center. That's the place.

The war in Vietnam was raging, and Kent was a peace activist. Some say they can see evidence of Kent's antiwar sympathies hidden in the tank. Look at the middle stripe. See the profile of Ho Chi Minh? Who? Ho Chi Minh, the former leader of North Vietnam and a busboy at Boston's Parker House Hotel in the 1920s. Others say the roadside Rorschach test contains the image of the devil, Osama Bin Laden, or Fred Flintstone. And then there are those who say that sometimes a tank is just a tank.

Be careful: Don't use the access road leading to the tank. It's private property. There are remote cameras watching you, and the property owners will call the police if you are on the road.

You Definitely Save on Wall-to-Wall Carpet

Boston

Jennifer Simonic; her husband, Spence Welton; their daughter; and their dog and cat live at 44 Hull Street in Boston's North End. This 200-year-old, four-story town house has been beautifully restored, but it is easy to miss. The house is just 10 feet 5 inches wide. The home is so narrow that the front door is located on the side. The ceilings are 6 feet 4 inches high. (Spence Welton is 6 feet 1 inch tall.)

Photo by Bruce Gellerman

The house at 44 Hull Street in Boston is the skinniest house in the city, and perhaps in the entire commonwealth.

The Skinny House, as it is called, is the narrowest home in Boston—if not the entire commonwealth. Legend has it that the house was built out of spite to block the view of neighbors behind it. Admittedly, that's a pretty thin story. More likely it is the last of a series of similar homes built in the area around 1800. At one time eleven people lived in the house. Ironically, the Skinny House has a spacious, 1,000-square-foot backyard, one of the largest in the densely populated North End.

The Skinny House is located directly opposite Copp's Hill Burying Ground. The house number is on the side.

Ether or Either

Boston

Boston printer Gilbert Allen never knew what hit him. After a few whiffs from an ether-soaked sponge, he was out. When he woke up, the human guinea pig learned he had made medical history. It was October 16, 1846, and Gilbert Allen was the first person to be successfully operated on while under anesthesia. Before then, undergoing an operation had meant enduring excruciating pain. Now, the ether-assisted surgery proceeded in silence as an astonished crowd of physicians looked on. Afterward, Dr. John Warren, the surgeon who performed the operation, told his incredulous colleagues, "Gentleman, this is no humbug."

Bah, humbug, indeed. The operation touched off a controversy of competing claims over who actually had invented the potent stuff, with two Boston dentists taking credit. When city authorities proposed a monument memorializing the inventor, they consulted

Photo by Erik Sherman

Patients breathed a lot easier after the invention of ether. This monument in the Boston Public Garden pays homage to the painkilling gas.

31

Harvard physician and wordsmith Oliver Wendell Holmes. It was Holmes who coined the term *anesthesia* and, acting Solomon-like, suggested dedicating the statue to "Either or ether."

When Mark Twain learned that neither man would be named on the statue, he proclaimed that the ether monument "is made of

Stars, Stripes, and Bars

In 1941, to commemorate the tenth anniversary of the "Star Spangled Banner" as the U.S. national anthem, Russian émigré Igor Stravinsky reorchestrated the song. Unfortunately for the composer, the song, originally penned by Francis Scott Key, was reharmonized off key and violated a Massachusetts law forbidding any "tampering" with the national ditty. Stravinsky's performance reportedly left the audience "stunned into bewildered silence." And Boston's finest visited Stravinsky at a later concert to make sure there wasn't a repeat performance. One Boston newspaper quoted Captain Thomas Harvey as saying, "Let him change it just once and we'll grab him."

The law is still on the books in Massachusetts.

In 1918 German-born Karl Muck, conductor of the Boston Symphony, also got stung by the "Spangled Banner." Muck was nabbed by federal agents for refusing to lead the orchestra in the tune. Muck said it wasn't in accord with the serious compositions in the schedule. The BSO stripped Muck of his position and he was interned during World War I as an enemy alien.

hardy material, but the lie it tells will outlast it a million years." Well, either it will or ether it won't, but it has lasted since its unveiling in 1868 in the Boston Public Garden. It is the oldest monument in the country's oldest public park. The Ether Memorial can be found facing Arlington Street. Atop the red marble columns is a rendition of the Good Samaritan. Be sure to check out the weird reliefs behind the granite arches.

The surgical amphitheater in which the first anesthesia-assisted operation took place is called the Ether Dome. It was designed by the great architect Charles Bulfinch. Until 1873 it was used as an operating room. Then it served as a storage area, a dormitory, and a dining room for nurses. It is now a classroom. The Ether Dome is open to the public and is located at Massachusetts General Hospital, 55 Fruit Street.

The Gardner Museum: What You Don't See Is What You Get
Boston

The magnificent Isabella Stewart Gardner Museum contains an eclectic collection of 2,500 paintings, sculptures, tapestries, pieces of furniture, manuscripts, and rare books. Mrs. Gardner, the grande dame of Boston's Brahmin high society, spent thirty years assembling the renowned collection and built a fifteenth-century Venetian palace with courtyard garden to house it.

But today what makes the collection a must-see for many tourists is what you do not see, as evidenced by the empty frames that hang on the walls. On St. Patrick's Day 1990, the Gardner Museum was the scene of the biggest art heist in U.S. history. Two men wearing fake mustaches and Boston Police uniforms stole thirteen priceless works of art. Among them were three Rembrandts (including the master's only seascape), five Degas sketches, a Manet, and Vermeer's *The Concert*. Despite a $5 million reward, none of the pieces has been recovered. The empty frames continue to hang on the walls because Mrs. Gardner stipulated in her will that everything in the house was

forever to remain exactly as it was or all her possessions would pass
to Harvard University.

The Isabella Stewart Gardner Museum is located at 280 The Fenway. For more information call (617) 566-1401 or visit www.gardner
museum.org. The Gardner is closed on most major holidays and usually on St. Patrick's Day.

Gillette Employees Get Worked Up into a Lather
Boston

Back in 1901 traveling salesman King Camp Gillette developed the
world's first double-edged disposable blade, and the hirsute have
never been the same. Today, from its World Shaving Headquarters
in South Boston, where Gillette founded his international empire,
the company turns out blades by the billions. To ensure that the
company lives up to its claim that Gillette's razors are "the best a
man can get" and that they get even better, Gillette employs 500
engineers and scientists in laboratories around the world who send
their improvements back to Boston for evaluation.

More than 300 volunteers at the South Boston factory sign up for
the shave-in-plant program to test-drive the latest experimental models. Each morning men from a select group take off their shirts, enter
one of twenty booths, and lather up. Technicians in white lab coats
register their reactions as the men shave the right side of their faces
with one unmarked razor and the left side with another. The results
are entered into a computer. After decades of studying shaving and
blades under electron microscopes and in slow motion, Gillette has
come to understand that making a blade shave smoother than a
baby's bottom takes a lot more than science and technology. Because
it sells blades from Armenia to Zanzibar, Gillette has to be sensitive to
the different kinds of skin and hair types, and to cultural differences
as well. Over the years, shaving scientists have learned that what
constitutes a great shave is really a subjective experience; there's the
sound of the blade slicing through whiskers, the feel of the razor in

the hand. After all the testing and experimenting, it turns out that when it comes to shaving, beauty is in the eye of the beard holder.

You Need This Museum Like a Hole in the Head

Boston

The Warren Anatomical Museum is the kind of place to which Alfred Hitchcock might have brought a first date. The museum is fascinating in a macabre sort of way, and not without humor, with a vast collection of medical instruments, photos, anatomical models, machines, gadgets, specimens, body parts, and medical memorabilia. In all, more than 13,000 artifacts detail the evolution of modern medical science from the nineteenth century. You'll be astonished by how far medicine has come in such a short period of time . . . and perhaps be unnerved by just how primitive it was until not too long ago.

Dr. John Collin Warren started collecting unusual anatomical specimens in 1799, when he was just twelve years old. In 1848 he hung up his stethoscope (there are scores of models on display) and resigned his Harvard professorship, donating his world-class collection of weird artifacts to the medical school. His own skeleton is now part of the collection.

On display is the phrenological collection of Dr. Johann Gaspar Spurzheim, who studied skull bumps for clues about personality and brain function. In 1832 the famed German doctor died unexpectedly in Boston while on a lecture tour. His body is buried in Mount Auburn Cemetery in Cambridge, but his unusually large skull is on display at the Warren Museum.

The most popular exhibit is the skull of Phineas Gage. An on-the-job accident sent a thirteen-pound steel bar flying through Gage's cheek into his brain. Unexpectedly, Gage survived. His memory was intact, but his personality took a turn for the worse. He became mean and lost his social constraints. Scientists studied Gage's skull for clues about personality. Seems they needed just such an accident, like a hole in the head, to discover the inner workings of the brain.

The Warren Anatomical Museum Exhibition Gallery is on the fifth floor of the Countway Library of Medicine, 10 Shattuck Street; (617) 432-6196.

Spurzheim's tomb is at the intersection of Fountain and Lawn Avenues, left sides, adjacent to the road in Mount Auburn Cemetery, Mount Auburn Street, Cambridge. Watch out for the bumps in the road.

Americans "In-vest" in an Insect

Boston

Since 1742, a 52-inch-tall, 38-pound copper grasshopper with glass doorknob eyes has looked down onto a good deal of American history. The 'hopper has watched from his weather-vane perch 80 feet above the ground as the winds of change turned the colonies into a nation and the nation into a world superpower. From the grasshopper's vantage point atop Faneuil Hall, the insect has been an eyewitness to the Boston Massacre and the Boston Tea Party and watched as patriotic conspirators gathered at the Old Meeting House. Over time the grasshopper has survived wars, hurricanes, earthquakes, fires, and vandals.

But the grasshopper is more than a priceless piece of Americana. It is also a time capsule. Inside the insect's stomach vest area is a copper container. Each time the grasshopper has been handled and restored, people have placed objects into the vest and taken things out.

In 1761, following a devastating fire and an earthquake, a note inscribed "food for the Grasshopper" was inserted into the copper time capsule by the restorer. The note, detailing the gilded insect's trials and tribulations, is now in the Boston Public Library's archives.

In 1842 the weather vane was restored again. This time it was filled with papers and coins. It is believed that the first contents were removed and sold at auction in 1885. In 1889 some newspapers and coins from the period were deposited in the capsule, and in 1952 Boston's mayor inserted one of his business cards and a message in the copper vest.

★ ★

In 1974 the grasshopper was reported missing and a massive insect hunt was started.

The 'hopper was discovered weeks later in the Faneuil Hall belfry underneath a pile of old flags. Seems painters had taken it down and forgot to put it back up. A tip from an ex-steeplejack who worked on the vane and was trying to beat a drug rap led to its recovery. Before the grasshopper was restored to its proper perch, Boston's mayor resealed all of the items in the vest, adding a letter of his own and two bicentennial coins.

The third floor of Faneuil Hall still houses the Ancient and Honorable Artillery Company. Founded in 1638, this is the oldest military company in the United States and considered the third oldest in the world. Among its collection is one of the grasshopper's eye sockets. Faneuil Hall is adjacent to Quincy Market.

Now, Where Did I Put That Key?

Boston

The giant Fortress padlock is a familiar, neck-bending icon for motorists on Interstate 93. When fully inflated, the 700-pound lock is 32 feet tall and 20 feet wide. To make sure the blow-up lock doesn't blow away, it's taken down for the winter and stored—where else?—in the super-secure, climate-controlled Fortress storage facility.

The eight-story Fortress building at 99 Boston Street is also unique. Fortress, the

Photo courtesy of the Fortress Corporation

The giant padlock can be seen from Interstate 93, just south of downtown Boston.

largest provider of high-security storage in the United States, invented a giant carousel device that suspends the room-sized safety deposit vaults in midair and automatically delivers them to clients waiting in the lobby. The giant lock is in good company. Many museums use Fortress to store their works of art.

A Thin Tome from the Tomb
Boston

James Allen's autobiography is one book you can definitely judge by its cover. It is awful, inside and out. Allen admits he was a rotten scoundrel, and the book cover testifies to that. His autobiography is certainly him; the book is bound in his skin.

In 1833 Allen attempted to rob John Fenno Jr. near Powderhorn Hill in Chelsea. Fenno fought back and was shot, but he survived because the bullet hit the buckle on his suspenders. Allen was arrested and sent to prison, where he wrote an autobiography of his troubled youth and his life as a highwayman.

Allen died on July 17, 1837, but before he did he asked to meet with Fenno, saying he wanted to shake the hand of a brave man. Then he made his fateful request. Figuring that once he was dead it would be no skin off his nose—or actually

Binding his autobiography was no skin off James Allen's nose. The cover came from his back.

Photo by Bruce Gellerman

his back—Allen asked that a copy of his autobiography, bound in his skin, be given to Fenno and a second copy be given to Dr. Bigelow of Boston, the physician he requested attend his death.

Allen's skin was removed, and bookbinder Peter Low tanned his hide and edged it in gold. The binding looks like pale gray deerskin and is inscribed in Latin: *Hic Liber Waltonis cute Compactus Est* ("This book by Walton bound in his own skin"). The full title of the book is: *Narrative of the life of James Allen, alias George Walton, alias Jonas Pierce, alias James H. York, alias Burley Grove, the highwayman. Being his death-bed confession, to the warden of the Massachusetts state prison.*

Allen's autobiography was donated to the Boston Athenaeum by one of John Fenno's descendants, and you can still find it there today, but the copy given to the doctor has never been found. The Boston Athenaeum (617-227-0270) is located at an address Harry Potter would love: 10½ Beacon Street in Boston.

The Athenaeum's collection includes 600,000 volumes. James Allen's autobiography is the one most often requested. You can access the text of the thin tome on the Athenaeum's Web site at www.bostonathenaeum.org.

The Plywood Palace

Boston

Building the sixty-story John Hancock Tower, Boston's tallest sky-scraper, was a real "pane in the glass." In 1973, soon after workmen began installing the first of 10,344 windows, the panes began to crack, and many of the windows fell to the ground. Luckily, no one was killed or injured.

The entire exterior of the 790-foot building had been designed to be covered in special mirror-glass, but by April 1973 plywood had replaced more than an acre of the tower's high-tech windows. The building became known as the Plywood Palace.

Needless to say, lawyers had a field day—or, in this case, field years. There were lawsuits and countersuits and counter-countersuits. Scientists and engineers were perplexed. After much high-tech sleuthing, the problem was identified. However, the judge in the case imposed a gag order on the aggrieved parties that lasted seventeen years. It was not until 1990 that the public learned what was wrong. It seems that the bonding material that was supposed to hold the dual layers of insulated glass together, didn't.

All 10,344 windows were replaced with single sheets of tempered glass. Sensors were installed on each pane to provide an early warning if any pane began vibrating too much. Five thousand undamaged windows were sold to the public for $100 each. As for the plywood? It was used to board up abandoned buildings in the city.

Photo courtesy of Peter Vanderwarker

The Hancock building was dubbed the Plywood Palace after workers replaced fallen windows with sheets of wood.

The Hancock Tower is located on Clarendon Street and St. James Place near Copley Square. You can't miss it. It's the one with all the shiny windows.

Curiosity of the Month
Boston

When Jeremy Belknap founded the Massachusetts Historical Society in 1791, he asked the public to submit unusual contributions to the organization's collection. Since then, the Society's "curiosity collection" has grown to hold some very unusual artifacts, including a five-dollar bill featuring Santa Claus, issued in 1850 by the Howard Banking Company (it was legal tender back then); a letter from Boston native Benjamin Franklin describing his attempt to electrocute a turkey; and a World Series medal from the 1912 Boston Red Sox. Little is known about the medal, but it is obviously very rare. After 1918 the Red Sox did not win the World Series again until 2004, finally overcoming the championship drought attributed to "the curse of the Bambino" when the Sox traded Babe Ruth to Boston's archrival, the New York Yankees.

The Massachusetts Historical Society is at 1154 Boylston Street, (617) 536-1608. The society maintains an "object of the month" online showcase of some of its more unusual artifacts at www .masshist.org/welcome.

Signs of the Times
Boston

Soaring 200 feet high over Kenmore Square, seemingly floating in midair, is one of Boston's more obvious and beloved landmarks: the Citgo sign. Built by City Services Oil Company in 1965, the giant ad measures 60 by 60 feet.

Originally, the two-sided sign was lit with 5,878 orange, red, and white neon tubes. In 2005 they were replaced with more efficient LEDs.

★ ★

Photo by Bruce Gellerman

The Citgo sign sits atop 600 Beacon Street in Kenmore Square. The building, originally known as the Peerless Motor Car Building, now houses a
bookstore.

Appropriately enough, the brightly lit sign is located on Beacon
Street and is used by Bostonians to orient themselves around the city.
However, in 1973 residents wandered around confused and direc-
tionless when the lights were turned off for a year as a symbol of
conservation during the energy crisis. Then from 1979 to 1982 there
were again lost souls in the streets when the sign was turned off
once more to save electricity.

Just how important the Citgo sign had become to residents
became clear in November 1982, when workers arrived to dismantle
the sign. Before they could remove a single bulb, the Boston Landmark Commission intervened, saying the sign was a "prime example
of roadside culture." There was talk of designating the sign an

official city landmark, but Citgo would have had to pay to move it. Instead, the company paid $450,000 to refurbish the sign and return it to its original glow. On August 10, 1983, as the song "You Light Up My Life" filled the air in Kenmore Square, 750 people attended the relighting ceremony.

"The British are coming. Open wide. The British are coming. Bite down."

Trying to get sleepy colonists awake and aware that the British were coming must have been like pulling teeth for Paul Revere. It's a good thing, then, that our alarmist, patriotic midnight rider wasn't only a highly skilled silversmith but talented in the art of oral health and hygiene as well. On August 20, 1770, five years before his midnight ride, Revere took out this ad in the *Boston Gazette and Country Journal*:

> Paul Revere Takes this Method of returning his most sincere Thanks to the Gentlemen and Ladies who have employed him in the care of their Teeth. He would now inform them and all others, who are so unfortunate as to lose their Teeth by accident or otherways, that he still continues the Business of a Dentist, and flatters himself that from the Experience he has had these Two Years (in which Time he has fixt some Hundreds of Teeth) that he can fix them as well as any Surgeon-Dentist who ever came from London. He fixes them in such a Manner that they are not only an Ornament, but of real Use in Speaking and Eating. He cleanses the Teeth and will wait on any Gentleman or Lady at their Lodgings. He may be spoke with at his Shop opposite Dr. Clark's at the North End.

Bridges That "Lie" Over Waters

As far as we're concerned it's all water under the bridge, but just to set the record straight, the Boston guidebooks have it wrong. Despite what they say, the iron bridge that crosses the swan lagoon in Boston's Public Garden is not the world's smallest suspension bridge. When it was built in 1866, the span, a quaint fifty-six paces long, was indeed a suspension bridge, but repairs in the early 1900s turned it into a plain old bridge.

Photo by Bruce Gellerman

The world's shortest suspension bridge, isn't.

Boston's newest bridge, the Leonard P. Zakim Bunker Hill Bridge, emerging from the underground Central Artery near Causeway Street, may also look like a suspension job, but it's not. It's a cable-stayed bridge. In fact, it's the widest cable-stayed bridge in the world. Both a suspension bridge and a cable-stayed bridge use two towers, but there is a difference in how the cables are attached to the towers. In a cable-stayed bridge, the cables run directly between the roadbed and the towers, and the towers bear the load. Suspension bridges have the cables slung over the towers, and they transfer the load to the anchorages on the other side.

While you are trying to figure out the difference, check out the new bridge's towers. They look just like the Bunker Hill Monument to the east. The bridge is named after the famous battle and for Lenny Zakim, a Jewish activist who tried to bridge the difference of Boston's many racial, religious, and ethnic communities. For his work, Zakim was even named Knight of St. Gregory by Pope John Paul II in 1999.

★ ★

Lady Madonna
East Boston

Not far from Suffolk Downs Racetrack and overlooking Logan Airport is the Madonna, Queen of the Universe National Shrine. The 35-foot bronze-and-copper statue was created by Italian-Jewish sculptor Arrigo Minerbi and set on the site in 1954.

Driving up the winding road to the shrine, you will see a 50-foot cross atop a hill. The hill is where the second battle of the American Revolution was fought. The views of Boston and the airport from the top of the hill are terrific. A gift shop near the shrine offers unusual religious object for sale.

The Madonna, Queen of the Universe National Shrine (617-569-2100) is at 111 Orient Avenue, East Boston. Follow the signs on Route 1A.

The Leaning Tower of Boston
Boston

Soon after the New Old South Church was completed in 1873 the massive 260-foot-tall tower or campanile began to tilt. By the 1920s the tower was 3 feet out of plumb and threatening to topple onto Boylston Street. In 1931 the leaning tower of Boston was dismantled stone by stone and rebuilt slightly shorter to its present day 240 feet.

The church is a world-class example of Northern Italian Gothic Architecture but it's a Yankee Doodle original. The exterior façade is made of Roxbury puddingstone and the structure was designed by two local architects: Charles Amos Cummings of Boston and Willard T. Sears of New Bedford.

The exterior is decorated in a stripe and checkerboard style and features carvings of squirrels, owls, and birds among the vines. Architects Cummings and Sears were so proud of their design they immortalized themselves in stone. Look at the arch way to the right of the main door on Boylston Street. Above you'll see the biblical message,

★ ★

"Behold I have set before thee an open door." Carved into the pillars holding up the porch under the words "have" and "thee" you'll find the faces of Cummings and Sears. The one on the left has a beard.

The New Old South Church in Boston isn't new and it isn't in the South. The original congregation met at The Old South Meeting House in downtown Boston, which was in what was then Boston's South. The meeting house is famous as the site where rebellious "Indians" launched the Boston Tea Party.

Photo: Bruce Gellerman

Come see the structure at 645 Boylston Street (corner of Boylston and Dartmouth). For information call (617) 536-1970.

2

The Technology Ring around Boston

Got food on the brain? *Have a smokin' good time at the Museum of Burnt Food, at the home of Deborah Henson-Conant in Arlington. Among the fire-fossilized delectables on display are Forever Shrimp Kebab and Well, Well Done Soy Pups.*

If you are more inclined toward pheasant under glass, a pair of the birds given to George Washington by the Marquis de Lafayette is on display—post taxidermy—in a glass corner case at Harvard's Museum of Natural History.

Over at MIT distance is sometimes measured by the "smoot," 5 feet, 7 inches, after Oliver R. Smoot Jr., class of '62, who just happened to be that height. And if you've always wanted to travel to Bhutan but couldn't, visit the Acme Bookbinding Company in Charleston, where the world's largest commercial book ever published, Bhutan: A Visual Odyssey, *is on display. It's 5 feet high and when open, almost 7 feet wide.*

You can find out if "The Riddle of the Universe [was] Solved" by visiting MIT's Archive of Useless Research in the Hayden Library. If you prefer to spend a little quiet time with those who might already know, head out to Concord's Sleepy Hollow Cemetery and stroll along the Authors Ridge where Henry David Thoreau, Nathaniel Hawthorne, Ralph Waldo Emerson, and Louisa May Alcott are buried near one another.

And don't forget Walden Pond; it is only a short drive away.

The Technology Ring around Boston

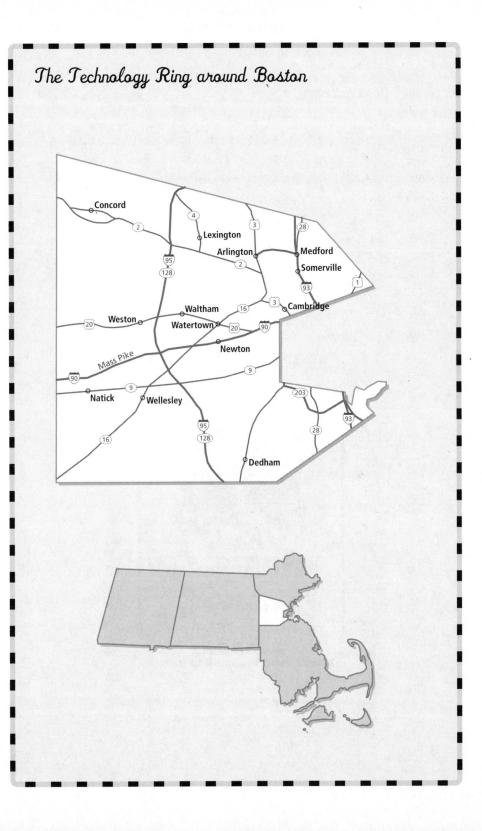

A Well-Done Museum
Arlington

Where there's smoke, there's Deborah Henson-Conant. Put a harp in her hands and boy, can she cook! With her long beaded hair and leather halter top, she plays the heaven-sent instrument with the fire of a bat out of . . . well, you-know-where.

Doc Severinsen calls Henson-Conant a wild woman of the harp, serving up blues, jazz, Celtic, and folk music with a generous serving of humor. But put her in the kitchen of her Arlington, Massachusetts, home and the menu changes dramatically.

Photo courtesy of Deborah Henson-Conant

For a meal Smoky Bear might love, check out the Museum of Burnt Food.

Henson-Conant is the founder of (and curator, and primary contributor to) the Museum of Burnt Food, an ever-expanding collection that celebrates the art of culinary disaster. Sometime in 1989, while heating a pot of apple cider on her stove, she was distracted from her task by a lengthy telephone call. By the time she returned, the cider had turned to cinder (exhibit A). She proudly mounted and displayed the piece and, voila, the Museum of Burnt Food was born. The museum's motto: "To cook the museum way—always leave the flame on low . . . and then take a long nap."

There's nothing half-baked about this eccentric collection of fire-fossilized food. Over the years Henson-Conant has cooked up, entirely by accident, the Forever Shrimp Kebab; Well, Well Done Soy Pups; and Trice-Baked Potatoes.

The entire collection is on limited public display in Henson-Conant's home by invitation only, but it can be viewed by the masses at http://burntfoodmuseum.com.

Brain Bank
Belmont

The Scarecrow in *The Wizard of Oz* would have loved this place. It's the world's largest brain bank. Officially known as the Harvard Brain Tissue Resource Center, the warehouse holds more than 4,000 brains. The brains were donated by individuals and used by medical researchers to study Alzheimer's, Parkinson's disease, schizophrenia, and other neurological disorders.

On average one new brain a day is added to the repository. Some parts are preserved in formaldehyde and stored in Tupperware containers, others are flash-frozen.

It's a permanent place to rest a weary mind. Deposits are welcomed. Call ahead or check out http://www.brainbank.mclean.org/.

Finding Bert Cohen's Marbles

Brookline

Bertram Cohen readily admits he's crazy about his hobby, but obviously he hasn't lost his marbles. In fact, at last count he had 300,000, constituting what he believes is the largest collection of marbles in the world. He's got onion skins, Joseph's coats, sulfides, immies, aggies, and, of course, cat's eyes.

Bert has been a marble consultant and historian for more than forty years, collecting, swapping, and selling marbles large and small, old and new online. His largest marble is a custom-made job that

Bert Cohen has all his marbles . . . and then some.

★ ★

rolls in at thirty-three pounds; the smallest is just one-sixteenth of an inch in diameter. One of his most unusual and valuable marbles is 4,000 years old, which is kid stuff when you consider that the game goes back 10,000 years.

Bert doesn't play anymore himself; but he does give out mass-produced marbles by the shovelful to worthy causes, such as the Boy Scouts. He gets them from a factory in Mexico that rolls out fifteen million a day. Collectors who share Bert's mania for marbles gather at an annual event he has organized for the past quarter-century in, where else? Marlborough, Massachusetts.

Now, having the world's most stupendous collection of marbles might be enough for some people, but Bert Cohen is a well-rounded collector. The self-described pack rat also has an extensive collection of glassware and what must certainly be the largest, if not only, collection of toys made by the long-gone Irving Corporation, maker of some of the first plastic toys.

Bert recently packed up his buckets, bins, and barrels full of marbles and moved from Boston to nearby Brookline, Massachusetts. Visits to Bertram Cohen's marble museum and toy emporium are by special invitation only, but you can learn more about his marbles at his Web site at www.marblebert.com/publications.htm.

Hey, Citgo Sign, Clam Up!
Cambridge

Literally and figuratively sitting in the shadow of Boston's famous Citgo sign is one owned by competitor Shell Oil, just across the Charles River. Built in 1933 and in operation continuously ever since, the giant scallop-shell neon is one of two that were constructed for Shell's regional headquarters on Commonwealth Avenue in Boston. In 1944, possibly in response to wartime restrictions, the company removed the signs. One was dismantled; the surviving spectacular neon sign was relocated to the existing Shell gas station on Memorial Drive. The Cambridge Historical Commission deemed the sign

★ ★

Photo by Bruce Gellerman

Memorial Drive in Cambridge is home to the giant Shell Oil sign.

an artifact of early commercial development in the city. The commission designated the Shell sign a historic and protected landmark, and in 1994 the sign was put on the National Register of Historic Places.

The Shell sign is at the intersection of Magazine Street and Memorial Drive, Cambridge.

It's MIT by a Smoot
Cambridge

The techies who attend Massachusetts Institute of Technology (MIT) deal with precise standard units of measure: the angstrom, the meter, the light year, and the smoot. The latter, while perhaps unfamiliar to laypersons, is an exacting measure: precisely 5 feet 7 inches.

There are just two things in the known universe measured in smoots: the Harvard Bridge connecting the MIT campus in Cambridge to Boston's Back Bay (364.4 smoots plus one ear) and Oliver R. Smoot Jr., MIT class of '62 (one smoot).

In October 1958, when O. R. Smoot Jr. was an MIT freshman pledge to the Lambda Chi Alpha fraternity, a fraternity brother decided it would be useful if students walking back to campus from Boston during the fog and snow knew how much farther they had to walk. Smoot, the smallest of the pledges, was measured with a string, and the unit known as the smoot was born. The fraternity members marked off the smoots in paint on the bridge. When a police van appeared at about the 300-smoot mark, the measurers took off, returning later to finish the job.

Today the pledge class of Lambda Chi Alpha repaints the smoots with a new color twice a year, and the police are no longer a problem. In fact, officers use the markers to indicate locations on the bridge when writing up accident reports. To make matters easier, the

Trivia

Tee for Too-th

Harvard University dentist George Grant is known internationally for his invention of the oblate palate, a device used to help people with cleft palate. Never heard of it? Well, how about Dr. Grant's other invention: the wood golf tee?

Until 1899 when Dr. G came along with his tee, duffers carried buckets of sand to each hole, building up a pyramid-shaped mound that they could set their ball upon.

Dr. Grant received U.S. patent No. 638,920 for his invention and the eternal gratitude of greens maintenance crews. But he never mass produced his tees or made a penny from his invention. Instead, he had them manufactured by a local company and then gave them away to friends and fellow golfers.

George Franklin Grant was the son of a former slave and the first African-American awarded a scholarship to attend Harvard's Dental School and the university's first black faculty member.

The Harvard Bridge is measured in smoots . . . plus one ear.

Continental Construction Company of Cambridge now makes concrete sidewalk slabs 5 feet 7 inches long to coincide with the smoots, instead of the usual 6-foot increments.

Ironically, in 2005, Oliver Smoot retired as chairman of the American National Standards Institute. The organization sets standard units and measurement guidelines.

You can count the smoots yourself by walking over the Harvard Bridge from Massachusetts Avenue in Cambridge to Boston. (By the way, MIT named the span Harvard Bridge, even though it is located next to the MIT campus. The school considered it an example of inferior engineering and gave the dubious honor to its archrival down Massachusetts Avenue.)

George Washington's Pheasants under Glass

Cambridge

Harvard's Museum of Natural History is an eclectic and eccentric collection of stuffed stuff, embalmed animals, and mounted fossils. It includes a dodo, giant tapeworms, a thirty-five-million-year-old bee, the world's largest frog, and the only known *Kronosaurus,* a 42-foot-long prehistoric marine reptile. The museum is also home to the Ware Collection of Blaschka Glass Models of Plants. The unique collection of lifelike plants made out of glass was the life's work and passion of Leopold Blaschka and his son Rudolph. There are over 3,000 plants representing more than 800 species.

A pair of George Washington's pheasants reside in a glass corner case, a gift to the founding father from the Marquis de Lafayette. When the pheasants died, a taxidermist had them stuffed and mounted. The birds must have overheard a foul (or is it fowl?) mouthed visitor, because they were recently put on indefinite loan to a museum in Philadelphia.

The museum building itself, at 26 Oxford Street in Cambridge, belongs in a museum. It's a nineteenth-century throwback to the days when museums had rich wood paneling on the walls, high ceilings, and white frosted globe lights. Set aside a couple of hours to see all of the exhibits, and be sure to stop by what may be the most curious oddity in the entire museum: the antique wooden telephone booth on the second-floor staircase. It may be the last of its kind in Cambridge, if not in all of Massachusetts, and it still works.

It Makes *War and Peace* Look Like a Skirmish

Cambridge

If you wanted to snuggle up for a little bedtime reading with the book *Bhutan: A Visual Odyssey Across the Last Himalayan Kingdom,* you'd better have a very big bed. Actually, the book is so big it could *be* your bed. According to the *Guinness Book of Records,* the 114-page tome is the largest commercial book ever published. It is 5

★ ★

Photo by Paul Parisi/Courtesy of Michael Hawley

Michael Hawley, publisher and author of *Bhutan: A Visual Odyssey Across the Last Himalayan Kingdom*, standing next to the world's largest published book at Acme Bookbinding, where the books are made.

feet high, opens to nearly 7 feet wide, and weighs more than 130 pounds. Two gallons of ink are needed to print a single book, each of which costs $10,000. Most of the proceeds go to charity, to send students from Bhutan abroad to study.

The hefty read is the creation of Michael Hawley, director of special projects at the Massachusetts Institute of Technology. Hawley was inspired by numerous trips to the remote Shangri-La kingdom. He also wanted to demonstrate state-of-the art publishing technology.

Bhutan's leaders have charted a unique course for their country. The government's stated economic plan is to achieve the highest level of "gross national happiness." Television was not even allowed into the country until 1999, no doubt because the Bhutanese are very big readers.

The Acme Bookbinding Company in Charlestown, Massachusetts, is the exclusive builder of *Bhutan: A Visual Odyssey Across the Last Himalayan Kingdom.* Acme calls itself not only "the world's oldest book bindery," but also the world's "largest book" bindery. Acme has more information about the big book on its Web site, www.acme book.com/index/2003/12/15.

For Solving Really Big Problems

Cambridge

It's only fitting and proper that the nation's numero uno school for nerds—MIT—is the home to one of the world's largest collections of that icon of nerdom: the slide rule.

In 2005, after months of intense negotiations, the MIT museum became the permanent repository of the Keuffel & Esser Company Slide Rule Collection. The New Jersey firm was the largest producer of the anti-quated calculators in the United States. Among the

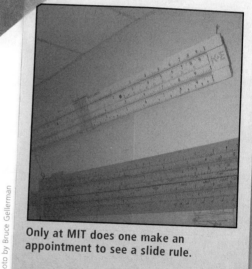

Photo by Bruce Gellerman

Only at MIT does one make an appointment to see a slide rule.

more than 600 historic slip slicks are a rare three-sided brass rule and giant 2.5-meter-long models used for demonstration purposes

Museum curator Deborah Douglas calls the slide rule the most important technology of the twentieth century that historians have not studied yet. Not far from the museum MIT engineers used slide rules to design the first lunar lander.

The slide rule collection is currently housed in the basement of the museum and can be see by special appointment. Bring a pocket protector and you'll fit right in.

For further information call (617) 253-4444 or visit http://web.mit .edu/museum.

Who Said Grime Doesn't Pay?

Cambridge

Since 1977, Elizabeth Magliozzi's sons have been driving radio listeners nuts and sending them reaching for their dials. Her boys, Tom and Ray, better known as Click and Clack of the weekly show *Car Talk,* are a public-radio phenomenon. These days they have two million listeners a week, from Sweden to Sheboygan. The gregarious grease monkeys are a mega-industry perpetually trying to unload their books, records, T-shirts, and whatever else they can get away with on their

Photo by Bruce Gellerman

Car Talk Plaza, appropriately located above the Curious George shop in Harvard Square, is the intergalactic headquarters of public radio grease monkeys Click and Clack.

shameless e-commerce Web site. The entire shenanigans come out of *Car Talk*'s dumpy offices high above Harvard Square in Cambridge, aka "our fair city," and can be found above the Curious George store at the intersection of Massachusetts Avenue and JFK Street.

Whatever you do, don't drive like these brothers.

The Thais That Bind
Cambridge

In Cambridge, at an intersection at the edge of Brattle Square (which is actually just an intersection on the edge of Harvard Square), you will find yet another square with a curious name. King Bhumibol Adulyadei Square commemorates the reign of the only monarch born on American soil. His Majesty, King Bhumibol of Thailand, was born at Mount Auburn Hospital in Cambridge in 1927 while his parents studied medicine at Harvard.

King Bhumibol ascended to the Thai throne in 1946, and in 2000 he became the longest-reigning ruler in the world. King Bhumibol is also the only reigning monarch ever to win a gold medal—or any medal, for that matter—at an international sporting event. He won a medal for sailing in the Southeast Asian Peninsular Games. The King was also the first member of a royal family ever to receive a patent. In 2003 he received his fourth patent, for inventing an artificial rain-making technique.

A photograph of the King can be found next to the elevators on the maternity floor at Mount Auburn Hospital.

If you want to learn more about the Cambridge-Thailand connection, ask for Joe at the Union Oyster House in Boston. In addition to being the owner of the restaurant, Joe Milano is Honorary Consul of Thailand.

Harvard University's Famous Overachieving Non-Grads
Cambridge

Some of the most distinguished people in the world have earned diplomas from Harvard University, including seven U.S. presidents, poet T. S. Eliot, authors Norman Mailer and John Updike, educator W. E. B. DuBois, jurist Oliver Wendell Holmes, Senator Elizabeth Dole, and many more household names.

And then there is the list of equally distinguished Harvard students who walked the same hallowed halls but never graduated. Among those who dropped out of Harvard or were otherwise "excused" are actor Matt Damon; poets Robert Lowell, Robert Frost, and Ogden Nash; and Edwin Land, inventor of the Polaroid camera and holder of more than 500 patents. R. Buckminster Fuller dropped out twice— once during midterms so he could take a dancer and her entire chorus to dinner. William Randolph Hearst got the boot after sending personally inscribed chamber pots to his professors while they were considering his academic probation, and bazillionaire Bill Gates left Harvard in his junior year to devote his energies to his fledgling start-up, Microsoft.

Pop singer Bonnie Raitt never made it through. Neither did folk singer Pete Seeger, although he was honored years later with the Harvard Arts Medal, telling the crowd that he "was tempted to accept [it] on behalf of all Harvard dropouts."

The Archive of Useless Research

Cambridge

At last count, there were fifty-six current or former members of the MIT community who had won a Nobel Prize. MIT is a center for superb scholarship, intellectual excellence, innovative entrepreneurship, and some of the craziest, crackpot pseudoscientific research you will ever find in one place. In room 14N–118 of the Hayden Library's Special Collections, collection number MC 187 consists of six large boxes known as MIT's Archive of Useless Research. It's a reminder that sometimes scientific exploration respects no boundaries, even when it should.

The archive began at MIT's Engineering Library as "the American Institute of Useless Research," a collection of crank files sent to the

Hasty, Not Tasty, Pudding

Harvard University's Hasty Pudding club was founded in 1790 as a secret social society. The club is named after a traditional American porridge made with milk and corn, which is required to be served at every meeting. Membership in the Pudding is selective and includes five U.S. presidents (John Adams, John Quincy Adams, Teddy Roosevelt, FDR, and JFK).

In 1881 the club formed The Hasty Pudding Theatricals club and, today, is the nation's oldest theater company. For the past few decades male members of the organization have dressed up in drag and awarded man and woman of the year awards—a hasty pudding pot. Recipient John Wayne showed up in Harvard Square in an M-113 armored personnel carrier. Other winners of the pot include John Travolta, Bob Hope, and Samuel L. Jackson. Female winners include Katharine Hepburn, Mamie Eisenhower, Jane Fonda, and Cher.

Hasty pudding has played a role in the school's history from the very start. Harvard College's first schoolmaster was fired for allegedly beating one of his students, and his wife reportedly served students pudding with goat dung in it.

★ ★

school's researchers over the years. In 1940 Albert Ingalls, an editor for *Scientific American,* began adding useless but invaluable research that had come his way, and the Institute morphed into today's current archive. Although the archive stopped adding to the collection in 1965, it certainly was not for lack of ongoing kooky research.

The collection is a celebration of screwball science, unpublished articles, self-published books, and rejected theories sent to MIT researchers over the years and deemed deserving of preservation for posterity. Included are such breakthrough studies as "Darwin as a Pirate" and "The Riddle of the Universe *Solved*."

The archive can be seen at the Hayden Library, 160 Memorial Drive, Cambridge. The archivist suggests you call ahead at (617) 253-5690 so they can retrieve this fascinating collection in advance of your visit.

Bring your aluminum foil helmet.

It's Kismet, the Robo Sapien
Cambridge

Kismet is a moody infant. One minute sad; the next happy; a few seconds later, angry; then calm, bored, or surprised. If Kismet were a baby with colic, you could understand, but Kismet isn't a baby. Kismet is a robot—more accurately, a seven-pound robot head. Still, that is enough to land Kismet in the *Guinness Book of Records* for being the most emotionally responsive robot ever built.

Created by Dr. Cynthia Breazeal at the Massachusetts Institute of Technology, Kismet has movable facial features that can express basic human emotions, and electronic eyes and ears to interact with its environment and people. If you stop playing with Kismet, it acts bored; shake a doll in front of the dismembered head and it looks agitated. Kismet's gremlinlike features are powered by twenty-one motors and fifteen huge computers.

It is a good thing that Kismet has been retired to the MIT Museum, or it would have the look of envy that comes with sibling

★ ★

Photo by Bruce Gellerman

Kismet is the world's most expressive robot, but MIT robo-scientists did not quit while they were ahead. They have built a robot with a body, too.

rivalry. Back in the lab, Kismet has a big brother, COG, a 7-foot-tall artificial humanoid with arms, hands, a sense of touch, and the ability to talk. To make COG even more humanlike, researchers are working on a biochemical system to run it. Ultimately, it is hoped that COG will have the intelligence equivalence of a two-year-old child.

It's the stuff of science fiction, complete with profound philosophical implications. Of course, there are also practical concerns. Perhaps robo-researchers will know they have gone too far when the machines they create in their own image start asking for the car keys.

You can see Kismet and videos of it interacting with its creator at the MIT Museum, 265 Massachusetts Avenue. For more information, check out the museum's Web site, http://web.mit.edu/museum/ or call (617) 253-4444.

MIT Eager Beavers Reach for the Brass Rat
Cambridge

Graduates of the Massachusetts Institute of Technology receive a special badge of honor and symbol of intellectual distinction and achievement for studying day and night, sweating through brain-bending tests, and ruining their social lives. It's a brass rat. That's the

By tradition, the Brass Rat contains secret codes and symbols. In this design, hidden in the waves of the Charles River along the MIT campus, are the letters "A=B=C=P," representing the fact that the class of 2005 was the last to have pass/no record in their entire freshman year. Notice the hand of the student drowning in the river. The "ZZZ" to the right of the beaver's tail is for the constant attention to the student's lack of sleep. See if you can find the letters IHTFP.

name affectionately bestowed on MIT's class ring, which, since 1930, has featured the MIT mascot, the beaver. After all, like MIT students, beavers are nocturnal, industrious, and master builders, but on the ring, the beaver, which is an aquatic rodent, looks like a rat. Hence the nickname.

The design changes each year, created by a committee from each class that spends the better part of a year meeting in secret. By tradition the design contains the letters *IHTFP,* an acronym with a number of interpretations underscoring the love-hate relationship MIT students have with their school. Some say it means "I Have Truly Found Perfection." Others say it stands for "I Hate This !$@#% Place." Both camps proudly wear the brass rat; nearly 95 percent of the student body buys one.

Another tradition is the way the students wear their rings, which they purchase in their sophomore year. As undergraduates, the bottom of the beaver faces in toward the student; at the graduation ceremony, the class *en masse* removes the rings and turns them the other way. The saying is that while they are students, the beaver excretes on them, but after they graduate, it excretes on the world.

Truth Be Told, Harvard's Statue Is a Liar
Cambridge

For a university whose motto is "Veritas," you would expect the truth, the whole truth, and nothing but the truth. But check out the statue of the venerable school's namesake, John Harvard, standing right in front of University Hall. It's a pack of lies. In fact, it is called the Statue of Three Lies.

The inscription beneath the statue reads JOHN HARVARD, FOUNDER, 1638. Not a word of it is true.

The college (it was a college back then) was founded in 1636 by the Massachusetts Bay Colony in what was then the village of Newtowne and later became Cambridge. John Harvard was an early benefactor to the college, he was its first professor, he erected Harvard's first

The Statue of Three Lies sits in Harvard Yard.

Photo by Bruce Gellerman

building, and planted its first apple orchard. One thing John Harvard wasn't? He wasn't the founder. The college was named for him in *1639* after he donated his library to the school. Nor is the statue a likeness of John Harvard. There were no pictures or images of him, so the sculptor Daniel Chester French chose a student at random as his model and dressed him in seventeenth-century garb.

And truth be told, the statue actually contains four, not three, lies. The statue is NOT of John Harvard, who was NOT the founder of Harvard University, which was NOT founded in 1638, and does NOT stand in Harvard Yard in front of University Hall. He sits.

While John Harvard's non-legacy lives on, his original bequest of 400 books, which got the school named after him, was destroyed in a fire in 1764. Only one book survived: *Christian Warfare Against the Devil, World and Flesh.* It's on display at the Houghton Library in Harvard Yard.

What You Get When You Cross Einstein with the Three Stooges

Cambridge

You have to hand it to those techno-nerds at MIT: They sure know how to hack. Since the technical institute first opened in 1861, the brainy students have been pulling creative practical jokes that are both technically challenging and devilishly clever. Over the years the ever-more-ambitious hacks, as they are called, have become an institution.

Some pranks have been elegantly simple, like the stoplight altered to read "don't walk—chew," instead of "walk." Others were more scientifically challenging. In 1976, for example, hackers consulted an arachnologist and used an electron microscope to study spider webs before weaving a wicked-big one out of 1,250 feet of wire and rope and installing it in a campus building. The real trick, as with all hacks, was not to get snared by the police.

In 1982, during the Harvard-Yale football game, hackers hid a weather balloon inscribed with "MIT" under the turf of Harvard's 40-yard line. The pranksters inflated the balloon by remote control. The crowd and teams looked aghast as the balloon grew to 6 feet in diameter and exploded in a burst of white smoke. MIT one, Harvard-Yale zero.

MIT's famed domes have long been favorite places for hackers to pull their pranks. One Halloween, hackers dressed the Great Dome in a 20-foot-tall witch's hat. Another year the huge dome was transformed into the Star Wars robot R2D2. The dome has been topped with a working telephone booth that rang when officials tried to remove it. Hackers also turned the

Photo by Bruce Gellerman

The 1982 weather balloon inflator that disrupted the Harvard-Yale football game.

pinnacle into a parking space for a full-size replica of a campus police car, complete with working lights, with a box of doughnuts on the front seat.

Hacks have to be harmless as well as humorous. Self-deprecating humor works well. In 1996 MIT student hackers transformed the Great Dome into a giant, working propeller beanie. Who says nerds have no sense of humor?

A Place to Be Caught Dead In
Cambridge

There are almost as many people buried in Mount Auburn Cemetery in Cambridge (93,000 and counting) as there are living in the city (101,000). The historic cemetery is a popular place for very permanent residents and visitors alike. More than 200,000 people a year visit the burial grounds, making it one of Cambridge's most popular tourist destinations.

Founded in 1831 by the Massachusetts Horticultural Society, Mount Auburn was the first landscaped cemetery in America. Its creation marked a dramatic change in the prevailing attitudes about death and burial, as it was designed not only to be a decent place of interment but also to serve as a cultural institution. Mount Auburn, unlike other early city cemeteries, utilized landscape architecture in its planning. This influenced the creation of no less than fifteen other park-cemeteries in the United States. Besides its obvious function, Mount Auburn also serves as a museum, a sculpture garden, an arboretum, and a wildlife sanctuary.

Among the notables making the 175-acre garden their final residence are Oliver Wendell Holmes, Winslow Homer, Fanny Farmer, B. F. Skinner, and Buckminster Fuller.

The grave site of Mary Baker Eddy, founder of the Church of Christ, Scientist, is one of the more spectacular. And contrary to long-standing rumors, she did not have a telephone installed in her crypt. During the construction of her monument, Eddy's body was kept in the cemetery's receiving vault. A guard was hired to stay with the body until it was interred and the tomb was sealed. A telephone was installed at the receiving vault for the guard's use during that period. There was never a phone at Eddy's monument.

Mount Auburn Cemetery is open every day of the year from 8:00 a.m. to 5:00 p.m. During daylight saving time hours are extended to 7:00 p.m. Drive-by and walking audio tours are available on tape for rent or purchase at the entrance gate or the office. The cemetery is located at 580 Mount Auburn Street, Cambridge. For additional information call (617) 547-7105.

The Original Airhead and His Ignoble Ig Nobel Prizes
Cambridge

Marc Abrahams is an airhead and proud of it. In fact, as publisher of the *Annals of Improbable Research,* or *AIR,* Abrahams is head airhead. *AIR* is what would happen if the editors of *Mad* magazine and the *National Lampoon* conspired to publish *Scientific American.* And lest you think being an airhead is somehow an ignoble distinction, the magazine has eight Nobel Prize laureates on its editorial board.

Since 1990 *AIR* has injected spoofs, parodies, and satires into the otherwise straitlaced world of science and scientists. Examples of typical articles include: "Why the Chicken Must Come First," "Mass Strandings of Horseshoe Crabs," and an inquiry titled "What Does Crime Taste Like?" A regular feature queries Nobel Prize winners with the most pressing questions of our time, such as, "Do you shave with a blade razor or electric?" and "Do you often give people nicknames?"

The highlight of the year for Abrahams and *AIR* is the annual Ig Nobel Prize ceremony, honoring people whose achievements "cannot or should not be reproduced." This takeoff on the Stockholm proceedings includes some of the pomp, along with a heavy dose of Swedish slapstick. Abrahams sports a tuxedo and top hat to announce the winners, including a biologist who studied how various flavors of chewing gum affect brain waves. Karl Kruszelnicki of the University of Sydney received his Ig Nobel Prize for his comprehensive survey of human belly button lint: who gets it, when, what color, and how much. Chris McManus of University College, London, was honored for his excruciatingly balanced report, "Scrotal Asymmetry in Man and in Ancient Sculpture." The 2007 Ig Nobel in Medicine went to Brian Witcombe of Gloucester, England, and Dan Meyer of Antioch, Tennessee, for their penetrating study, "Sword Swallowing and Its Side Effects." That year's Peace Prize went to the Air Force Research Laboratory in Dayton, Ohio, for instigating research and development on a chemical weapon—the so-called "gay bomb"—that will make enemy soldiers become sexually irresistible to each other.

The Ig ceremony, featuring opera, interpretive dance by Nobel laureates, and drama, takes place in Sanders Theatre at Harvard University the first week of October and is broadcast on National Public Radio's *Science Friday,* the day after Thanksgiving. Check your local listings and be prepared to fall out of your seat.

Heard on the Grapevine:
Sometimes You Don't Reap What You Sow
Concord

Ephraim Wales Bull is buried in Concord's Sleepy Hollow Cemetery alongside some very distinguished company. Here, along Authors Ridge, you will find the grave sites of Henry Thoreau (1862), Nathaniel Hawthorne (1864), Ralph Waldo Emerson (1882), and Louisa May Alcott (1888) and her father, Bronson Alcott (1888). Okay, admittedly Ephraim Wales Bull's name is not as familiar as these literary greats, but his contribution to the nation looms just as large. You see, Ephraim Wales Bull is the "father of the Concord grape." Today U.S. grape farmers harvest more Concord grapes than all other varieties combined.

Now, by all rights you should not even be able to grow grapes in Massachusetts. The grape killing frost comes early in fall and lasts until late spring. Nevertheless, Bull was, well, bullheaded. He persevered for ten years to develop his plump, purple berry, testing thousand of seedlings on his Concord farm before he came across his hardy, all-American variety.

Bull sold cuttings from his divine vine for $1,000 each, yet despite the horticultural breakthrough he died a poor man. His gravestone is inscribed, "He sowed—others reaped."

Among those who reaped was Vineland, New Jersey, dentist Thomas Welch, who began squeezing Bull's grapes with vigor in 1869. His company, Welch's, began producing unfermented sacramental wine. In 1913 Secretary of State William Jennings Bryan served Welch's Grape Juice instead of wine at a state dinner for the outgoing British ambassador. The uproar in the press resulted in months of free publicity.

Ephraim Wales Bull's farmhouse, Grapevine Cottage, still stands on Lexington Road. The original vine from which all of the world's Concord grapes are descendants can still be seen.

An interesting note: A Massachusetts law regulates the taking of photographs and movies in a public cemetery for commercial purposes. To receive permission to do so, contact the cemetery department at (978) 318-3233.

Sleepy Hollow Cemetery is on Bedford Street just off the rotary in the center of Concord.

Dead Pet in Dedham
Dedham

Founded in 1907 Pine Ridge Cemetery for Small Animals is the oldest continuously operated pet cemetery in the country. It's run by the Animal Rescue League of Boston.

The bucolic twenty-eight-acre site is the final resting place for over ten thousand animals including many celebrity pets. Among the notables are horses from Boston Police Department's mounted unit and Lizzie Borden's beloved bowsers: Donald Stuart, Royal Nelson, and Laddie Miller. Oddly Borden's dogs' tombstone is an exact replica of the one belonging to her parents in Falls River, Massachusetts.

Polar explorer Richard Byrd's terrier Igloo is also buried in the cemetery. A pinkish stone chiseled in the shape of an iceberg with the carved inscription IGLOO marks the spot. Byrd's faithful companion accompanied him on expeditions to both the Arctic and Antarctic.

For information contact the Pine Ridge Animal Center, 238 Pine Street, (781) 326-0729.

Art Too Bad to Be Ignored
Dedham

The Museum of Bad Art (MOBA) is testimony to the wisdom of writer Marshall McLuhan, who said, "Art is anything you can get away with." The museum is dedicated to "the collection, preservation, exhibition, and celebration of bad art in all its forms and all its glory." In short, it's a permanent repository for art too bad to be ignored.

What started out in 1995 in a suburban basement as a humble assemblage of spectacularly awful artwork has evolved into a full-fledged museum, complete with the requisite gift shop. The MOBA

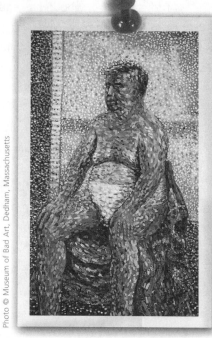

Photo © Museum of Bad Art, Dedham, Massachusetts

Sunday on the Pot with George sits in the Museum of Bad Art.

holds a special place near and dear to connoisseurs of misunderstood masterpieces. It's also located within earshot of the men's room at the Dedham Community Theater.

To qualify for an esteemed place in the museum's collection, an artist should display ambition that vastly exceeds his or her ability. One classic museum piece, for example, portrays a naked woman in stiletto heels and red leg warmers sitting on a stool milking a unicorn. The unicorn looks startled but not displeased by the experience. It's truly a head-snapping, jaw-dropping sight.

MOBA curators are constantly searching Salvation Army stores and landfills in search of the highest-caliber bad art. The majority of the collection came from bequests of the public refuse system. Submissions are always welcome. The curators have imposed a $6.50 limit on acquiring new works but once offered twice that amount as a reward for a piece that was stolen. (Alas, even at that price the painting was never recovered.)

MOBA's permanent gallery is in the basement of the Dedham Community Theater, 580 High Street in Dedham Center. For more information visit www.glyphs.com/moba.

Tunnel Vision on a Hill
Lexington

It's called the Big Dig House because it was constructed using 6,000 tons of concrete and steel recycled from Boston's major underground highway project. Built in 2003 the unusual home weighs more than a million pounds, three times that of an average home of comparable size.

Paul Pedini built the hefty house because he thought it would be a shame if that part of history—the giant steel girders and 100-foot long pre-fab, concrete slabs, used in constructing temporary ramps for Boston's Big Dig Project—were to be scrapped. Instead, Pedini, an engineer who worked for one of the Big Dig's major contractors, got the materials for free and brought them to this hilltop in Lexington. Fellow workers thought he was crazy.

The 4,300 square foot contemporary home has won numerous design awards and features four bedrooms, a thousand-square-foot kitchen/family room and twenty-six-foot ceilings. In keeping with the "waste not, want not" philosophy, the Big Dig House is eco-friendly. A 600-gallon cistern below the garage floor provides water for the rooftop garden. The super-strong roof supports three feet of soil, boulders, and two Foo Dog statues made of marble that once stood guard in Boston's Chinatown.

Boston's Big Dig project was supposed to take less than 5 years and cost 5 billion dollars. Instead, it took 15 years and 15 billion dollars. In comparison, the Big Dig House cost $645,000 to construct, it went up in just a few days, and unlike the tunnel, the home doesn't leak. The house is located at 8 Bird Hill Road.

The Man Who Invented Money
Lexington

Charles Ponzi was a small man with a taste for the finer things in life. He loved luxurious houses and large automobiles, and he dressed in the finest suits, with top hat and walking stick. Too bad he couldn't afford them. No matter; the former dishwasher, convicted smuggler, and scam artist was "the man who invented money." At the peak of his pyramid scheme in 1919, Ponzi was raking in a million dollars a week. He created 40,000 "millionaires" and at one point sauntered into the Hanover Trust Company, opened a suitcase with $3 million in cash, and bought a controlling interest in the bank.

The pyramid scam is probably as old as, well, the pyramids. But it took Charles Ponzi, an Italian immigrant living in Boston, to raise it to new heights in the world of modern finance. The scam is simple: Borrow from Peter to pay back money you borrowed from Paul. Repeat over and over again and, voila: You have a Ponzi scheme. A bit like Social Security, the system works as long as you bring in enough new investors at the bottom to support those at the top of the pyramid.

Ponzi employed a new twist on the old scam. He promised investors a 50 percent return on their money in ninety days if they purchased international postal reply coupons, which were coupons he bought overseas for a penny and exchanged in the United States for six cents. (Unfortunately, it wound up costing more money to ship and exchange the coupons than they were worth here, but that was a minor detail to Ponzi.)

Ponzi's house of reply coupons finally collapsed when a Boston newspaper questioned the con. Ultimately, five banks went belly-up in the scam. Ponzi wound up spending seven years in a Boston jail and died penniless in Rio de Janeiro. He left behind an unfinished manuscript for a book, appropriately titled *The Fall of Mr. Ponzi*.

As Ponzi's wife, Sophie, watched, investigators searched their twenty-room mansion in Lexington, Massachusetts, for securities and evidence of fraud. All they found were one hundred gallons of home-made Italian wine.

The stucco house in Lexington still stands. It's the third on the right on Slocumb Street, off Massachusetts Avenue.

Black Dahlia Monument
Medford

One of the stranger monuments in Massachusetts was designed and paid for by documentary filmmaker Kyle J. Wood, whose film *Medford Girl* chronicles the life and death of Elizabeth Short, "the Black Dahlia." Short was born in Hyde Park, Massachusetts, in 1924 and grew up in Medford. She quit school at age sixteen, seeking fame and fortune in Hollywood. Her mutilated body, severed in half at the waist, was found in a vacant lot in Hollywood in 1947—one of the most celebrated unsolved mysteries of its time. In 2006 director Brian De Palma made a feature film about the case.

The Black Dahlia monument is located at 115 Salem Street in Medford.

Jumbo in a Jar
Medford

Although students at Tufts University are called Jumbos, it's not that they are especially big. They hold that nickname because the school's

★ ★

original mascot was P. T. Barnum's famous elephant, Jumbo. Born in Africa in 1859, Jumbo grew to 12 feet high at the shoulder and weighed more than six tons. Barnum, ever the showman, billed the huge pachyderm as the largest land animal ever in captivity. Big as he was, today all that remains of Jumbo are some ashes stored in a fourteen-ounce Peter Pan peanut butter jar locked in the safe of the school's athletic director.

A jar of crunchy Peter Pan peanut butter is the final resting place of Jumbo the Elephant.

Photo by Bruce Gellerman

The story of how Jumbo went from circus center ring to a crunchy peanut butter jar at college begins in 1882, when Barnum bought Jumbo from the London Zoo for $10,000. Jumbo traveled the circus circuit in a specially built railroad car until 1885, when he was hit by a train and died. The pachyderm underwent taxidermy, and the stuffed hide was taken on a four-year world tour. Jumbo then came to his final resting place at the Barnum Museum at Tufts University, where the ringmaster was a school trustee. Jumbo stood there for eighty-six years, while generations of students stuffed his trunk with pennies and pulled his tail for good luck on tests. In 1942 Jumbo underwent an overhaul, and his original over-tugged tail was archived at the school's library.

All was well until 1975, when a fire destroyed the Barnum building, rendering everything, including the elephant, into a pile of ashes. Mindful of the mascot's importance to Tufts, a member of the school's athletic department scooped up what he assumed were Jumbo's ashes and put them into the container he had on hand—an empty peanut butter jar—which is now kept in a safe in the athletic director's office. To this day Tufts Jumbos rub the jar for luck just before a big game.

The tail on Jumbo's tush is in Tufts' Tisch Library Digital Collections and Archives. Say that three times fast and win a Kewpie doll.

Elephant Man Has a Herd Instinct

Medford

It's probably a good thing that John Baronian did not attend the University of California–Santa Cruz or Cal State–Long Beach. Otherwise, you might be reading about the world's largest collection of banana

Photo by Bruce Gellerman

"Mr. Tufts," John Baronian, with members of his mini-elephant menagerie.

★ ★

slugs or dirtbags. Baronian, you see, collected miniature models of his alma mater's mascot. As luck would have it, he went to Tufts University, home of Jumbo, the elephant, and so for fifty years Baronian collected elephant figurines.

Baronian began gathering his mini-menagerie of mini *objets de pachyderm* soon after graduation. Today he has more than 4,000 figurines in his collection—probably the largest assemblage of pachyderm art on the planet. (If you've heard of a bigger herd, let him know.) He has elephants made out of wood, glass, bronze, porcelain, and yes, ivory. He even has an elephant crafted out of camel hide. There are elephant ashtrays, mugs, jewelry, and bookends and a pachyderm jigsaw puzzle.

Baronian is not just any Jumbo alum, he's *the* jumbo Jumbo supporter. On campus he is known as "Mr. Tufts" for his long volunteer service and generosity to the university. A man with a big heart and a herd to match, he ran out of space for the collection in his home, so he donated it to the school. It now resides in the Remis Sculpture Court at the Aidekman Arts Center, 40R Talbot Avenue on Tufts's Medford campus. Call ahead for hours at (617) 627-3518.

This Sign Will Sleigh You

Medford

We hate dashing your Christmas spirit, but one of the most popular songs sung around the holiday has nothing to do with Christmas. "Jingle Bells" was written by Medford resident James Pierpont in 1850, inspired by the annual one-horse open-sleigh races on Salem and Pleasant Streets between Medford Square and Malden Square. Pierpont penned the racy little ditty in Simpson's Tavern, a boardinghouse that had the only piano in town. The lyrics tell the story of picking up girls while hot-rodding through the snow.

The song was originally titled "One-Horse Open Sleigh," and initially it was a flop. But after a Boston publishing house released it as "Jingle Bells" in 1859, the rest was history, albeit controversial history. It seems that Savannah, Georgia, thinks it's the "Jingle Bells capital of the world" because Pierpont was living there when the song was released and is also buried there. However, a plaque at 21 High Street near the corner of Forest Street in Medford sets things right. As residents in Medford are quick to point out, Pierpont wrote the tune while in Massachusetts . . . and racing a sleigh in snowless Savannah doesn't make much sense, anyway. (In fairness to Savannah, it too has a plaque commemorating the composer of "Jingle Bells.")

The Big Skinny

It takes big bucks to attend Harvard University, so perhaps it's only fitting that Harvard Square was the scene for showing off the world's largest wallet. Dubbed The Big Skinny, the back-pocket-busting wallet measured 10 feet high and 21 feet long when opened, but was only a quarter-of-an-inch thick.

The weird wallet was sewn from Harvard crimson-colored microfiber made by the Cambridge, Massachusetts, based Big Skinny Corporation. The family owned firm, which claims it makes the world's thinnest, smallest, and lightest wallets, created The Big Skinny to encourage people during the Christmas season in 2010 to open up their wallets to non-profit organizations and local charities.

It took 160 hours for company seamstresses to sew The Big Skinny. They suffered 452 pin pricks while stitching together 171 feet of material, 90 feet of velcro and 20 feet of clear plastic. When done the wallet weighed 128 pounds, requiring 8 wheels to make it portable. A notary witnessed and measured the finished product, certifying it for the Guinness Book of World Records. The previous record holder was a paltry 6.5 foot by 4 foot.

★ ★

Medford is also where the lyrics for another famous festive song were written. Town resident Lydia Maria Child's poem "Boy's Thanksgiving" became the song "Over the River and Through the Woods." Child lived in the Greek Revival house at 114 Ashland Street on the corner of Salem Street, not far from where Pierpont sleighed them with "Jingle Bells." Behind Child's house are the woods she went through and the Mystic River over which she traveled to get to Grandfather's house. We're told the horse knows the way.

The Cockroaches That Almost Ate Natick
Natick

On the battlefield of the future, it may be the suit that makes the soldier. The uniforms warriors will wear decades from now are being designed at the U.S. Army Soldier Systems Center in Natick, about 20 miles due west of Boston.

The center is a high-tech laboratory that designs and develops everything a soldier wears, carries, or consumes. Established in 1954, the lab created the technology that led to freeze-dried food. During the Vietnam War it created a boot sole in the shape of a barefooted Vietcong soldier to confuse the enemy, and it designed a camouflage Jewish prayer shawl.

The Natick lab is best known for developing the field combat rations called MREs, or Meals Ready to Eat. The MRE menus provide high-calorie, relatively palatable foods with a shelf life that rivals enriched uranium.

In 1974 army scientists were experimenting with a new way to control pests by zapping them with ultraviolet rays. Unfortunately, the experiment went out of control. The zapped bugs were put in plastic bags with a chemical, then disposed of at a local dump. The chemical ate through the bags, and the bugs' eggs hatched and escaped into Natick. The insects, 4-inch flying Madagascar cockroaches, drove residents buggy. The cockroaches were resistant to most pesticides, and the army had to call in the "big guns" and use DDT.

Researchers at the Natick facility are now working on projects designed to protect our men and women in uniform with fabrics that change color depending on their surroundings, and spray-on clothing.

Due to budget cuts and the cost of fighting current wars, the Soldier Systems Center is not conducting tours for the public. However, its Web site, www.natick.army.mil, provides a good overview of the ongoing research. The bugs won't get out as easy that way, either.

Newton's Contribution to Cookiedom

Newton

In 1891 James Henry Mitchell invented a contraption that could squish figs into jam and smear the substance between two layers of soft, crumbly cookie dough. The cookies were a smash hit, and soon the Kennedy Biscuit Works in Cambridge was turning them out by the truckload.

The famous cookie got its name from the plant manager at the bakery, who liked to name his cookies and crackers after surrounding Massachusetts towns. Thankfully he didn't decide to dub his latest concoction after Cow Yard, Massachusetts, or Marblehead, and instead settled on the suburban city of Newton.

Photo courtesy of Newton History Museum at the Jackson Homestead

The Big Fig, as usual, is right in the middle of things.

An apartment building now stands at 129 Franklin Street on the site near MIT where the original factory baked Fig Newtons by the billions. Several of the original biscuit ovens have been preserved there, and above the front door is a giant rendition of the cookie itself.

Nabisco Brands eventually bought the Kennedy Biscuit Works, and to commemorate the one-hundredth anniversary of the Fig Newton, it threw a bash for the cookies' namesake community. The Big Fig acted like the fruit he is and, of course, was right in the center of things.

Beautiful Blabbermouth Bridge
Newton

Echo Bridge is one of the highest stone arches in the world—its crown is 51 feet above the Charles River—but what makes it truly remarkable is that, as the name implies, the bridge talks back to you, and back to you, and back to you.

Built in 1876 to carry water to Boston, the 500-foot-long aqueduct consists of seven arches. The largest segment, spanning the Charles, is 130 feet long, and it is this arch that produces the remarkable reverberation. It's said that on a still day the granite walls can bounce a human voice back and forth as many as eighteen times. (Be forewarned: You might not always like the responses you get. Try yelling the word *July* under the archway.)

For a spectacular view of the Charles River, stand atop the bridge's pedestrian promenade. The span is located at the end of Chestnut Street, north of Route 9 in the Upper Charles River Reservation. It is open from dawn to dusk year-round.

Marathon Man
Newton

John Kelley liked to run and run and run. Between 1928 and 1992, John "the Elder" Kelley, a Massachusetts native, ran the Boston Marathon sixty-one times, finishing all but three races. He came in first in two races (1935 and 1945), took second place a record seven times, and finished in the top ten eighteen times.

Photo by Bruce Gellerman

At the foot of Heart Break Hill is the monument to Boston Marathon man John Kelley.

Kelley ran his last marathon when he was eighty-five and became the first road runner elected to the National Track and Field Hall of Fame. Officials waived the retirement rule because they figured he might never retire. Kelley died on October 6, 2004, at the age of 97. He was selected "Runner of the Century" by *Runner's World* magazine.

A statue dedicated to the amazing marathoner as a young man and as an older participant is located at Heart Break Hill, on the corner of Walnut Street and Commonwealth Avenue in Newton, across from City Hall.

In the 1996 centennial running of the Boston Marathon, 39,708 official entrants participated in the race. According to the *Guinness Book of Records,* this is the largest number of runners in a single race in history.

Maybe It Was So the Worms Didn't Have to Use the Stairs?
Newton

It's called simply the Old Stone Barn, but don't let the plain name deceive you. This is one strange structure. Built in 1839, the huge stone building (100 feet by 50 feet) has an architectural feature you don't see every day: All four stories have access to ground level. The architectural feat was accomplished by building the barn into dirt

Photo courtesy of Newton History Museum at the Jackson Homestead, Newton

The Old Stone Barn has access to ground level from all four stories.

embankments. The sub-basement faces the east; the basement, the south; the first floor, the west; and the second floor, the north, off Cliff Road.

Historians are not sure why the barn was built this way, or even if it was originally intended to be a barn. The owner, Otis Pette Sr., never told anyone why he had it constructed. After it was built it lay empty for years, until it was used as a stable. Some speculate that Pette meant for the barn to house a silkworm hatchery and constructed it out of stone because his textile factory had burned to the ground earlier that year. However, the silkworm industry quickly unraveled in colonial New England. (The cold killed the mulberry bushes.)

The Old Stone Barn, or whatever it was, still stands and is used as a warehouse. It can be seen at 38–44 Oak Street, off Cliff Road in Newton Upper Falls.

What the Fluff

Somerville

Sure Somerville is the birthplace of Betty Davis and it's where the first telephone wire was installed, but the city's real claim to fame is for what resident Archibald Query concocted in 1917: Fluff. You know the marshmallow spread that forms the backbone of the fluffernutter sandwich?

Query whipped up the first batch of the goo in his basement kitchen on Springfield Street just off

Photo by Bruce Gellerman

The What The Fluff festival is held the last Saturday of September in Union Square, Somerville.

87

of Union Square. He sold the recipe three years later to H. Allen Durkee and Fred L. Mower, whose company continues to crank out the stuff in their Salem, Massachusetts, factory.

In 2006 then state senator Jarrett Barrios raised a flap over fluff when he proposed an amendment to a junk food bill that would have limited the serving of the white stuff in schools. A representative from Somerville countered the proposal with a suggestion to name the fluffernutter as the official state sandwich.

Nothin' became of the idea but on the last Saturday in September residents of Somerville pay homage to Query's contribution to tooth decay and celebrate WTF "What The Fluff" day. There's a cooking contest for the most creative fluff desert recipe, a fluffernutter eating contest, and dance routines featuring the Fluffettes.

Any Seat in a Storm

New England nor'easter snowstorms are legendary for their ferocity. So are folks from Somerville, Massachusetts. After residents shovel out their parking spaces along the city's narrow streets, they jealously guard their clearings by putting lawn chairs, chaise longues, even sofas in the street to hold "their" spots. It's not unusual to see bundled-up Somervillians sitting on their furniture, waiting for the family car to return.

Saving shoveled-out spots in the snow is a time-honored winter tradition in Somerville, and heaven help those who violate the unwritten rules of the road. If you do, make sure you have towing insurance and are prepared to buy four new tires.

One Artist You Definitely *Don't* Want to Paint Your Portrait

Watertown

Part of the permanent collection at the Armenian Library and Museum of America in Watertown, Massachusetts, are pictures painted by Dr. Jack Kevorkian. Known to many as "Doctor Death," Kevorkian is a controversial physician who promotes assisted suicide and has been jailed for practicing what he preaches. Kevorkian is also an oil painter of some note, and being an ethnic Armenian, he has donated a number of his works to the

Photo by Bruce Gellerman

Dr. Jack Kevorkian's *Very Still Life* hangs in the Armenian Library and Museum in Watertown.

Armenian Library and Museum. Two of his oils, *Very Still Life* and *Genocide,* are hanging in the museum at 65 Main Street, Watertown. For more information, call (617) 926-2562.

As the World Doesn't Turn

Wellesley

One of the largest worlds in the world can be found on the campus of Babson College in Wellesley. The giant Babson Globe was built in 1955. It weighs 21.5 tons and is 38 feet in diameter. It is literally meant to provide an out-of-this-world experience, to give you an idea of what Mother Earth would look like if you stood 5,000 miles away in space. Each inch on the steel ball represents 24 miles. The globe rotated on its base and spun on its axis until sometime in 1993,

Photo by Bruce Gellerman

The 21.5-ton globe at Babson College
stopped revolving in 1993.

when the mechanical turning-and-spinning device broke. The earth
has stood still ever since.

Truth be told, there are larger globes. The Unisphere, from the
1964 New York World's Fair in Queens, is 120 feet in diameter. The
world's current world record holder, Eartha, installed at the DeLorme
Map company in Yarmouth, Maine, is about 41 feet in diameter.

To get up close and personal with the Babson Globe, the onetime
largest world in the world, go to Babson College in Wellesley sometime during daylight hours. It's that giant round thing fixed in space
outside the Coleman Map Building. There is no admission charge.
Who says nothing in the world is free?

Understanding the Gravity of the Situation

Wellesley

It was Roger Babson's dream that what went up would not necessarily have to come down. To accomplish this gravity-defying feat, Babson created the Gravity Research Foundation in 1948. Its goal was to investigate ways to block and harness the force of gravity.

The idea of violating a basic law of physics may sound far out, but Babson was a man who had his feet firmly on the ground. A self-made millionaire who earned his money revolutionizing the financial services industry, Babson also founded two universities, ran for president of the United States against FDR (he came in third out of eight candidates), and authored forty-seven books.

In one of his books, *Gravity—Our Enemy No. 1,* Babson explained his quest to tame the pull of the earth. It was a personal battle, as he blamed gravity for his son's death in an airplane crash and for his sister's drowning, writing of the latter, "She was unable to fight gravity, which came up and seized her like a dragon and brought her to the bottom."

The Gravity Research Foundation, which recently relocated to Babson College in Wellesley, holds an annual convention and essay contest. Although the contest does attract its share of crackpots, it also receives submissions from some of the best minds of our time. Famed cosmologist Stephen Hawking has won the foundation's cash prize five times.

The foundation has also installed a number of granite monuments on college campuses where distinguished anti-gravity research was being done. One monument was installed in 1961 on the Tufts University campus in Somerville, Massachusetts, where it soon became a source of myth and mirth. THE INSCRIPTION READS: THIS MONUMENT HAS BEEN ERECTED BY THE GRAVITY RESEARCH FOUNDATION. IT IS TO REMIND STUDENTS OF THE BLESSINGS FORTHCOMING WHEN A SEMI-INSULATOR IS DISCOVERED IN ORDER TO HARNESS GRAVITY AS A FREE POWER AND REDUCE AIRPLANE ACCIDENTS.

The Massachusetts Vikings

Three public monuments in eastern Massachusetts lay claim that it was Viking Leif Eriksson in 1000, not Christopher Columbus in 1492, who was the first European to step foot on North America. The monuments were built by Eben Norton Horsford, a Harvard professor of chemistry turned amateur archaeologist who was convinced that "Leif the Lucky" was the first European in the New World.

Professor Horsford made a fortune in the mid-nineteenth century selling "Horsford's Cream of Tartar Substitute," a new-formula baking powder, and used the money to fund excavations in Cambridge, Weston, and Watertown. According to Horsford, Eriksson landed on Cape Cod, sailed up the Charles River, and built a house in what is now Cambridge. Horsford said he found some buried Norse artifacts near the intersection of Memorial Drive, Mount Auburn Street, and Gerry's Landing Road. He built a small monument there marking the spot.

Farther upstream stands Norumbega Tower. Horsford built the structure in 1889 to commemorate the site on which he believed the Vikings had constructed the legendary Norse settlement of the same name. A summary of Horsford's theory is engraved on a plaque on the tower. To see it, take Route 128 to Route 30 West to River Road North.

The third monument to Horsford's fanciful theory is located at Charlesgate East on Commonwealth Avenue, near Kenmore Square in Boston. It was unveiled in 1887 and depicts Leif the Lucky on a pedestal scanning the distant horizon. The back of the memorial is inscribed: LEIF THE DISCOVERER SON OF ERIK WHO SAILED FROM ICELAND AND LANDED ON THIS CONTINENT AD 1000.

Leif Eriksson near Kenmore Square.

Horsford's theories of Vikings in Cambridge were later debunked as just bunk, and he's considered a crackpot today. But recent scientific analysis of a controversial parchment drawing, the so-called Vinland Map, and an accompanying manuscript called "The Tartar Relation" seem to suggest that maybe the chemist was onto something archaeological after all.

A year after the monument's installation, a group of students dug a hole around the stone to test whether it would defy gravity. (It didn't.) Another group dug it up again and moved it to a different location. Thus began a cycle of burying and digging up that lasted several years. In 1968 Tufts groundskeepers dug up the stone to make way for a sidewalk and buried it in a secret locale. It remained hidden until 1971, when members of the Mountain Club unearthed it by sheer accident. In 1975 it was moved again. Then in 1977 the administration confiscated the stone and moved it to an undisclosed location after students had used it to block the doors of (P. T.) Barnum Hall. In the 1980s the stone was finally set to rest in its present location between Eaton Hall and Goddard Chapel.

A Chip Off the Old Block

Wellesley

The story about how Sir Isaac Newton got clunked on the noggin and discovered gravity isn't as far-fetched as it may sound. On the campus of Babson College stands a fifth-generation apple tree grown from a cutting of a tree from young Isaac's home in Woolsthorpe Manor, Lincolnshire, England. You'll find the area around the fenced-in tree littered with apples, proving Sir Isaac correct.

Photo by Bruce Gellerman

A chip off Newton's block grows on the campus of Babson College.

Babson College founder Charles Babson was fascinated with gravity and Newton. In addition to the Newton apple tree now growing in the center of campus, Babson also purchased the fore-parlor from the great mathematician's last London residence. He had the room disassembled and rebuilt in the Babson College library.

3

Northeast Massachusetts

Something magical seems *to happen as you head northeast from Boston. Check out "Le Grand David," in Beverly, the world's longest-running magic show, played in two wonderfully restored vaudeville theaters.*

If you want to get closer to God, head for High Rock in Lynn, a spiritualist mecca since the early nineteenth century. It was here that John Murray Spear began to build his God Machine, with the help of Ben Franklin from the "other side." Alas, Spear took the God Machine to New York State, where unbelievers wrecked it!

Salem takes its witches to heart. Laurie Cabot is the official town witch, and a statue of Samantha, the witch from TV's Bewitched, *has been erected in newly renovated Lappin Park. Those who are more serious about witches and witchcraft should head over to the Salem Witch Trials Memorial near the Charter Street Old Burying Point.*

If you like to find your magic a little closer to nature, there's the Singing Beach of Manchester-by-the-Sea, or the wolf habitat run by the North American Wolf Foundation near Ipswich, Wolf Hollow.

If you're in Gloucester in June, there's no excuse for missing the St. Peter's Fiesta's Greasy Pole Contest. Buon appetito!

A drive along Route 1 from Saugus to Peabody will put you in touch with roadside America, circa 1960, its restaurants, and cuisine. Dine at the Hilltop Steakhouse with its 68-foot neon cactus or at the life-size, two-masted Weathervane restaurant. Different is better!

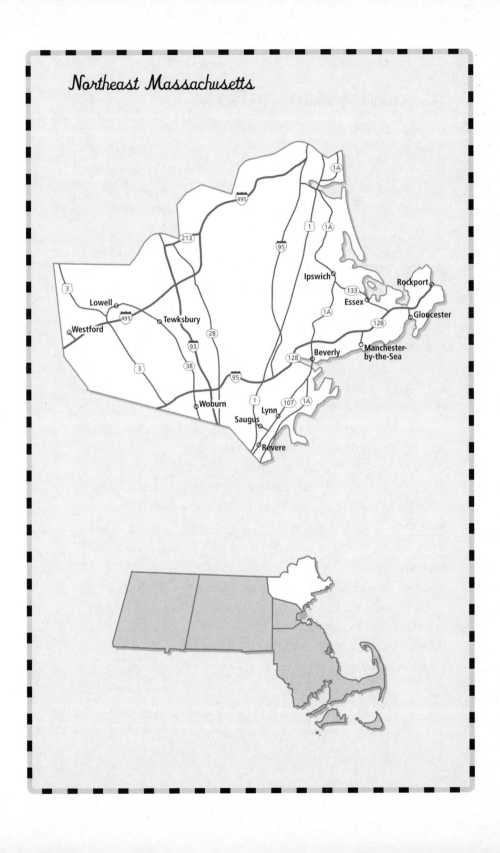

Northeast Massachusetts

★ ★

There's Definitely Something Up His Sleeve

Beverly

It seems the only thing magician Cesareo Palaez can't make disappear is his magic show. In 1972 Palaez conjured up "Le Grand David and his Own Spectacular Magic Show" out of thin air, little money, and a bunch of volunteers. Today the act is the longest-running stage magic show in the world.

The magic is not limited to the stage. It begins as soon as you enter the theater. Palaez and his troupe perform Le Grand David in two vaudeville theaters that they have meticulously restored to their former gilded glory. In the lobby, members of the troupe, many of whom have been with Palaez since the very beginning (and, in some cases, their children and even grandchildren), entertain patrons before the stage performance starts. It's multigenerational, multitasking magic. The sets are magnificent, the costumes opulent. Members of the cast make both.

Taking center stage, of course, is Palaez, who says it's his passion for "wonder, mystery, and enchantment" that brings so many people under his spell. A professor emeritus of psychology, Palaez is also a past president of the Society of American Magicians and was voted Magician of the Year several times. He came to the United States from Cuba, hoping to re-create the magic shows he had watched as a boy. He left his home just after Castro took power, in what he calls his greatest escape.

Palaez, starring as Marco the Magi, performs on select Thursdays at 7:30 p.m. at the Larcom Theater, 13 Wallis Street, and Sundays at 3:00 p.m. at the Cabot Street Theater, 286 Cabot Street. For more information, call (978) 927-3677. Every performance is another record-breaker.

Aw, Shucks, I Do

Essex

The fried clam is the claim to fame at the restaurant Woodman's of Essex. It was here on Main Street, along a marshy road, that Lawrence and Bessie Woodman say they invented the world's first munchy mollusk. Although others make the crunchy clam claim, they don't have the evidence the Woodmans have. Right on the back of their marriage certificate, it says they dunked the first mollusk into a deep-fryer on July 3, 1916. They said "I do," and they did. If anyone claims otherwise, let them come forward or just clam up.

The idea certainly wasn't half-baked. Come during the summer and expect a line out the door. Woodman's of Essex is on Route 133, Main Street. For more information, phone (978) 768-6057 or (800) 649-1773 or visit www.woodmans.com. (Or is it "dot-clam"?)

Photo by Bruce Gellerman

A deep fryer and clams are a marriage made in heaven at Woodman's.

Hunting for Babson's Big Boulders
Gloucester

By 1830, Dogtown, Massachusetts, had literally gone to the dogs. First the men left, then the women, leaving behind their canine companions. The abandoned, unincorporated town was purchased by philanthropist Charles Babson, founder of Babson College. Babson hired Swedish stone carvers to chisel words to the wise into huge glacial boulders that littered the property. And today Dogtown is best known for the big boulders bearing their messages. The messages include: "Never Try, Never Win," "Be on Time," "Help Mother," and our favorite, "Get a Job."

Photo courtesy of Don Noll © 2004 (www.don.noll.com)

Words to the wise can be found in Dogtown.

Dogtown is now part of Gloucester and has become a favorite haunt for trail-riding bicyclists. You may have to hunt a bit to find the place. (Don't forget to take insect repellant with you.) Take Route 127 just outside of Gloucester to Reynard Street. At the end of Reynard, turn left onto Cherry Street. You'll see a small sign for Dogtown Commons. Hey, never try, never win.

★ ★

A Greasy Pole and a Tough Italian

Gloucester

Since 1931, Gloucester's Italian-American fishing community has paid homage to the patron saint of fishing by holding its annual Saint Peter's Fiesta. Here, commercial fishing is a way of life and, too often, death. Gloucester was the hailing port of the *Andrea Gail,* which encountered the Perfect Storm.

According to Alphonse Millefoglie, vice president of the Fiesta Committee, the celebration's most unusual event is the Greasy Pole Contest. A heavily greased, 45-foot telephone pole is extended over the water, 200 feet off Pavilion Beach. Contestants must wiggle and squirm their way along the pole and capture a red flag nailed to the

Photo by Bruce Gellerman

Each year contestants squirm along this greased pole to capture a red flag.

end. The winner then swims back to the beach. All the other contestants lift the victorious pole walker onto their shoulders and parade around the town.

The first round is traditionally a trial run without capturing the flag. In 1979 one contestant broke the courtesy rule and was quickly confronted by a contest enforcer, Anthony "Matza" Giambanco. Matza presented the offender with a knuckle sandwich, the flag was once again nailed to the pole, and the competition commenced.

The fiesta is a five-day event held on the June weekend closest to the Feast of Saint Peter. It's a time for prayers, food, a parade, food, sporting events, and food . . . sometimes a knuckle sandwich. For more information, visit www.stpetersfiesta.org.

The greasy pole is a permanent fixture and can be seen year-round. It's offshore, in the harbor right behind the Cape Ann Chamber of Commerce on Commercial Street.

The Inventive Genius with an Itch for Discovery
Gloucester

Couch potatoes everywhere owe a debt of gratitude to their patron saint, John Hays Hammond Jr. This inventive genius was one of the early pioneers of radio electronics and is considered "the Father of the Remote Control." Dr. Hammond patented more than 430 inventions, second in number only to Thomas Edison. Hammond's inventions reflect his wide interests, whimsical sense of humor, and taste for the flamboyant. In 1914 the good doctor spooked sailors and spectators when he guided a crewless "ghost ship" by remote control on a 130-mile round-trip cruise from his home in Gloucester Harbor to Boston. Among his other inventions was a hypodermic meat baster, a stove that cooks food without using a pan, and a magnetic bottle cap remover. Alas, his cure for baldness failed, succeeding only in turning his scalp green.

Most of Hammond's creations had military applications. During World War II he offered the United States and Great Britain his pat-

★ ★

Photo by Bruce Gellerman

A knight in shining armor and a pipe organ reside at the eclectic castle built by inventor John Jay Hammond Jr.

ent to a fire bomb. Although the Allies turned him down, Hammond was arrested for treason when Germany subsequently used it on England. He was freed only after one of his staff members admitted to selling the weapon to the enemy.

Hammond did much of his inventing in a medieval-style castle he constructed in Gloucester from 1926 to 1929. In the Great Hall Hammond designed and built the largest pipe organ in a private residence in the world. It has more than 10,000 pipes. (No, he's not *that* Hammond.)

When Dr. Hammond died in 1965, he was buried with his mummified cats, who tour guides claim were placed in mayonnaise jars, in a crypt not far from the castle. According to his instructions, the spot was covered in poison ivy. However, despite the fortification, someone broke in to the burial chamber, smashed one of the mayo jars with a cat mummy, and stole Hammond's head. A ransom was paid, and the skull was eventually returned.

The castle, complete with pipe organ, drawbridge, and a dungeon, is open to the public at 80 Hesperus Avenue in Gloucester. Directions and hours of operation are available at www.hammondcastle.org or by calling (978) 283-7673.

A Real Hatchet Job

Haverhill

In downtown Haverhill you'll find the first public statue in the United States honoring a woman. The statue depicts Hannah Duston getting her revenge against members of the Abenaki Indian tribe.

On March 15, 1697 Indians attacked Haverhill where Duston lived with her husband and nine children. Duston, her infant daughter Martha, her midwife, and a fellow captive, fourteen year old Samuel Lennardson, were abducted

Photo by Stephen Hamel

The Hannah Duston statue is on the eastern end of Haverhill common facing the public library.

and forced to march towards Canada. Along the way the Indians murdered Duston's one week old baby. Along the route, in New Hampshire, Hannah led a revolt while the Indians slept. She stole the Indians' tomahawks and scalped ten of her captors, taking their scalps as proof of her revenge.

Cotton Mather and later Henry David Thoreau wrote of the event and in the late 1870s this statue was erected to honor Haverhill's favorite heroine. Four plaques at the base of the statue depict the captives' ordeal. You can find artifacts from the event, including one of the tomahawks and a scalping knife Duston used, at the Haverhill Historical Society.

Hannah Duston's ancestors meet each year on the second Saturday in August to commemorate her heroism. Duston's courageous act stands in stark contrast to her sister Elizabeth Emerson's exploits, who was hanged in 1693 after being found guilty of murdering her illegitimate twin infants.

For more information contact the Haverhill Historical Society, 240 Water Street; (978) 374-4626; www.haverhillhistory.org.

Dances with Wolves. Not.

Ipswich

If Little Red Riding Hood had traveled to Wolf Hollow, she would have learned a lot more than Grandma without having to take a single step into the forest. Wolf Hollow was founded in Ipswich in 1988 to allow people to experience wolves in the animals' natural habitat and to dispel the many myths surrounding the much-maligned creatures.

Wild wolves once populated all forty-eight contiguous U.S. states. Today they're nonexistent or endangered in forty-seven of those states. Humans are the wolves' only predators. The North American Wolf Foundation, which runs Wolf Hollow, contends that the wolf can harmoniously co-exist with humans and other mammals; it is a matter of understanding wolf behavior and the pack's social order. According to the foundation, there is not a single documented case of a healthy wild wolf attacking a human. But just in case, the pack at Wolf Hollow is enclosed in a large meadow protected by a 12-foot-high chain fence. Visitors are cautioned not to stare a wolf

★ ★

in the eye or to show their teeth. The founders of Wolf Hollow, the late Paul Soffron and his wife, Joni, learned firsthand the laws of the pack. They even slept with young pups to create a lifetime bond.

Wolf Hollow is open year-round, and there are one-hour structured presentations, weather permitting. Check ahead. There are also special seminars and events such as one observance that poet Allen Ginsberg might have enjoyed, "Howl Night." Grandma never had it so good.

Wolf Hollow is about 3 miles east of Ipswich on Route 133. For more information call (978) 356-0216 or visit www.wolfhollow ipswich.com.

On the Road On a Roll
Lowell

As literary lore has it, Lowell's legendary writer Jack Kerouac wrote his classic novel *On the Road* in a three-week typing marathon. To capture the essence of living in the moment, Kerouac taped sheets of paper together, enabling him to write uninterrupted. His inspiration, fueled by coffee and Benzedrine, drove him to write a 120-foot long manuscript.

Kerouac was born in Lowell on March 12, 1922 and is considered one of the pioneers of modern fiction. He lived in Lowell for the first seventeen years of his life and returned to the city later in life. The city holds the annual Lowell Celebrates Kerouac one weekend in October.

In 2001 James Irsay, owner of the Indianapolis Colts, purchased the original scroll for $2.4 million. It is currently on the road as a touring exhibit across the United States. The tour, scheduled to end in 2009, includes stops in San Francisco, Denver, New York, Orlando, and of course, his hometown: Lowell.

The National Park Service visitor center at 246 Market Street in Lowell has a daily screening of the film *Lowell Blues* about native son Jack Kerouac.

Coutesy National Park Service/Phil Lupsiewicz. http://www.nps.gov/lowe/historyculture/kerouac.htm

The National Park Service has an exhibit of Kerouac's life and times in Lowell.

Hey, If the Shoe Fits. . .

Lowell

Lowell is perhaps best known as the home of beat-generation author Jack Kerouac. But if you are on the road looking for something low-brow but upbeat and find yourself in the historic mill town, drop by the Lowell Historical Society. There you will find two curious items that have almost nothing to do with Lowell history.

The first is a helmet made out of a coconut and a sea urchin. It was worn by a Lowell soldier who served in the Philippine Insurrection of 1899–1901. The second item is a mummified ankle and foot.

No one seems to know how the preserved appendage got to the museum, where it came from, or what it really is. Until a few years ago, it was thought to be a mummified child's foot from ancient Egypt, but recently an expert identified it as being from South America and perhaps belonging to a woman.

Both items are in storage but are taken out on special occasions. The Lowell Historical Society is located at the Boote Cotton Mills Museum, 400 Foot of John Street. (No, we're not kidding, and no, it's not John's foot. That's just the address.)

Dungeon Rock
Lynn

Legend has it that in 1658 pirate Thomas Veal sailed up the Saugus River and anchored at Pirate's Glen. Although three of his buccaneers were captured and hanged by British soldiers, Veal escaped into the woods and hid in a cave all alone with a stash of ill-gotten gains. Suddenly a violent earthquake shook Lynn, entombing Veal and sealing his treasure trove in what has come to be called Dungeon Rock.

Over the centuries there have been numerous attempts by psychics and the certifiably insane to recover the loot. The most famous attempt began in 1852, when Hiram Marble, a spiritualist from Charlton, Massachusetts, his wife, and his son Edwin, purchased five acres in the area and, "guided by the spirit of revelation," started digging for the hidden treasure.

To help raise money for their project, the Marbles gave tours of the site and sold bonds for a dollar each, promising investors a share of the loot. The Marbles also sought guidance from the spirit of Pirate Veal, who perhaps advised the abrupt changes in direction apparent in the tunnel today. It is more likely that the spirits assured the Marbles that, like Moses wandering the desert for forty years, it was necessary for them to toil before reaching their reward.

Hiram Marble died in 1868. His son continued digging until his own death, in 1880. By that time the duo had dug 145 feet through solid rock, a rate of about a foot a month. Edwin's last wish, to be buried at Dungeon Rock, was granted. You will find a large pink rock marking his grave at the top of a set of stairs next to an old cellar hole.

While the gravel debris from the Marbles' blasting and remnants from many structures they built in the area can still be seen, the pirate treasure, if there ever was any, remains to be found.

Curiously, the Marbles were not seeking the treasure for themselves. Their first goal was to prove that the dead could communicate from the afterlife. They didn't have much luck there. Hiram Marble also hoped to use the pirate's treasure to purchase land in the area

Photo courtesy of Dan Small

Dungeon Rock is the site of two graves and supposed pirate's treasure.

for the people of Lynn to enjoy forever. He largely succeeded. Soon after Edwin's death the city of Lynn purchased the family's land for their new park, the Lynn Woods.

The entrance to Dungeon Tunnel is sealed with an iron gate but open to the public from May through October and by request. Bring a flashlight; it's really dark and scary.

In late October the Friends of Lynn Woods hold a Dungeon Rock Day celebration, where people dress as pirates and tell stories.

The shortest walk to Dungeon Rock is from the Rose Garden entrance to Lynn Woods. Maps are available at the entrance. For more information check out the Lynn Woods Reservation Guide at www.flw.org or call the rangers at (781) 477-7123.

The God Machine

Lynn

The era of the 1850s was a high-water mark for spiritualists in the United States, and High Rock, with its commanding view of Boston to the south, was something of a magnet for séances and spiritualists. Molly Pitcher, said to be clairvoyant, lived at the base of High Rock until her death in 1813. She was legendary among sailors whose fortunes she foretold before they set sail. In 1846 a man named Jesse Hutchinson bought High Rock and erected Stone Cottage on the side of the hill. It became home to Hutchinson and his eleven brothers and sisters, who formed the world-famous group the Hutchinson Family Singers. Jesse Hutchinson was a social activist and spiritualist who organized a meeting of spirit-minded people on High Rock. Reportedly, in 1852 spirits from twenty-four countries gathered on the mound. A year later nineteenth-century spiritualist John Murray Spear made the High Rock scene.

Although many say High Rock is as close to heaven as a Lynn poet can get, it obviously wasn't close enough for Spear.

In 1853 Spear and a group of philanthropic spirits he called the "Band of Electricizers" gathered atop the 170-foot-tall granite hill to build "Heaven's last, best gift to man." They set about constructing the New Messiah.

The Electricizers, led by the spirit of Benjamin Franklin, provided Spear and his followers with step-by-step instructions to build the New Messiah. It was later dubbed the God Machine.

Slowly the God Machine took shape on a dining room table. It was a mass of metal spheres, magnets, and coils of zinc and copper. There was a flywheel in the center of the contraption, with wire connections. When it was complete Spear encased himself in a shroud of metal plates and gemstones and for about an hour came in contact with the machine. Not much happened, although later a follower of Spear's went into labor while touching the God Machine, even though she claimed she wasn't pregnant. Spear insisted that at the moment of the baby's birth the machine became animate for an instant.

The contraption was later dismantled and moved to upstate New York, where an angry mob of nonbelievers reportedly mauled and mangled the God Machine. No trace of it has ever been found.

Today High Rock is still a place for those looking toward the heavens. Atop the tower built on the summit in 1906 are an observatory and a new computerized telescope. The observatory is open to the public on Tuesday nights or by appointment for large groups. For more information visit www.ci.lynn.ma.us/public_documents/lynnma_resources/highrock27.

To get to High Rock, take Essex Street and make a left on Rockaway Street. Turn up High Rock Street to Circuit Avenue and park at the end of Circuit.

Carrying a Tune in a Bucket
Manchester-by-the-Sea

Dinah Shore it's not, but Singing Beach really does sing . . . sort of. Shuffle your feet over the sand or pull your hands through it quickly and you'll hear a squeaking sound, not unlike a high-pitched violin

★ ★

(or Dinah on a bad day). To get the full experience, try the sand clos-est to the bathhouse. It seems to be the most mellifluous.

Naturalist and writer Henry David Thoreau wrote about the sono-rous sands of Manchester-by-the-Sea in the mid-nineteenth century, but scientists are still not sure of the exact mechanism of its tonal quality. It's thought that the uniform size and round shape of the grains is responsible for the phenomenon. Whatever the cause, even if you could never carry a tune in a bucket, now you can.

Singing Beach is at the end of Masconomo Street off Route 127 in Manchester-by-the-Sea. Parking is limited to town residents with spe-cial stickers, so you will have to park your car in town about a half-mile away and walk to the concert that awaits you.

Billions of Sweet Nothings
Revere

Back in the 1920s there were at least thirty-two candy manufactur-ers in the Boston area churning out sweet stuff by the megaton. One is still going strong. The New England Confectionery Company, or NECCO, recently celebrated its 150th anniversary, making it the old-est continuously operating candy company in the United States.

Until 2003 NECCO was located in a huge building next to the MIT campus in Cambridge. It was the largest factory in the world whose entire space was devoted to candy production. The company has since moved to Revere, north of Boston.

NECCO is literally a sweetheart of a company. Besides its signature Necco Wafers, it produces eight billion Sweethearts Conversation Hearts a year. They're the chalky-tasting, heart-shaped candies bear-ing saccharine sayings such as "Kiss Me," "Be True," and "Be Mine."

The Valentine's Day *amore* mottos have been updated in recent years to include "Girl Power," "Swing Time," and "Got Love." For a minimum order of $7,600, you can even have a custom-made cupid-saying printed on the hearts. You will have a whole lot of loving to go around. That's about 1.6 million candy hearts.

★ ★

Extra! Extra! Read All About It!
Rockport

At 52 Pigeon Hill Street in Rockport is an unusual home you not only can read about; you can actually read the home itself.

The house and most of the furnishings are built out of old newspapers. Elis F. Stenman constructed the house as a hobby. Perhaps his talent for paper construction had something to do with being a mechanical engineer who built machines to make paper clips. Certainly he had a passion for newspapers. He read three a day.

In 1922 Stenman started experimenting with newspapers as insulation for the cottage he was constructing. The material proved so strong that he decided to varnish it. The outer walls are 215 pages thick, and the roof is lined with newspapers but has a wood outer

Photo by Bruce Gellerman

The Paper House is black and white and read all over.

shell. It took Stenman two years to build the house and eighteen years to construct the clock, chairs, tables, and piano that furnish it. Although the fireplace is made of bricks, the mantelpiece is built from the magazine sections of Sunday newspapers.

The Paper House is located at 52 Pigeon Hill Street in Pigeon Cove in Rockport. Take Route 127 to Pigeon Cove; after the Yankee Clipper Inn, take the second left onto Curtis Street and then turn left onto Pigeon Hill Street. On Curtis Street you will see handwritten signs on telephone poles directing you to the house. Of course, they're written on paper.

Visitors are on the honor system to make a contribution. To read an interview with Elis Stenman, go to www.rockportusa.com/paper house/.

Bewitched, Bothered, and Bewildered
Salem

Salem, Massachusetts takes its witches very seriously. In 1692 fourteen women and five men were hanged and two dogs were executed for being witches. Another man, 80 year old Giles Corey, was crushed to death under heavy stones for refusing to enter a plea.

Today, Salem is Halloween Central year-round and witches and things of the occult are big business, attracting hundreds of thousands of tourists a year. The city even has an official witch. In the 1970s then governor Michael Dukakis bestowed upon Laurie Cabot the state's Patriots Award and named her the official witch of Salem. Recipients of the Patriots Award have the privilege of grazing cows on Boston Common, and wearing a tri-cornered hat.

Cabot, an ordained High Priestess of Celtic descent, founder of the Witches League for Public Awareness, opened the first Witch shop in America and currently owns the store The Cat, The Crow and The Crown.

Seems Salem is a place steeped in historic, real, and fictional witches. One of the newest attractions is the statue of Samantha, that nose-twitching witch from the goofy 1960s sitcom *Bewitched*. While the program ran for just eight seasons and just two shows took place in Salem, in 2005 executives of that rerun cable network TV Land decided the city was the perfect place for a 9-foot statue honoring the show starring the late actress Elizabeth Montgomery.

Many local denizens were bothered by the bronze monument featuring Montgomery astride a broom flying through a crescent moon. Opponents were bewildered and feared that the tragic events that took place in their city would be trivialized. The cable company got its way, providing the monument for free and paying to renovate Lappin Park where the statue now stands and has become a favorite among visitors.

For a more moving monument, visit the Salem Witch Trials Memorial near the Charter Street Old Burying Point, the second oldest cemetery in the country. The monument, dedicated in 1992, consists of twenty large granite stones and a low wall. The names of those who died during the witch hunt are inscribed in the stones.

Photo by Bruce Gellerman

Sam watches over Lappin Park.

The *Bewitched* statue is in Lappin Park at the corner of Washington and Essex Streets. The Charter Street Cemetery is one block south of the park off where Washington turns into Hawthorne Boulevard. The Cat, The Crow and The Crown is located at 63R Pickering Wharf, Salem, Massachusetts (978-744-6274).

★ ★

Route 1: The (R)Ode to Individuality
Saugus

Ten miles north of Boston you will find a major dose of roadside
America circa 1960. The strip of Route 1 stretching from Saugus to
Peabody is a six-lane tabernacle to garish taste and unbridled indi-
viduality. It is a road that tells it like it was; a time when your mother
wore a bouffant, your dad motored happily with a tiger in his gas
tank, and the family saw the U.S.A. in a Chevrolet. You'll want to
yell, "Hi, Dad, hi, Mom, hi Beaver" as you pass the Bel-Aire diner
and the Fern Motel, a place where Norman Bates would feel right at
home. And if you want to whack a few balls, stop at Route 1 Miniature Golf, where an orange *Tyrannosaurus rex,* a national landmark,
guards the links.

In its heyday, Route 1 had more restaurants per mile, serving more
people, than anywhere else in the nation. The eateries were an exu-
berant celebration of tacky taste and entrepreneurial chutzpah, and
the road was a mecca for marketing meals run amok. Different was
better. Biggest was best.

Atop a hill overlooking Route 1 in Saugus, you can still see the
huge pagoda-shaped Weylus, once said to be the largest Chinese
restaurant on the planet. It featured cuisine from every Chinese can-
ton in a style you might call "Saugus Early-Elvis Dynasty." They could
serve up egg foo yung for 1,400 with no sweat. Alas, the last egg roll
left the Weylus kitchen in the late 1990s. But fear not; you won't go
hungry along the Route 1 kitschway today. If you have a hankering
for a slab of beef the size of Plymouth Rock, you can still head to the
Hilltop Steakhouse, the place with the 68-foot neon cactus right next
to the giant fiberglass grazing cows. Feel like Italian? A bit farther
north is Prince Restaurant. It's the one with the three-story leaning
tower of pizza sign, just across the road from Kowloon, a humon-
gous grass-hut Polynesian restaurant with giant tiki statues out front
and a bubbling volcano inside. Diners looking for a nautical motif

★ ★

The Hilltop Steak House cactus.

Photo by Bruce Gellerman

can chart a course a bit farther north to the life-sized, two-masted Weathervane restaurant. The "ship" is anchored between a Yankee Candle Shop and a Christmas Tree Shop. Guiding the way is a faux lighthouse in the parking lot. You can't miss it.

Yet despite the best efforts of kitsch preservationists, this roadway—architecturally littered with a kind of joyful abandon you just don't find much anymore—is slowly but surely giving way to staid chain stores and look-alike fast-food franchises. Nonetheless, there is enough of the old Route 1 still standing to make a trip down memory lane at forty miles an hour worth it. Just hop in your Chevy, put the top down, turn up Dean Martin on the AM radio, and cruise the road. It's *amore*.

The two-masted Weathervane restaurant.

Photo by Bruce Gellerman

Hey, Bartender, I'll Have Another One of Those Medicines
Tewksbury

In the old administration building of what is now known as Tewksbury Hospital is the only public health museum in the United States.

The hospital was established in 1852 as an almshouse for the
poor. Its most famous patient during the nineteenth century was
Anne Sullivan, later the tutor and companion of Helen Keller. In
1994 the bottom floor was converted into the unique public health
museum by Chet Kennedy, former art director for the Massachusetts
Department of Public Health, "to show to the world what a great
heritage we have in this part of the country" and to sing the praises
of public health pioneers. Colonial Massachusetts passed the first
laws to register births and deaths; it was the first state to require lead
testing in children; and it was the first with a tuberculosis hospital.
It's hard to remember now that in 1900 TB was a major cause of
death in the United States.

The Queen Anne–style museum building itself is an exhibit, listed
on the National Register of Historic Places. The eight rooms in the
museum include a nurses' classroom and a hospital room from the
1920s. The Mural Room features a four-wall mural from the Works
Progress Administration in the 1930s. The steep staircase up one wall
leads to a little room used to store records of venereal disease.

Massachusetts was also the epicenter for the patent medicine
industry, as evidenced by the museum's extensive collection of bottles
and advertisements. Included are bottles of Turtle's Elixir, Atwood's
Jaundice Bitters, and Bee's Laxative Cough Syrup. Prominently displayed are patent medicines produced by Lydia Pinkham. In 1876
Pinkham began manufacturing her nostrum, Lydia E. Pinkham's Veg-
etable Compound, in nearby Lynn promising to cure "the worst form
of 'Female Complaints'—everything from 'General Debility' to cancer." The elixir was based on a formula Pinkham's husband won in a
card game. Lydia Pinkham became known as "a lady's best friend"
during Prohibition, and no wonder: The elixir was 90 percent alcohol.

Photo by Bruce Gellerman

The Public Health Museum's collection of patent medicines might not be good for what ails you.

Pinkham's cure-all was a phenomenon and her salesmanship made her one of the most successful women in U.S. history. Indeed, although she died in 1883, customers were still encouraged to write to Mrs. Pinkham for medical advice. In 1905, twenty-two years after her death and countless letters later, the *Ladies' Home Journal* exposed the scam in an article that included a photograph of Mrs. P's tombstone, located at the Pine Grove Cemetery in Lynn within sight of the maintenance garage, 145 Boston Street.

The Public Health Museum in Massachusetts is located off Interstate 93 at exit 42 West. More information is available at the museum Web site, www.publichealthmuseum.org.

★ ★

What's a Knight Like You Doing in a Place Like This?
Westford

Historian Frederick J. Pohls says "fuggetabout" Columbus sailing the ocean blue in 1492. In his book, *Atlantic Crossings Before Columbus,* Pohls makes the case that it was a seafaring Scot in 1398 who first "discovered" America. According to Pohls' research, Henry Sinclair (Earl of Rosslyn, Prince of Orkney and Lord of Shetland, Duke of Oldenburg and Premier Earl of Norway) set out to explore newly discovered Newfoundland but wound up getting chased away by natives. It seems he then got caught in a New England nor'easter, sending Sinclair's armada to the coast just north of Boston, where he had better luck with the local inhabitants. Maybe it was all his titles, or maybe it was his kilt. In any case, Sinclair and his crew of one hundred were allowed to spend the winter on shore. In the spring they trooped inland and climbed what is now called Prospect Hill in Westford, perhaps seeking a place to hide the Holy Grail some say they carried with them. Historian Pohls writes that one of Prince Henry's men died there and the Scots memorialized him by carving a marker into a flat, 8-foot-square hunk of granite. Although the weatherworn carving is faint, you might be able to make out a roughly life-sized portrayal of a fourteenth-century knight with a sword, shield, and crest, wearing a helmet.

"Holy Grail, shmoly grail," say nonbelievers who contend that the Westford Knight is nothing but a weather-beaten rock. Decide for yourself. From the Westford Common, make a right on Lincoln Street onto Main Street and a left onto Depot Street. Park near the Abbot School and walk 50 yards up Depot. A commemorative marble marker marks the spot where Prince Henry may have left evidence of his discovery of the New World, or maybe not.

The Scoop on the Battleship *Maine*

Woburn

Do you remember the *Maine*? The USS *Maine* was the battleship that mysteriously blew up in Havana Harbor in 1898, setting off the Spanish-American War. To remember more, go to Main Street in Woburn, where you'll find remains of the *Maine,* specifically one of the ship's ventilator cowls (an air scoop that looks like a crushed tuba and is enshrined in a glass case).

When residents of Woburn had requested a piece of the *Maine* in 1911, Congress rejected them, stating that only nonprofit, patriotic organizations could apply.

Photo by Bruce Gellerman

Visitors can remember the *Maine* on Main Street in Woburn.

The citizens got Local Post 161 of the Grand Army of the Republic to submit an application, and it was approved by Congress. The 315-pound, barnacle-encrusted cowl was put on display in the front window of Whitcher's Drug Store (now a sushi restaurant) on Main Street. A year later it was encased on the Common and dedicated on July 4, 1913.

As they say, "from sea to shining sea."

4

Southeast Massachusetts and the Cape and Islands

New Englanders are *not afraid of going 'round and 'round to have a good time. Hull is home to the Paragon Carousel, one of eighty-nine carousels built by the Philadelphia Toboggan Company, famous for its realistic hand-carved figures. At Panhead Mike's Offshore Cycle, on Martha's Vineyard, there's the Flying Horse, the nation's oldest operating platform carousel, brought to the Vineyard from Coney Island in 1884.*

You can't visit this part of the world without seeing a lighthouse or two. Cohasset is home to the Minot's Ledge Light, known as "the most wave-swept lighthouse" in the U.S. lighthouse system. Hannah Thomas was the country's first woman lighthouse keeper. The light she tended, Plymouth Light, is located at the tip of Duxbury Beach.

Plymouth is the place for all things Pilgrim. There's a "piece of the Rock" on display under a portico on Water Street. How it got there is a tale for another time. The Pilgrim National Wax Museum offers a series of dioramas showing scenes from the Pilgrim past. Also in Plymouth are a working replica of the first corn-grinding mill in the colony, and the National Monument to the Forefathers, a freestanding granite monument.

Climb to the top of the Pilgrim Monument in Provincetown for a spectacular view of the Cape Cod National Seashore. It might be smart to pack a lunch—the monument is 253 feet 7 inches tall!

Worn out? Spend a night at the Lizzie Borden Bed and Breakfast Museum in Fall River. If you're lucky, the suite that includes Lizzie's room will be available. And enjoy that Ma and Pa Borden (last) breakfast!

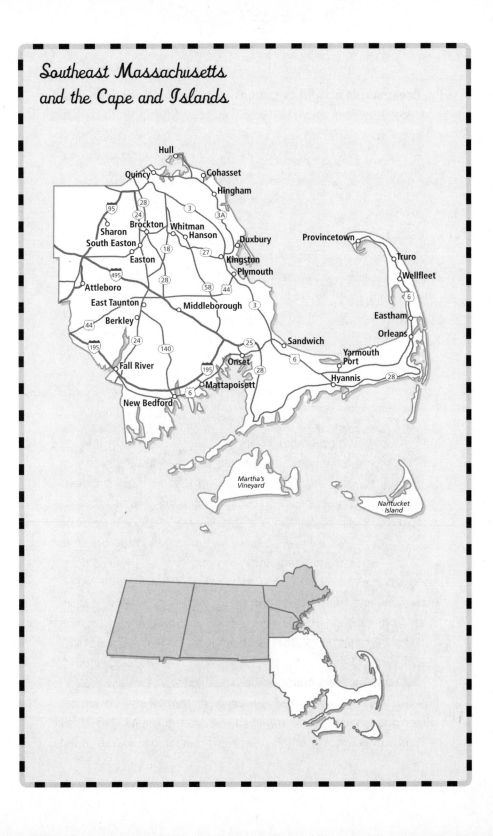

Southeast Massachusetts
and the Cape and Islands

I'm Dreaming of a Light Christmas
Attleboro

If you are of a certain age and cultural background, you spent many youthful hours among cloaked figures—silent, swift, certain. We're talking nuns here, those powerful and virtually omniscient harbingers of order, guilt, and swift retribution. Also of humor, teaching, an understanding ear, and a mean swing on the softball field. It all depends—hardly surprising—on the individual. But uniforms can be deceiving and even leveling. Part of the raiment, at least in the Northeast in the 1960s, was strands of rosary beads, which are a physical system for tracking a series of prayers, like a spiritual abacus. In those days, when you were six, those beads seemed large, far bigger than marbles. In Attleboro at the La Salette Shrine, however, you will find

At Christmas, visitors enjoy the lighter part of the shrine.

Photo by Erik Sherman

★ ★

a rosary that dwarfs those once sported by the nuns, with beads as big as bowling balls. The site, originally intended to be a sanatorium, was purchased in 1919 by the Methodist Church. It was called Attleboro Springs, named for the springs on the property. The Methodists used it as a retreat for a time, finally closing the facility in 1938. In 1942 representatives from a French Catholic order called the Missionaries of Our Lady of La Salette bought the property and, ten years later, began building a shrine commemorating a supposed appearance of Mary to two children in France. The Giant Rosary, which stretches over a walkway arch, is part of the scene, as are other religious statues and peaceful gardens.

A particularly bright and uplifting time to visit is during the annual Christmas Festival of Lights. Tens of thousands of miniature lights illuminate the trees and grounds and draw hundreds of thousands of visitors. The lights go on at 5:00 p.m. from Thanksgiving through January 1. To see the beads and lights, follow the blue-and-white signs on Route 152 in Attleboro or from exit 5 on Interstate 95. For more information visit www.lasalette-shrine.org.

American Graffiti

Berkley

Kids who "tag"—draw large and elaborate versions of graffiti on anything that doesn't move (and on some things that do, if you look at subways in New York)—might think they are on the cutting edge of generational revolt. Oh, if only they realized that the graffiti in this land even makes their parents look young. Dighton Rock is a noted bit of sediment: an 11-foot boulder covered in petroglyphs (fancy talk for lines carved into a rock) that was originally on the Taunton River at Berkley. Think that urban tagging can be hard to read? These ancient inscriptions were left by unknown people with a meaning that is more obscure than a political party's press release. Back in 1712, when Cotton Mather wasn't looking for witches, he was trying to figure out what the markings meant. He even made a copy of the

★ ★

figures and sent them to the Royal Society in London for a translation, but the experts there were undecided.

Was this the literary equivalent of crop circles and mysterious Mayan hieroglyphs? It could be that what you can see is actually the musings of an international group of ancient punks. Over the years many have argued that the petroglyphs aren't a single language, but several. Some scholars think that they have deciphered bits and pieces. One of those pieces is the name *Thorfinn Karlsefni* and the phrase, "Miguel Cortereal by will of God, here Chief of the Indians," along with the date 1511 and a Portuguese coat-of-arms. (Not all students of language and history agree with even these fragmentary—or is it figmentary?—translations.) What is clear, however, is that Dighton Rock became a veritable billboard for graffiti enthusiasts over many years. To avoid having the rock face damaged by tides and weather and the modern tagging practitioner, it now sits in a museum in Dighton Rock State Park.

We have our own theories on what was meant by the writing. Either this is an old variation of "Kilroy was here," or an early comic dramatic masterpiece, *Dighton Beach Memoirs*. If you visit, be sure to bring a picnic lunch for the eighty-five acres of grassy areas and shade trees. There is also boating, fishing, and hiking. Dighton Rock State Park is on Bay View Avenue; for more information, call (508) 822-7537 or visit www.mass.gov/dcr/parks/southeast/digr.htm.

A Lasting Impression
Brockton

Imelda Marcos has nothing on the city of Brockton when it comes to shoes. She only had hundreds of pairs at hand (or would that be "at foot"?) But the Brockton Shoe Museum lifts shoe obsession to an art. Those who are interested in fashion—whether leather or lace—can see how boots and sneakers can be a veritable foundation for a look. Not only does this shoe showplace examine the footwear-making craft from the sixteenth century on, but it also has entire theme col-

★ ★

lections, like military shoes from the Civil War to Desert Storm. If your mother wore combat boots, they may be here.

Then there are the celebrity shoes, including those worn by Ted Williams, Arthur Fiedler, and Rocky Marciano. (Marciano was a Brockton native.) There is even a pair, size 24, used by an Italian boxer of the 1930s. And don't forget those of the political persuasion: Mamie Eisenhower, President Gerald Ford, and President Bill Clinton, whose sneakers are fast enough to get out of almost any scrape. If you get tired of Shoes,

Photo by Erik Sherman

The Brockton Shoe Museum features the size 24 shoes worn by 1930s world champion Italian boxer Primo Carnera.

the Exhibit, then you can move on to Shoes, the Movie—actually, a video of shoes. We won't be heels and give the ending away. But we do have a bone to pick with the people who have designed the attraction's marketing message. The Shoe Museum bills itself as "the only authentic shoe museum in America." We beg to differ and offer as evidence the closets of virtually all the women we have ever known. You can judge for yourself at the Brockton Heritage Center, 216 North Pearl Street. For more information, or to find out if they have your size, visit www.brocktonma.com/bhs/shoe.html or call (508) 583-1039.

Heavy Lighthouse

Cohasset

Whoever said that watching over a lighthouse was easy work, let alone even safe? Sure, turn the switch on and turn it off—and make

★ ★

out your last will and testament. Just off the coast of Cohasset is Minot's Ledge Light. Erected in the mid-nineteenth century, it is the most wave-swept lighthouse of the United States Lighthouse System (USLHS). This is the Hawaii of the lighthouse set, where the biggest and baddest waves break—and, sometimes, so do the light keepers. After the lighthouse's initial construction, the first keeper complained about how dangerous the waves were and immediately quit. The next keeper also complained. The year after the lighthouse went up, it came down in an April storm, killing the two assistants who were on duty. The USLHS wanted a light there, since this was a dangerous stretch of water, so it rebuilt on the site. Some people can't take no for an answer. Replacing the building was quite the trick, using 1,079

Photo by Erik Sherman

The memorial of the Minot's Ledge Light honors the two men who died when the lighthouse collapsed.

Lady of the Lighthouse

Working in a lighthouse was always a lonely job, perhaps making the appearance of ghosts not all that unwelcome. Maybe previous occupants didn't want the new ones to feel isolated. One such place is Plymouth Light, formerly known as Gurnet Light, established in 1768 on the property of John and Hannah Thomas at the tip of Duxbury Beach. It was one of a dozen colonial stations, and John was the lighthouse keeper until he was killed during the Revolutionary War. That left Hannah as the first official female lighthouse keeper on the continent. According to accounts at the time, Hannah was good at what she did. She was also very loyal, refusing to leave the lighthouse during her life. She worked until her death, at which point her son took over. The original lighthouse is long gone, having been replaced in 1803, rebuilt in 1843, and then rebuilt again in 1924.

In 1994 Bob and Sandra Shanklin, world-famous lighthouse photographers, enthusiasts, and authors, came to photograph the building and stayed at the keeper's house. In the middle of the night, Bob woke and saw the apparition of a woman's face, dark clothing, and shoulder-length hair. Could Hannah be the lighthouse keeper emeritus?

Although Plymouth is technically the closest city to the lighthouse, the only way to approach is by four-wheel-drive or by foot from Duxbury Beach. The lighthouse is generally closed to the public, though it is open on such special occasions as the annual Opening of the Bay each May in Duxbury.

blocks of granite from Quincy—more than 3,500 tons in all—cut to fit together like a well-made joint on a dresser drawer. It took the USLHS five years to put all the blocks in place. Impressive, but the engineering wonder still left keepers wondering why, in the name of all that was holy, they should sit out there. People quit, right and left—that is, when they didn't become violent or literally lose their minds. Reports of hauntings include the mysterious polishing of lenses, odd noises, and a figure screaming in Portuguese for help while hanging off a ladder. Talk about your hostile working environments.

Amusingly, the Minot's Ledge Light is also known as the "I love you" light, because it flashes in a 1–4–3 pattern, mirroring the number of letters in each word. (Imagine what conditions would have been like if it hated you.)

These days the lighthouse itself is automated, working off solar power, and is closed to the public. The lighthouse keeper's abode has become a private club and a pleasant venue for functions. But you can read about the storm and the men who died (although not the ones who went off the deep end, so to speak) by going to the memorial at Cohasset Harbor. The memorial includes a replica of the top portion of the lighthouse on granite blocks from the original structure. The light keepers' residence also makes an interesting place for a social gathering. Set sail for a driveway that runs off Border Street, next to the small bridge.

Good Works and Good Eats
Eastham

Saving souls is serious work, but that doesn't mean that you can't have some fun while you do it. The Methodists have long understood that part of spiritual development was being in the proper atmosphere, and they have been drawn to beautiful seaside areas in the hot days of summer. In Eastham is Millennium Grove, an oak grove in which as many as 5,000 of the faithful would camp and pray with some 150 ministers. Henry David Thoreau witnessed this on one of his walking trips of the Cape and later wrote about it. While it's easy to build an image of what this must have been like, it's easy for that image to be wrong. Life at the camp was not one of deprivation; the worshipers were apparently open to sustaining the flesh as well as the spirit. Thoreau wrote of his visit: "I saw the heaps of clam-shells left under the tables, where they had feasted in previous summers, and supposed, of course, that that was the work of the unconverted, or the backsliders and scoffers. It looked as if a camp-meeting must be a singular combination of a prayer-meeting and a picnic." We can only imagine the difficulties the faithful must have faced: mounds of shellfish and not a drop of melted butter in sight. To get a feel for the old surroundings, let the spirit move you to Campground Road and look for the old lobster bibs.

Digging Culture

Easton

If you liked watching *Home Improvement,* or if going to Home Depot is your idea of a night out on the town, then the Arnold B. Tofias Industrial Archives at Stonehill College will give you fun by the spadeful. This special collection of the school's Stonehill Indus- trial History Center, located in the Cushing-Martin Building on the campus, is nicknamed the Shovel Museum. There's a good reason for the moniker, as this could well be the largest historic ret-

Photo by Erik Sherman

More than 800 shovels and shovel components are displayed at Stonehill College.

rospective of that most essential icon of earth movement. It's not to everyone's taste; according to a researcher, in 1995 only 200 people visited the collection. What do most people think it must be, a hole in the ground? Absolutely not: There are papers—diaries, sales ledgers, and catalogs—of the O. Ames Company, which happened to make shovels. And you will also find more than 800 shovels and shovel components, as well as trowels, trenchers, and other related tools.

★ ★

The business had its start in the Revolutionary War, when Capt. John Ames, a blacksmith by trade, made shovels and muskets in West Bridgewater. His son moved the business to an abandoned nail factory in Easton in 1803. Because merchandise from England was relatively cheap, Ames concentrated on making expensive, high-quality shovels. The company thrived in Easton until it merged with another in the 1950s and moved out of town. In the process of the move, the new owners managed to leave an attic full of shovels in the old building. Thus was born the collection. Family members are still in the area, and one donated the paperwork a few years ago. A gallery is open Monday through Friday, 9 a.m. to 5 p.m., where you can view the shovels through glass, but if you want to dig into the subject more, call the curator at (508) 565-1774 to arrange for a walk through the *objets de dirt,* or visit www.stonehill.edu/archives/sihc. The historical big dig is at the Cushing-Martin Building, Stonehill College, 320 Washington Street.

Pop-Top Art

East Taunton

College students who spend their hours hardly studying and partying heartily might seem to be wasting important intellectually formative years. Yet we'd like to think that an entire genre of beer art has been the result. Unlike much cultural philanthropy, this is not a category that owes much to wealthy patrons or even government underwriting. Beer art is something that the average person on the street supports, sip by sip. There are the nameless people who have done their small share, and then there are the heroic figures who, each like a modern Hercules, move and direct the rivers of frothy liquid. It is the latter category that features the East Taunton Beer Can and Breweriana Museum. Kevin "Kevbo" Logan, the owner and curator, was introduced to this collection pastime by his cousin in Galveston, Texas. Since then Kevin has collected more than 1,000 cans, along with roughly the same number of coasters, half a dozen beer trays, and

★ ★

assorted glasses and bottles from around the world. His best find was in 1980, cleaning out a woman's basement; she told him to keep anything he found. In an old running refrigerator were two rare Schaeffer 1964 World's Fair Special Steel Flattops, one of which now sits in the museum. (The other went to cousin Patrick, a belated but much welcomed, we assume, thank-you.) On his Web site, Kevin answers what might seem obvious: Why would someone collect beer cans? "Beer cans are pretty fascinating, really." We are sure that the display-preparation phase, which includes draining the contents (from the bottom) doesn't hurt. In fact, it's probably good for what ales you. The collection is large, but the number of visitors is only about forty a year. To arrange a visit or just to take a virtual tour, go to http://kevs log.tripod.com/beercanmuseum—it's the yeast you could do.

Shell Game
Fall River

The USS *Massachusetts* never lost a sailor in combat, but the government nearly lost the *Massachusetts*. In the early 1960s the Navy was going to sell the battleship—home to 2,300 sailors during World War II—for scrap. The ship, built in 1941 in the city of Quincy, Massachusetts, had joined the war in November 1942. In a battle with the ship *Jean Bart* during the drive into North Africa, the *Massachusetts* let loose the war's first American 16-inch shell. (This piece of artillery was nothing to trifle with—it was nearly a foot and a half in diameter.) On August 9, 1945, less than a month before the end of the war in Asia, the *Massachusetts* shelled the Kamaishi, Honshu, ironworks with, as it turns out, what were probably the war's last American 16-inch shells.

Luckily, before the Navy could sell the *Massachusetts*, a group of citizens organized a battle plan and turned the valiant ship into a museum worthy of the name. They rescued not only the *Massachusetts*, but an entire fleet, adding a destroyer, a submarine, two PT boats, a mechanized landing craft, and even some foreign craft, such as a Russian warship and a Japanese suicide-attack boat. Now the *Massachusetts* hosts camping adventures where youth groups can see what a sailor's life was like. That includes meals served on board, berthing in crew's quarters, movies about Navy ships and Navy life, and Morse code classes for those who want to join the signal corps and pursue radio licenses. There are even facilities for functions and meetings for those above the recruitment age. Stop by headquarters at Battleship Cove; the Web site www.battleshipcove.com gives directions, hours of operation, and other details.

Photo by Erik Sherman

Battleship Cove is home to the world's largest collection of historic naval ships, including the USS *Massachusetts*

★ ★

A Hatchet Job
Fall River

Forget television movie re-creations of sensational crimes or even reality shows. If you have an ax to grind with secondhand titillation, you might find a trip to the Lizzie Borden Bed and Breakfast Museum intriguing. This was the site of the double-hatchet murder of Andrew J. and Abby Borden and the trial of their spinster daughter, Lizzie. Legal authorities not only charged Lizzie with the murder of each parent, but they also accused her of an additional charge of killing both of them—sort of a double double-homicide.

Photo by Erik Sherman

The old Borden house is now a bed-and-breakfast.

Lizzie was tried and eventually acquitted—whether fair or not we couldn't say, as that would be splitting hairs. But much of the defense's success seemed to lie in excluding testimony Borden gave during the inquest that contradicted what she said at the trial, as well as having certain other testimony labeled inadmissible. Oh, and there was that mysterious man who had been hanging around the Borden home. No matter about the verdict, though, as the town didn't forgive her. That rhyme about "giving her mother forty whacks and when she was done giving her father forty-one" had to hurt, and it was untrue—Mom got nineteen and Dad, only eleven.

Now, thanks to the time-honored commercial tool of exploiting the macabre, you can experience the Borden house up close and personal by spending the night in the very dwelling that was the site

of the deeds. You can even have a suite that includes Lizzie's room.
The meal portion is actually similar, so we read, to the ones the
Borden parents had the morning of that . . . uh . . . unfortunate incident: bananas and johnnycakes, washed down with coffee and sugar
cookies.

There are tours of the house on weekends in May and June, and
daily in July and August, but the hours vary. For more information,
go to www.lizzie-borden.com or call (508) 675-7333. To reach that
(hopefully not) final resting place, go to 92 Second Street.

Ship's Chapel
Hingham

On an elevated site to one end of Hingham's tony downtown stands
the Old Ship Church, the oldest religious meetinghouse in continuous
use in the United States. Originally the First Church in the town, the
congregation was organized in 1635 and eventually built a meetinghouse. Starting in 1681, that structure was replaced with the central
part still standing today. Through the 1700s the members added a
couple of wings, did some plastering, put in a ceiling to hide the top
beams, and added pews to replace the original benches. Talk about
getting your money's worth from a building fund.

In the late 1800s the members got a little wild. Just about as the
last pew was put into place in 1869—obviously no one was in a
rush—the congregation decided to tear them all out and install cush-
ioned benches. In the 1930s a restoration began to bring back the
feel of the seventeenth and eighteenth centuries—including bringing many of the original pews back in. Would people please make
up their minds? Not only is the architecture old, but so are some of
the furnishings, including a christening bowl that probably dates to
before 1600.

For more information you can call (617) 749-1679 or go to www
.oldshipchurch.org. Or, if you want, you can take a drive down to
90 Main Street, see the church, and then stroll through the pleasant

downtown area that is only a block away. And if you can't get there right away, don't worry—the church isn't going anywhere.

Ready Oar Not

Hull

Most museums are happy with just telling about the past. The Hull Lifesaving Museum does that and goes a bit further, though with a twist. The U.S. Life Saving Service, established in the 1870s to assist mariners in distress, had stations up and down the East Coast, and the branch in Hull was certainly busy. But the present-day museum actually has a program for putting people into the water, not taking them out. It sponsors various open-water rowing races, and you have to wonder about the conditions when you hear some of the names: the Snow Row and the Icebreaker. (Undoubtedly the museum staff doesn't have to worry about people falling out of the pilot boats, dories, wherries, and whaleboats, as they would probably just bounce off the frozen surface.)

If you don't catch one of the races, there is still a lot to see—and to think about. This part of the state has had a long relationship with the sea, and the loss of life in its waters has been real and historic. Sometimes the rescuers from the local station would take boats out to pull mariners from the rough waters off the shore. When the weather was too rough, a canon would shoot a ball and line out to sea so those in trouble could pull themselves back to land (if they were lucky).

The Hull Lifesaving Museum is open year-round and has both artifacts and hands-on exhibits. Be sure to go up into the children's space and climb into the cupola, which, on a clear day, offers a view of the harbor and the neighboring lighthouse that can't be beat. Row, row, row your way to 1117 Nantasket Avenue. Just don't forget your life preserver. For information, call (781) 925-5433, or go to www.lifesavingmuseum.org.

Old Tech

Is he a curator, or simply a pack rat? We're not sure, but Mark Vess of Hanson certainly has come up with the best excuse for keeping an overwhelmingly large collection of old stuff. Calling his obsession with antiquated technology a "museum" seems unfair. After all, it's not a public institution and you can't drop by to see it. But the founder and curator does give a few tours each year to school groups and collectors.

Vess started saving old radios and phones when he was a child, and if his own mother couldn't stop him, who can? Now, decades later, he keeps the bulk of the collection in the hayloft of his barn, though it does spill out into other parts of the house, and some things—a tractor, a number of antique autos, and a player one-man band (piano with other instruments)—require a bit more space planning.

A number of the items, such as the Edison wind-up phonograph and the manual typewriters, are obvious in their function . . . or they would be, for those old enough to remember records and carbon paper. Then there are things that could use descriptive panels, like the electrical coils that doctors of the late-nineteenth century used to (unsuccessfully) treat stomachaches and bad pregnancies. But not everything is hand-powered: Vess also has a selection of handheld transistor radios. Those lucky enough to tour past the wooden display tables will also see cameras, flashlights, telegraph keys, lightbulbs, sewing machines, and even antique shaving blades. The world may be waiting for a better mousetrap, but when society moves on, you can bet that Mark Vess will have the old model.

Dizzy Displays

Hull

Ever feel like you're going around in circles? It's an unpleasant hazard of modern life. Instead of giving up, try a little sublimation: Head to the end of the small boardwalk-like strip in Hull, and check out of the rat race and into childhood at the Paragon Carousel. Before the turn of the twentieth century, this area was a major New England resort, complete with an amusement park. In 1928 its owners installed this carousel, number eighty-five of the eighty-nine built by the Philadelphia Toboggan Company, known for its realistic hand-carved figures. Back in those days Hull was a resort town, and people would flock to

Photo by Erik Sherman

The carousel in Hull is a taste of summer, whether you ride or watch.

the shore to enjoy a vacation in the cool breezes. Times changed, and the seaside community became a bit rundown. It transformed into a blue-collar residential area as plane travel became more prevalent and could take the wealthy to real tropical destinations. The Paragon Amusement Park, long a fixture, finally came down in the mid-1980s, the victim of a condominium development. Most of the history is just a paper memory, but thanks to the efforts of community activists and sentimental supporters, three investors purchased the carousel and set it up on land provided by the state. Fate does have a way of going in circles, and the owners decided that they wanted "off" the merry-go-round when their interests changed. They put the carousel on the market again, and it appeared that it was going to be dismantled and sold piecemeal to antiques buyers. Rather than let the beloved amusement be taken for a ride, its fans from neighboring towns raised more than a million dollars to purchase the carousel and save it for posterity. Today the carousel's mighty Wurlitzer band organ plays on. The sixty-six wooden horses and two Roman chariots have been taking turns undergoing restoration, and today they await to take you away from care. Just hop on and enjoy the satisfyingly long ride. Next to the carousel is a great local ice cream store, and the beach across the street has its own appeal, as long as you aren't horsing around. The carousel is at 205 Nantasket Avenue; call (781) 925-0472 or visit www.paragoncarousel.com for information.

Parallel Parking
Kingston

We like straight lines—they're so orderly. And what better order do they provide than when arranged as longitude and latitude, giving direction and guidance to us all? Okay, okay, so the latitude bands that run parallel to the equator and the longitude lines passing through the poles are actually big circles, and not straight at all. The point is that without them, we'd be totally lost. Those who appreciate the niceties of navigation can enjoy the pure mathematics of the way the numbers look. And one of the coolest things for the aficionados is finding a spot where either latitude or longitude is a complete whole number, with no fractions. Think of it as directional geek chic. You can enjoy a small sample of it by driving down Loring Street in Kingston, between Parks and River Streets. On the east side of the road, look for a granite slab celebrating the 42nd parallel. On that spot, you are at exactly 42 degrees latitude. Isn't it good to know where you are?

Hog Wild
Martha's Vineyard

Some motorcycle lovers says that Harley Davidsons make a deep-throated rumble that is music to their ears. It seems that the people at Panhead Mike's Offshore Cycle have taken that idea to an extreme. Sure, they tune Hogs—and totally rebuild and restore vintage bikes as well as giving attention to the more ordinary examples. But how many cycle shops expand into more cultural aspects of life? Panhead Mike's is also the rehearsal space for a local band that ended up taking its name—the Offshore Cycle Band—from its digs. And Panhead Mike's is also the official mechanic and enabler of the Flying Horses, the nation's oldest operating platform carousel. The merry-go-round was brought from New York's Coney Island to Oak Bluffs on the Vineyard in 1884. If you were born to be wild, thanks to the shop, you can still take a spin from Easter Sunday through Columbus Day and grab for the brass ring that gives a free ride. You'll be on a hand-carved horse, but if you'd rather try a Hog, head to the shop at 348 State Road, Vineyard Haven, call them at (508) 693-7447, or go to www.offshorecycle.com. For the carousel, go to the end of Oak Bluffs Avenue near the beach in Oak Bluffs . . . and don't forget the leather jacket.

★ ★

What Religion Hath Wrought
Martha's Vineyard

We'd love to tell you when you can enjoy Illumination Night in Oak
Bluffs—really, we would. It's a warmly glittering affair celebrating
the end of summer. After a sing-along concert, the oldest member
of the community lights a Japanese lantern. Then hundreds of similar
lamps are lit as they hang on the Tabernacle, a wrought-iron open-
air auditorium seating more than 3,000. (The Tabernacle was built
for religious services by the Methodists, who knew a good location
for a religious revival when they saw one.) And there are even more
lanterns on the nearby gingerbread cottages. These brightly painted
wooden structures once housed those attending the camp and are
now private homes. Footpaths lead all around the courtyards, so you
can take a stroll and appreciate the colorful dwellings in the glow.

So why don't we cough up the details of when you can see all
this? It's because we don't know. The event takes place sometime in
late August, but the exact date is kept a secret until about a week
before it happens. You can try to pry the secret out of someone, or
at least get the schedule for concerts and other activities at the Tabernacle, by calling (508) 693-0525 or going to www.mvcma.org/tab
.htm. And if you do miss the celebration, you can still have some fun
near the Tabernacle. See the cottages in the daylight or learn about
the life of the early fervent inhabitants at the Cottage Museum, One
Trinity Park in Oak Bluffs.

"Sea" the Big Horse
Mattapoisett

If you are traveling along the main drag in Mattapoisett, an aqua-
equestrian sight might leave you crying, "Whoa, Seabiscuit!" More
than fifty years ago, a gift shop owner wanted something to attract
attention and customers, so he asked sign maker Theodore Tetreault
to build an 8-foot-tall sea horse to place on the road. And build it he

★ ★

Photo by Erik Sherman

Salty the giant sea horse has gone from kitsch to landmark.

did. But in the grand scheme of things, how impressive is that? The finished product was hardly taller than some professional basketball players. Once it was finished, the original owner thought that the landscape swallowed it up. So Tetreault, with the help of his two sons, went back to the stable (or was it the fishing hole?) and built a 38-foot plywood sea horse. When done, it looked almost the way it does today. (Tetreault returned later with some boat builders to add a fiberglass layer, the better to protect the steed from its native element in liquid or frozen form.) Long after the original business owner was gone, the icon stayed. After all, where does an almost 40-foot sea horse sit? Anywhere it wants.

A few years ago the sea horse came down for some rest, recreation, and rehabilitation. The decades of exposure to the elements had been hard, and eight months of work were a wonderful restorative: a new tubular frame, the removal of rotted material, fresh sherbet-colored paint, another coat of fiberglass, and a new name: Salty. Tetreault died in 2001, but his monument lives on. The land around it is now a park. How fitting: After years of working to bring in the customers, the sea horse is happily put out to literal pasture. To see it, take a drive down Route 6 by North Street.

It's a Small World
Middleborough

The lesser things in life are usually those that qualify for small talk, and these days, the public is interested in bigger and better. However, today's small was the mid-nineteenth century's big. Mercy Lavinia Warren Bump, born in Middleborough, was more—or is it less?—than diminutive. At 32 inches tall, she was one of the two most famous midgets in the country. (The other was her husband, Charles Sherwood Stratton, otherwise known as "General" Tom Thumb.) Lavinia had a sister who was also only 32 inches tall. Her other sister was normal size, and all four of her brothers grew to over six feet. Yet she gained a level of fame that towered over that of her siblings. She spent a few years working on a relative's steamboat show on the Mississippi, then was hired by P. T. Barnum when she was 21 and dubbed "the Little Queen of Beauty." Although we're sure she was attractive, to be fair, there probably weren't a lot of contenders to the crown. Her future husband already worked for the master showman, and it would seem destiny that the two should marry, or at least form a conglomerate of their interests. Barnum turned the engagement announcement into a money-maker, putting the future bride on display for tens of thousands of people. The

★ ★

wedding, in 1863, was a major event in New York City, with more than 2,000 guests. The honeymooners spent time touring the world. As the years passed, both grew to 40 inches tall. After her husband's death, Lavinia lived in retirement until her marriage to Count Primo Magri, an Italian dwarf. She lived until the age of sixty-four and is buried in South Amenia, New York. But some of the personal effects of both Lavinia and Charles are on display in the Middleborough Historical Museum, which has the world's largest collection of Tom Thumb memorabilia, including his 12-inch walking stick. The collection is behind the town police station, on Jackson Street. Call ahead (508-947-1969) for the hours, though the management has been known to set up appointments at other times.

Thermometer Man

Onset

What's the difference between a personal collection and a museum? Maybe just a degree of interest. Some people get all hot and bothered about a subject, but Richard Porter could be called positively mercurial—literally. He has assembled thousands of items in what he claims is the world's largest—actually, he claims that it's the world's only—thermometer museum, which sits in the basement of his home. It's also, at last check, the only museum in Onset on Cape Cod. Here are big thermometers, little thermometers, thermometers shaped like animals. There are two pill-sized thermometers that John Glenn had to swallow on his last mission on the space shuttle, which match the backup model that traveled to the moon on *Apollo 9*. There is a thermometer that came as a prize in a Cracker Jack box, and another used in deep-sea studies. A model from Alaska reads to −100 degrees F. Some float; some are scientific instruments. Many came from flea markets, and others are from Porter's travels in the United States, Europe, South America, and Africa. Porter, a retired science teacher, started his collection decades ago after a friend told him, "If you don't collect something in retirement, you may just collect dust." His teaching activities have not been left out in the cold. He regularly gives presentations at schools, museums, and conferences. You can see the collection yourself by traveling to Onset, where the museum's motto is "Always open and always free with over 3,000 to see." Check www.members.aol.com/thermometerman for information or to inquire about visiting.

Cable Entertainment
Orleans

Sociologists and economists would argue that the telecommunications industry leaves a mark on society. We have learned that this is literally true. Just check the French Cable Station Museum, which celebrates what was a straightforward business investment of the day. Despite the reputation Yankees have of being taciturn and uncommunicative, Massachusetts became a hub of firsts in communication. Granted, this was largely because the innovators were from Europe. Alexander Graham Bell, a Scot, invented the telephone in Boston, and although the weather was against him, Italian Guglielmo Marconi looked to Cape Cod to provide a base for the first transatlantic radio broadcast—probably a good excuse to write off a vacation. But what the French Cable Museum commemorates is the time when the French, in 1869, laid their first transatlantic telegraph cable. It ran from the western tip of France to Newfoundland, to Orleans, and finally over to Duxbury. Given the difficulties of ocean travel, this was an impressive engineering feat. It was also a slow one, as the Atlantic Telegraph Company had managed to make a transatlantic hop a few years before. Yet being in second place didn't hinder the cable's usefulness. It was the mechanism by which the United States learned of Charles Lindbergh's successful landing in Paris. News from the French end was cut off in the spring of 1940 with the message "Les Boches sont ici—The Germans are here." The sister station in Brest finally resumed transmission—in 1952. (We figure that one of those famous

French labor strikes might have slowed things down after the end of the war.)

The museum is not the only legacy of the cable. To this day, you will find many Norgeots, Deschamps, and Ozons in local phone directories. These are the descendants of men who came from a French-owned set of islands near Newfoundland to work at the station. To check out the museum, go to 41 South Orleans Road, which is near the intersection of Cove Road and Route 28. It's open various hours, though not at all times of the year, so call (508) 240-1735 ahead of time to be sure.

Photo by Erik Sherman

The French Cable Station Museum in Orleans celebrates the French connection.

★ ★

Were the Pilgrims Really Stiffs?
Plymouth

The Pilgrims have a reputation for being unbending—religious, industrious, and no fun at all. Yet there is stiff, and there is . . . stiff. At
the Pilgrim National Wax Museum, you can find representations of
the sect that are entirely unmovable. Interest in our national forerun-
ners is hardly unusual, and wax museums are common enough. But
how many wax museums are completely devoted to the people who
landed at Plymouth Rock? This one is located on Cole's Hill, where
the *Mayflower* immigrants secretly buried their dead after their first
winter on this continent so that the Wampanoag Indians would not
know how their number had dwindled (amusing, as the group would
have disappeared had the natives not helped them). Here, though,
the dead still live. A series of dioramas show scenes of the Pilgrim's
past: being jailed in England, signing the Mayflower pact, the first
Thanksgiving, the blossoming love of John Alden and Priscilla Mullins.
There are twenty-six scenes in all and a total of 180 figures. That's a
lot of wax. If you get tired of the educational tour, then step outside,
cross the street, and take in the salt air of the harbor. Just remember
that this is a unique experience. In fact, you might say that no other
attraction holds a candle to it. The museum is at 15 Carver Street.
You can get more information at (508) 746-6468 or by checking
www.falmouthvisitor.com/plymouth_national_wax_museum.htm.

Pilgrim's Grind
Plymouth

Let's thank the Pilgrims for all they have done: opening a new land
to colonization, kicking out anyone who didn't agree with their religious views, and introducing the concept of the public utility. That's
right: The next time you get angry at the electric company, remember
that you have people from the seventeenth century to thank. When
the Pilgrims almost starved and froze to death their first year here—

obviously not having read the visitors' information—the Wampanoags taught them to grow and store corn. But the settlers had increasing numbers of residents to consider, and the process of grinding corn with a mortar and pestle was either too inefficient or had become an entirely too overwhelming drag. Enter John Jenney, who knew that he could make use of the settlers' laziness. In 1636 he received permission to build a grinding mill, starting a tradition of disputed charges and poor customer service that has lasted to this day. At least reliability was there—although the original burned down in 1847, a 1970 reconstruction brought it back to working order; it still grinds corn, and you can buy bags of meal. Next to it is a fish ladder, so the herring can go upstream to spawn.

If you want to see where it all started and take a tour, head to the corner of Leyden and Water Streets. Walk through the park area, called Brewster Gardens; look for the small footbridge. Cross it, continue down the path along the stream, and you will see the building at the end. Or, if you are feeling lazy, go directly to the mill at 6 Spring Street. For more information call (508) 747-4544, or go to www.jenneygristmill.com. Sorry, but the complaint department isn't open today.

Plymouth Pebble?

Plymouth

Anyone in the United States who has sat through coloring paper turkeys at Thanksgiving has heard of Plymouth Rock. But few know how lucky they are to have any rock at all. First there is the question of what the rock actually was. According to the Pilgrim Hall Museum, none of the documents from that time mentioned a pebble, let alone a rock. The two books of the time written by participants said only that they had landed. It wasn't until a hundred years later that any written works mentioned Plymouth Rock, yet somehow a local legend became "fact." Okay; for the sake of grade school teachers everywhere we'll be nice and say that it was the stepping-stone. However,

★ ★

Photo by Erik Sherman

A local legend became fact when Plymouth Rock was turned into a memorial.

that anything remains of the rock is a wonder. It was in the nineteenth century that people decided to make a monument of the rock, and the object of public affection barely survived. It had become embedded in a wharf, and attempts to move it with a team of oxen actually split Plymouth Rock into two pieces. So the people took the small piece from the top and placed it prominently in front of the town hall. At that point, all manner of people snuck in to chip away at the stone for a souvenir. The townsfolk decided to protect this remaining shard by carting it off to sit behind a fence at the Pilgrim Hall Museum. Whoops—the rock popped off the cart and cracked on the way. And at some point, someone carved the date *1620* into the rock. (Gee, we thought the Pilgrims found it that way.) It's just not easy being a legend.

If you visit today, you'll find Plymouth Rock behind walls and under a fancy portico on Water Street, near the end of North Street. Or you could seek out the local hotel that advertises a hot tub with a plastic replica of the big stone—a regular chip off the old granite, and maybe even as authentic.

Taken for Granite
Plymouth

The Pilgrims stand tall in American history and imagination, and even taller on a hilltop on Allerton Street—81 feet tall, to be precise. The largest freestanding granite monument in the world, the National Monument to the Forefathers is a massive edifice commemorating the arrival of the *Mayflower* and its occupants and visited by a quarter million people annually. The designer was Boston artist and architect Hammat Billings—the original illustrator of *Uncle Tom's Cabin*—while the sculptor was Joseph Archie, a Spaniard.

The monument, at a cost of $150,000, wasn't finished until 1889, some fifteen years after the death of Billings. But you don't realize just how long it took to erect the monument until you realize that the cornerstone went into place in 1859. The builders managed to make the trip to the New World look short, and no wonder. The amount of detail and ornamentation was enough to make the plain-loving Puritans on the boat blush. Seated figures representing education, liberty, law, and morality surround an eight-sided base. At the top stands Faith, and panels on the sides depict Pilgrim history, or at least what we'd like to think was Pilgrim history. The names of all those who came over on the *Mayflower* are on two plaques, and a front panel reads, "Erected by a grateful people in remembrance of their labors, sacrifices and sufferings for the cause of civil and religious liberty." Hopefully someone remembered to thank whoever made it possible to haul the granite into place. Sometime after the construction came the walk paths, a driveway, and fancy fence and entry posts. All it needs is a neat little house, a white picket fence, and the American dream will have come to fruition. To learn more about the monument, go to www.mass.gov/dcr/stewardship/rmp/rmp-forefatheres.htm.

Gender Bender
Provincetown

Those with an aversion to the unusual in gender roles should avoid Provincetown in mid-October when the town hosts the Fantasia Fair, also known as TransGender week. An annual event since 1974, the fair would more accurately be called a conference or convention. It is meant to help the transgendered live in the midst of regular society while providing "positive reinforcement and encouragement." Participants pay and register for either a half week or full week of sessions such as Daytime Makeup Tips, Trans in the Workplace, and Hormones 101. There is information for MTF (male-to-female) and FTM (female-to-male). Aside from information sessions, there are breakfasts, lunches, and dinners, and even a fashion show and musical review. This is not an occasion for gawkers, as the fair costs a pretty penny. Those attending have paid hundreds of dollars for the full week or a discounted rate for four days and three nights, not counting lodging. Many bring partners and spouses, who pay a lower rate to take part. If you aren't part of the scene, then remember that October is past the summer season and a great time to visit a beautiful part of Cape Cod in relative quiet. Just try not to get rattled and use the wrong public restroom. For more information see www.fantasiafair.org.

Why? Whydah Not?
Provincetown

Some people climb mountains, some swim the English Channel, and some seek shipwrecks. There is nothing else that can describe the drive that Barry Clifford has when it comes to finding boats that sank in the ocean. What can only be called an obsession of Clifford's with

★ ★

the pirate ship *Whydah* started when he heard stories in his youth. As an adult, he put together an expedition that had one of the great "in the nick of time" endings. After almost two years of searching, and down to his last dollar and tank of fuel, Clifford's group found the famous pirate ship, whose sunken fortunes raised Clifford's. Since then he has found the remains of one of Captain Kidd's ships, as well as a French fleet. Now Clifford thinks that he's found the *Santa Maria*—the flagship of Christopher Columbus.

At the time of this writing, there is nothing definite about the identification of Clifford's latest find, but you can visit the museum that commemorates his most famous discovery to date. The Expedition *Whydah* Sea Lab and Learning Center at 16 MacMillan Wharf features some of the 200,000 artifacts that Clifford's team brought up. Also take time to learn more about the ship, the lives of pirates, and the methods that put the jolly back in the roger. Call (508) 487-8899 or visit www.whydah.com for hours and other information.

Grudge Granite
Provincetown

The words *Pilgrim* and *Plymouth* have a historic alliterative American accent. Yet before the *Mayflower* neared the famous P-rock, it stopped at the very end of Cape Cod, at what would eventually become P-town. (They must have been the first Provincetown tourists.) They even managed to sign the Mayflower Compact during their brief stop on their way to Plymouth. Not that you would know it from the way history is taught in schools. To almost everyone, the first, last, and only stop the Pilgrims made was north of the Cape. This must have left the good folks of Provincetown feeling slighted. To make sure that they got their due, the townspeople erected the Pilgrim Monument. Work began in 1907 and ended three years later.

The Pilgrim Monument is the tallest granite monument in the country, at 252 feet 7 inches. The design was copied from the Torre del Mangia in Siena, Italy. Okay, so maybe someone was confusing the England of the Puritans with the Italy of Columbus. No matter: The view from the top can be spectacular, with Cape Cod Bay, Provincetown Harbor, and the sand dunes of the Cape Cod National Seashore visible. On a clear day you can even see Boston. To get to that lofty sight, however, you must gain the lofty height, climbing 116 stairs and sixty ramps. After all that work, you might want to take a brief rest, which you can do in the museum while enjoying the current exhibition and remembering not to take the first Pilgrim landing spot for granite. It's not open year-round, so check http://pilgrim-monument.org or call (508) 487-1310 for information. Then drive to One High Pole Hill Road.

Photo by Erik Sherman

The Pilgrim Monument, the highest point in Provincetown, celebrates the area's highest point in American history.

A Tale of Two Presidents

Quincy

Like father, like son? There is a long tradition of offspring following parents into a line of work, except when it comes to being president of the United States. The Bushes have managed it, but before them the only case was that of John Adams and his son, John Quincy Adams. There are a number of similarities, such as both the fathers serving only one term and the sons taking office after losing the popular vote in a disputed election. But the presidents Adams were far closer, at least physically, in their origins and ends. They

★ ★

were born within 75 yards of each other in the same house, and both are buried, along with their wives, at the United First Parish in Quincy, also called the Church of the Presidents. The church keeps the Adams crypt open to visitors and is actually part of the Adams National Historical Park, although it receives no public funding. The rest of the park includes the birthplace of the presidents as well as the Stone Library, which includes the entire book collection of John Quincy Adams. During the season, April 19 to November 10, there are guided tours of the homes. Go to the visitor center in the Galleria at Presidents Place for the first-come, first-served, first in the hearts of their—sorry, wrong president—tours. There is validated parking and a free trolley between the center and the historic homes about every thirty minutes on the quarter hour. For more information call (617) 770-1175 or visit www.nps.gov/adam.

Will the Real Peter Please Hop Up?

Sandwich

Know the name Thornton W. Burgess? This native of Sandwich may not sound familiar, but chances are that you know some of his creations: Peter Rabbit, Hooty Owl, Grandfather Skunk, and Jimmy Skunk. Naturalist and author Burgess wrote more than 170 books and some 15,000 stories—enough to keep a child out of trouble for at least part of the formative years. Now you too can avoid some trouble in two facilities: a museum and a nature center.

The Thornton W. Burgess Society runs a museum in a house once owned by Burgess's Aunt Arabella. It is filled with memorabilia, art, and other items of interest; an herb garden and pond are out back. (There is a nominal entrance fee during the open season of April through October.)

Yet while looking into the museum's history, we ran into a bit of a problem. One Burgess character was Peter Rabbit, as his books and the Society Web site show. Yet there is a different Peter Rabbit, written by author and animal lover Beatrix Potter. According to a bit of

Kilroy Was in Quincy

Anyone whose parents lived through World War II has likely heard of Kilroy. Like an armed forces Mary and her lamb, anywhere the military went, the mysterious man was sure to go. But unlike the nursery rhyme, Kilroy was a pioneer, not a follower. Wherever GIs went, the bet was more than even money that they would find written on a wall, a monument, or even a latrine that "Kilroy was here," often accompanied by a cartoon face peering over a wall. It got to be a race among soldiers and sailors to see if they could chalk the presence in a spot before others.

What might have surprised most of those GIs was that there actually was a Kilroy: James J. Kilroy, to be exact. The man worked at the Fore River Shipyard in Quincy, once a major building facility. He was an inspector, seeing how many holes riveters would fill in a day. To avoid double-counting by some worker trying to make the job rosier, Kilroy would mark his passage by writing "Kilroy was here" with a yellow crayon. Once a ship was finished and sent overseas, the expansive presence of Kilroy continued as it sailed around the world. However, no one bothered to explain the cryptic notation to the troops on the ships. Kilroy eventually got around in a big way: The name has supposedly been found on Mount Everest, the torch of the Statue of Liberty, the underside of the Arc de Triomphe, a girder on the George Washington Bridge, and in the dust on the moon. According to one probably apocryphal story, during the Potsdam Conference, in which the United States, Great Britain, and the Soviet Union set the surrender demands for Japan, Stalin was the first to use an outhouse built for the occasion. Upon exiting, the leader reportedly turned to his aide and asked, "Who is Kilroy?" He was just this guy in Quincy. Chalk it up to a triumph of international relations. Although Kilroy is no longer there, you can see the shipyard and the United States Naval Shipbuilding Museum, which is housed on the old USS *Salem*, at 739 Washington Street. For information and hours call (617) 479-7900 or visit www.uss-salem.org.

★ ★

online snooping, it seems that Potter's first book, *The Tale of Peter Rabbit,* appeared in 1902. The Burgess Peter Rabbit was in part of a set of syndicated children's stories illustrated by Harrison Cady, which appeared in 1910 as newspaper columns. So the timing is close, but the two characters are different in age and temperament, and the two authors were separated by the Atlantic Ocean. We guess that Peter is a common enough name, even among rabbits.

One difference between the two animal worlds is that Burgess's Peter Rabbit lived in a briar patch. If the kids, or the kid-in-you, want to move around more, wander over to the Green Briar Nature Center, open all year and situated next to a briar patch—yes, the one in the stories. You can find workshops, natural history programs, and some pleasant walking trails in a fifty-seven-acre conservation area, all open to the public. And while you're there, take a peek into the Green Briar Jam Kitchen. Call ahead and you may be able to catch a jam-making workshop. The Robert S. Swain Natural History Library, containing books, magazines, and other materials on the flora and fauna of the Northeast, rounds out the visit. For more information visit the museum at 4 Water Street (Route 130; 508-888-4668) or the Green Briar Nature Center and Jam Kitchen, 6 Discovery Hill Road in East Sandwich (508-888-6870).

Corn Hill

Truro

Pilgrims? Plymouth Rock. It's a match made in the history books. But that town wasn't the ship's only stopping place. Right before landing there, the immigrants stopped on Cape Cod in the areas that would become Eastham, Provincetown, and Truro. After making some sojourns for supplies and a break for washing clothes—inspiring, we are sure, the Laundromat—a group of men went exploring. While tromping about, they stumbled upon some fields cleared for farming and a store of corn, as well as a metal kettle that looked as though it came from Europe. After taking as much corn as they could carry to

Photo by Erik Sherman

Corn Hill was once the site of perfidious provisions pilfering.

plant later, they buried the rest in the kettle. We can hear the conversation now: "Jumping Jehoshaphat, Brother Ephraim, look at all this corn. Good thing there's nobody here that it belongs to. Let's scram." That corn was a literal life saver; roughly ten bushels provided a crop for the spring and a welcome source of food after a winter that would kill a frighteningly large percentage of the party. So the successful colonization of Massachusetts started with an act of larceny. Good thing there were no laws making it illegal.

The Pilgrims vowed to make restitution, having a sneaking suspicion that the corn belonged to someone. Eventually they put two and two together and realized that it was Indian corn. The restitution came in the form of the weeklong feast that we now commemorate as Thanksgiving (to say nothing of disease, war, and land-grabbing). You can see the historic spot, called Corn Hill, and a commemorative

Revolutionary Feminist Fighter

When we hear the phrase "daughters of the American revolution," the images that come to mind include petticoats, churning butter by hand, sewing clothes, and picking up the eggs for breakfast from under the hens. But Deborah Samson, descended from Gov. William Bradford of *Mayflower* fame, would tend to wearing trousers, shooting guns, and fighting. Blame it on poverty and a father who abandoned her, but this was a woman who could take care of herself. This native of Plympton also became the first woman to masquerade as a man and fight in the Revolutionary War.

Samson's father went to sea and her mother couldn't make ends meet, so Samson lived with relatives and, at age ten, became an indentured servant to a family of ten. She stayed in this position until she was eighteen. Hard labor developed her strength, and she learned to shoot a musket as well as to spin, weave, and cook. In other words, this was a woman to be reckoned with. When two of the sons of the family that she lived with were killed, her fate was decided.

Samson borrowed clothes from a man named Samuel Leonard, disguised herself as a boy called Timothy Thayer, and joined the Continental Army. Then in 1782, at age twenty-one, she enlisted in the Fourth Massachusetts Regiment under the name of Robert Shurtleff. She was 5 foot 7 inches tall, and she bound her breasts to look like a lad. Other soldiers assumed that "Robert" was too young to have started shaving. Good thing they didn't check her legs. Eventually an illness revealed the truth, and she had her honorable discharge personally handed to her by George Washington. Obviously he knew better than to make her mad.

Samson even received a pension eventually, thanks to the intercession of Paul Revere, and her husband was granted a widow's pension after her death at age sixty-six, to complete the tale of gender reversal. In 1983 she was named the official heroine of Massachusetts. A plaque honoring Samson is on the Plympton Town Green; go to 11 North Main Street in Sharon to see a statue of her.

★ ★

marker near Corn Hill Road off Route 6, which is a darned sight harder to find than the corn was. While you are there, enjoy the beach.

Towering Talent
Truro

Every age has its superstars. Even before music videos, CDs, and movies, there were performers who could command enthusiastic mayhem. One of them was Jenny Lind, the soprano known as the "Swedish Nightingale." She started playing piano at age four and eventually attended the Royal Theater School to study music, dance, and acting. She had her first big opera role at age seventeen, and she soon became

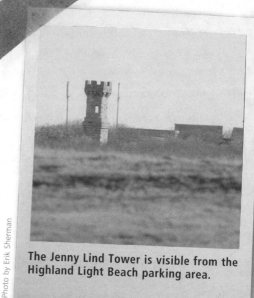

Photo by Erik Sherman

The Jenny Lind Tower is visible from the Highland Light Beach parking area.

the leading singer in Europe. Taking into account the slower pace of communications and travel, it is difficult to appreciate the furor that could bubble up about Lind's performances. When she came to New York for a concert tour promoted by showman P. T. Barnum, nearly 40,000 suckers . . . ah, adoring fans . . . lured by the artful publicity packed the docks to welcome her arrival by ship.

As part of her tour, Lind was scheduled to sing in Boston in 1850, but someone massively oversold the concert, and many of the people who paid their money could not fit in the building. According to legend, which seems to be unsupported by newspaper accounts at the time, Lind climbed to the top of an adjoining 55-foot tower to sing to

★ ★

the people in the street. Perhaps another piece of Barnum's hokum? Could be. However, in 1927, the tower was slated for demolition. Harry M. Aldrich, supposedly a serious Jenny Lind fan, bought the structure. He had it moved, stone by stone, to North Truro by train, and then by horse-drawn cart to its present location in Truro. The building, which came to be known as the Jenny Lind Tower, was deeded in 1961 to the Cape Cod National Seashore by Aldrich's daughter-in-law. You can't get to the tower without trespassing on private land, but you can drive up Highland Road and park at the Highland Light Beach parking lot to take a look and a bow.

A Place Made for Radio
Wellfleet

Guglielmo Marconi was the first person to make it big in radio. First he invented it; then he demonstrated the first transatlantic broadcast in 1901. Too bad that he couldn't have staged his demonstration in Wellfleet, and moved to Canada instead.

Cape Cod was Marconi's preferred location, and his team was erecting transmission equipment there in 1901. Unfortunately, the quality of construction left something to be desired. In August, just two months after building had started, a stiff breeze bent the heads of the antenna mast, and the Italian inventor moved north, where men were men and radio towers were sturdy. It was the first case of cheaply made electronics equipment with no written warranty in sight. So much for history.

In the fall of 1901, the masts totally collapsed. It wouldn't be until January 18, 1903, that the station finally was put back into commission. A transmission occurred from the United States, with President Theodore Roosevelt sending a message to King Edward VII of England. The Wellfleet station remained in operation until the U.S. Navy closed it in 1917 for safety reasons. (How surprising.) The area became a military camp and, eventually, part of the Cape Cod National Seashore. Today some tower footings and a bit of the station's foundation are all that is left. There is an informative display as well as a pleasant beach, which is good because you will probably tire of the placards even faster than the towers fell. Head over to Marconi Site Road and drive down, following the signs to the beach. For more information call (508) 255-3421, or see www.nps.gov/caco/planyourvisit/marconi-beach.htm.

Belly Confusing
Wellfleet

The Wellfleet town clock confuses the uninitiated. When its bell rings four times, it is 6:00 in the morning . . . unless it is 10:00 a.m., 2:00 p.m., or the middle of the night. No, the mechanism is not broken. Wellfleet has the only town clock that rings on ship's time. It's a complex system in which the day is broken into watches and then subdivided into hours marked by anywhere from one to eight bells.

The story of how the clock ended up here is happily simpler. It was the brainchild of a town selectman in 1952, Lawrence Gardinier, who was a brilliant tinkerer without a formal education. Because of the maritime history of the area, he wanted a town ship's clock. After convincing others to go along with the idea, Gardinier proposed a budget of $500 to create a striking mechanism for the three-faced clock in the steeple of the First Con-

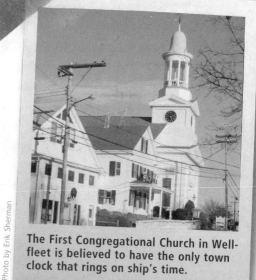

Photo by Erik Sherman

The First Congregational Church in Wellfleet is believed to have the only town clock that rings on ship's time.

gregational Church, which was just ornamental. Combining motors, relays, wire, mechanisms, and other bells and whistles, he rigged a device that would ring the church bell the proper number of times at the correct hours. His contraption was used for twenty years before it was replaced for the most part by an electronic system. However, on special occasions, the old bell system still delivers on time, every time. You can see and hear the time at 200 Main Street.

Letting the Chips Fall
Whitman

Most roads lead somewhere, and most signs are put in place to draw attention to something. But there is the odd dead end and at least one carefully tended sign advertising a business that has been gone since the mid-1980s.

The story of the phantom sign has a uniquely sweet beginning. Most cookies don't have the prominence to deserve a history. Not so the original chocolate chip cookie—the toll house—which really came about by accident. Kenneth and Ruth Wakefield ran the Toll House Inn in Whitman. The building had originally been a toll booth on the road between New Bedford and Boston. One day in 1930 Ruth was baking a batch of cookies for customers. She usually chopped up baker's chocolate for this particular recipe, and the dark chunks would melt into the dough. One day she ran out of her usual ingredient and instead turned to the next chocolate thing she had: a bar of Nestlé semi-sweet. But instead of melting in, the bits of chocolate kept their shape. The cookie became a hit, her recipe was published in some newspapers, and sales for the chocolate bar went through the roof. Ruth then approached Nestlé. She struck a deal with the company, and the recipe appeared on the candy bar wrapping. Sales continued to improve and the company eventually started scoring the bar and including a special chopper. In 1939 Nestlé finally created a bag of special chocolate pieces that worked well in the recipe, and smart business met culinary history.

★ ★

Photo by Erik Sherman

Pay no attention to the pointing hand. You can't get there from here.

The Toll House Inn went through several owners and finally burned down on New Year's Eve in 1984. Ruth Wakefield died in 1977 and is buried in the Mayflower Cemetery at 774 Tremont Street (Route 3A) in Duxbury. However, you might call the one remnant of the late Toll House Inn the marketing equivalent of a headstone. To this day, if you go to Route 18, right near the intersection of Route 14, standing proudly between two fast-food emporiums is the sign.

Golf Grave

Yarmouth Port

We come into the world alone and we leave alone—unless we have company. Many old graveyards in Massachusetts are filled with figures from politics, literature, and the arts. They tend to be crowded, as free space is scarce. But in Yarmouth Port on Cape Cod, there is a

★ ★

singular phenomenon: a cemetery with a single gravestone sitting on a golf course. In December 1801, a sixty-four-year-old resident, John Hall, died. The cause of his death was smallpox, which, although long since controlled, was a scourge of the world at that time. It was contagious and a killer. In those days, people figured that the safest thing was to keep everyone, and every corpse, with the disease far away from the uninfected. And so, John Hall had a solitary grave in the woods, as happened in other towns on the Cape.

Eventually, someone decided to build the Kings Way Golf Club in that same patch of woods. In clearing the trees, they found Hall's final resting place. It was neither a natural hazard nor something that could be moved, so it became part of the scene. Was John Hall married, and if so, can we call the Widow Hall the first literal golf widow in this country?

Protecting the grave is a low, heavy chain supported by short posts. We assume that should a ball stray onto the grave, it must be considered dead, with the player losing a stroke. Here's hoping that Mr. Hall continues to find peace—and maybe a mulligan or two. To pay your respects to the late Mr. Hall, and to any wayward golf balls, go to the course by taking King's Circuit off Route 6A. Follow the large circular drive around the course, look for the sign that says "13," take the side street, and look for the parking area on the right. The grave is past the trees, on the right-hand side of the green for the par-three hole.

Photo by Erik Sherman

John Hall's compact abode rests behind a sand trap.

5

Central Massachusetts

A museum tour of Massachusetts might start right here in the central part of the state. There's the Top Fun Aviation Toy Museum in Winchendon, the National Plastics Center and Museum in Leominster, the Higgins Armory Museum (don't miss the armored dog) in Worcester, and if you are of a more musical turn of mind, the Frederick Historic Piano Collection in Ashburnham.

Happier collecting antiques than looking at them? Plan to go to the Brimfield Fair held for a week in spring, summer and fall. Five thousand or so antique dealers show their wares along a mile stretch of Route 20. Bring shopping bags, a knapsack, a wheelbarrow, and cash (the preferred medium of exchange), and haul those goodies home.

Yes, Podunk is in Massachusetts, but it's not as much fun as the state's very own "Second City," Worcester. Once "the shredded wheat capital of the world," it claimed America's first Nobel Prize winner—Albert Michelson of Clark University—as its own. Worcester is also the home of Buster, the world's largest inflatable crab, and was the site of professional baseball's first perfect game, pitched by left-hander John Lee Richmond in 1880. Eat your heart out, Chicago!

Feel like humming a tune? "Say Hello to Someone in Massachusetts" is the official state polka; Arlo Guthrie's "Massachusetts" is the state's official folk song. "The Great State of Massachusetts" is the official patriotic song. Whatever happened to "Please Come to Boston"?

Central Massachusetts

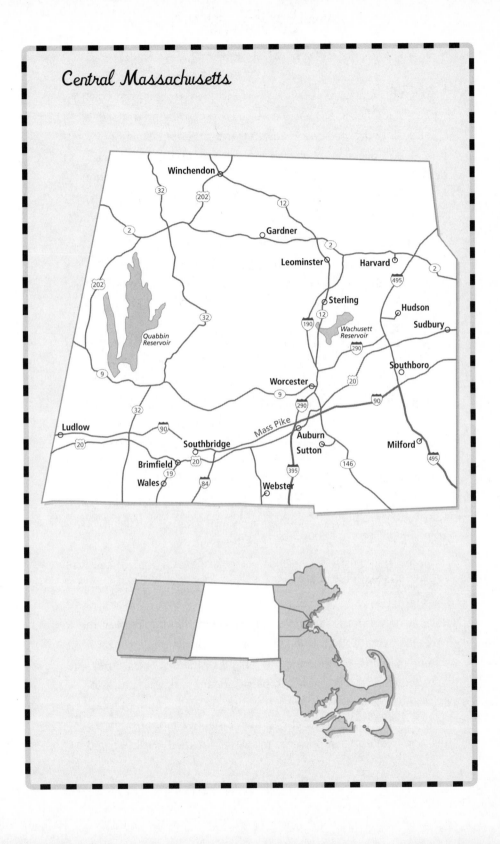

Keyed Up
Ashburnham

If you're a fan of the song "I Love a Piano," then the Frederick Historic Piano Collection is a place for you. Maybe it's a grand place
because it houses only grand pianos, or perhaps the real attraction
for musicians, students, and music lovers is the chance to hear major
piano work played on instruments like the ones the composers would
have known and used or preferred. The difference in sound can be
enormous, and a modern instrument may not let you hear pieces as
their creators envisioned. The oldest piano in the collection comes
from 1790, and the most modern trails off just over 200 years later.
The collection was the brainchild of Edmund Michael Frederick and
his wife, Patricia Humphrey Frederick. Both are musicians and still live
in the town. Rather than have a museum, they created what they call
a study center, with instruments available to scholars and musicians.
There are public tours on Thursday and Saturday all year. For over
twenty years the couple has also run a concert series, pairing music
with period-appropriate instruments on various Sunday afternoons.
To learn more about the instruments, the concert series, or even
about how a piano is made, go to www.frederickcollection.org. The
study center is at 30 Main Street, adjacent to the town hall at the
intersections of Routes 12 and 101. Most concerts take place at the
Community Church, about 3 blocks east.

. . . Seven, Six, Five, Fore!
Auburn

Halfway between the tee and the green on the ninth fairway of the
Pakachoag Golf Course in the town of Auburn is a unique hazard:
a stone marker commemorating the flight of the first successfully
launched liquid-fueled rocket. Robert Goddard, a physics professor
at nearby Worcester Polytechnic Institute, set off his 10-foot rocket
on March 16, 1926, on what was then his aunt's farm. Goddard's
gas- and liquid-oxygen powered missile, nicknamed "Nell," soared 41

feet into the heavens before landing in a frozen cabbage patch. The hometown newspaper's headline the next day read: "Moon rocket misses target by 238,799½ miles."

The successful, if not stratosphere-breaking, launch earned Goddard the title of "Father of Modern Rocketry," and today road signs leading into Worcester proudly honor the hometown scientist. Quite a different reception from the one the *New York Times* gave Goddard in 1929. The prestigious newspaper proclaimed him a crackpot who lacked "the knowledge ladled out daily in high schools." Everyone knew, reported the *Times,* that space travel as theorized by Goddard was impossible because without atmosphere to push against, a rocket could not move. Despite Goddard's certainty that Newton's law of action and reaction was with him, the article sent the scientist into a funk from which, despite his aeronautical achievements, he never really did recover. In 1969, after the first lunar landing, the *New York Times* published a correction.

Long after his death in 1945, Goddard received scores of honors, including the Congressional Medal and the National Inventors Hall of Fame Award. The awards are part of the extensive collection of Goddard memorabilia in the Goddard Library at Clark University. A time capsule containing a replica of a rocket Goddard built in 1940 and some dirt from his aunt's farm launch site is encased in concrete in the floor leading to the library. The rocket time capsule is to be opened in 2466, five hundred years after it was dedicated by Vice President Hubert Humphrey. You can find the library, at least, at 90 Main Street, Worcester, at (508) 793-7711, or at www.clarku.edu/research/goddard.

World's Biggest Garage Sale
Brimfield

Are you an inveterate collector? Is that being kind? Do friends and family more often use the term "pack rat"? If so, you will be in rat . . . uh, hog heaven three times a year at the Brimfield Fair. The fair is the work of a number of event producers, all of whom have their own staked-out spots. On a Tuesday through Sunday in late spring, summer, and early fall, 5,000 or more antiques dealers from all over the country converge here, lining a mile of Route 20. Add bargain-hunting crowds and you have something modern in the midst of the old treasures—a traffic jam.

Planning an outing through Brimfield on a show day is something like planning the Normandy invasion. If you are a serious shopper, do not—we repeat, do *not*—decide to "wing it." Go to www.brimfield .com and check out the pre-show schedule. Also, come prepared. You'll want a backpack to carry your swag. And, another must, don't claim to be with the Internal Revenue Service; cash is by far the pre-ferred currency. Another piece of advice: These dealers have paid good money to attend, and show organizers aren't inclined to offer refunds, no matter what the weather, so if it rains, quickly find an umbrella. Don't put off a trip until the last hours, as dealers often wrap up early. If you're so inclined, it's okay to buy some new things while you are there; they'll probably be antiques by the time you finally get out of traffic.

Sit Down and Be Counted
Gardner

They've been making chairs in Gardner since 1805. By 1837 they were turning out so many chairs that residents immodestly dubbed the place "Chair City of the World." Then in 1905 the town com-memorated the one-hundredth anniversary of its chairmaking industry by building a 12-foot-tall mission chair. But the folks in Thomasville, North Carolina, the self-proclaimed "Furniture and Hosiery Capital of the World," weren't about to take a back seat to Gardner. So in 1928 they built a chair that was a foot and a half taller.

Over the next seventy-five years, other cities built increasingly larger chairs to lay claim to the throne as the king of chairdom. In Bennington, Vermont, they built a 19-foot 1-inch-tall ladderback.

★ ★

Again, Thomasville wasn't about to take this sitting down. They built a chair 5 inches taller. Morristown, Tennessee, got into the fray with a 20-foot-tall green sheet metal recliner. Then in 1976, for the bicentennial, Gardner defended the North's honor by building a 20-foot 7-inch-high job. The local Rotary Club in Gardner commissioned Leon W. Plante to design the mother of all chairs. His creation, 10 feet wide and 9 feet deep, stands (or sits, as the case may be) in front of the Helen Mae Sauter Elementary School at 130 Elm Street. However, Gardner sat tall in the saddle for just a year, when its chair was upstaged by a 24-foot 9-inch tall ladderback in Binghamton, New York.

Photo courtesy of Yulia Govorushko

It may not be the largest chair in the world, but Gardner's 20-foot 7-inch model is the biggest in the Bay State.

In June 2002 rustic furniture maker Bim Willow of Michigan bent branches into a behemoth 55-footer and says he will build a 70-foot willow tree chair on request. It's left the competition weeping.

While you are in Gardner, you'll also see a 15-foot pretender to the throne on Route 2A.

Ye with Little Faith

Hudson

Apparently Rev. Louis Winthrop West was bored with retirement and wanted to do a little ministering. So in the summer of 1953, he began constructing a church on the front lawn of his house of

★ ★

worship. It didn't take long to build because it wasn't very big. In fact, Reverend West's Union Church of All Faiths was the smallest church in the world. The mini-sanctuary measured just 5 feet wide, 11 feet deep, and 10 feet high. Inside, on the back wall, a 20-square-foot painting depicted a sailing ship grounded on rocks. Its title: *In the Cross of Christ I Glory*. The nautical theme was continued atop the church, where the steeple housed a bell from a Coast Guard vessel. Reverend West also placed a golf ball under the church's mini–weather vane.

Over the years more than 10,000 people have signed the tiny church's guest books. More than 600 weddings have taken place in the petite structure. Obviously Reverend West thought small was beautiful, because a few years later he built an even smaller church, measuring just 5 feet by 9 and a half feet at his summer home in Wiscasset, Maine. It was later dismantled.

The smallest church in the world was built by Rev. Louis Winthrop West in Hudson.

Photo courtesy of the Hudson Historical Society

When Reverend West died in 1966, his son, Horace, took over the micro-nondenominational church. The church was open 24/7 year-round until vandals broke two crosses and left beer bottles on the floor. Then in the fall of 1977, the tiny chapel was moved down the street to the rear of the First Federated Church, where it was rededicated but little used. Eventually the steeple fell off.

Vic Petkauskos, a contractor from Hyannis who grew up in Hudson in the 1950s, always remembered passing Reverend West's tiny church. In the spring of 2003 Petkauskos bought what remained of the building, hauled it to his garage on Cape Cod, and began repairing "the whole shooting match." He installed a new floor and even built a new steeple with stained-glass windows. Petkauskos plans to place the church on a barge, decorate it with flowers, and hold weddings afloat off the coast of the Cape. The little church that could, still can.

The Sunny Side Up
Leominster

For years a giant frying pan that weighs 380 pounds, is 9 feet in diameter, and has an 8-foot-long handle, hung on the outside of Rob's Country Kitchen at 23 Sack Boulevard. Obviously, Rob couldn't stand the heat because in April 2004 he got out of the kitchen . . . and the restaurant biz. Today you will find Al Dente Pizzeria at the address. The giant pan still hangs outside, but now it holds several slices of very large pizza.

Featherstone's Flamingos
Leominster

Florida may have the real thing, but Massachusetts has the biggest flock of fake flamingos in the United States. Leominster is home to the plastic pink variety produced by Union Products from 1957 until 2006, when the company stopped production for financial reasons. The feather in the cap for the idea goes to Don Featherstone, who created the classic lawn ornament soon after he started working at the company. His first design for the firm was an anatomically correct duck, but it didn't fly. However, sales of the flightless 3-foot-tall birds immediately took off; more than 20 million of the Pepto-Bismol–colored birds sold.

Photo by Bruce Gellerman

Don and Nancy Featherstone hold flightless fancy birds of his design.

In 1986 Featherstone's signature was added to the statue to guarantee authenticity, but when he retired from Union Products in 2000, the company removed his John Hancock. Traditionalists flocked together and caused quite a flap when they heard the news, calling for a boycott against buying the statues sans his signature.

In the summer, Featherstone and his wife, Nancy, place fifty-seven of the birds in their cement-covered backyard. In the winter they install a pair of "snomingos" (albino models of the birds).

Nancy and Don are a strange pair of birds themselves. Every day for the past twenty-six years, they have worn identical outfits she sews. Two years prior to that, before they were married, they wore the same outfits only on weekends. To see the location where the pink plastic once flew out the doors, head to 511 Lancaster Street.

Say Hello to Someone in Massachusetts

Lenny Gomulka is no Lawrence Welk, but he has penned a high-stepping polka worthy of the bubble master himself. His tune, "Say Hello to Someone in Massachusetts," is the official polka of the commonwealth. Lenny wrote the catchy little ditty in a moment of inspiration. He was driving near his home in Ludlow when the tune just came to him. He grabbed his handheld tape recorder and thankfully preserved the polka for posterity.

Despite the fact that it is really, really hard to come up with words that rhyme with *Massachusetts*, the state has more than its fair share of official songs. Arlo Guthrie's "Massachusetts" is the official state folk song. "The Road to Boston" is the official ceremonial march. The official patriotic song is "The Great State of Massachusetts," and let's not forget the official state ode, appropriately titled, "Ode to Massachusetts."

While we're on the subject, Massachusetts has a penchant for making things official. The cranberry, for example, is twice blessed. It's the state berry and the official beverage.

Johnny Appleseed of Leominster is the state folk hero, and Deborah Samson is the state heroine. (Samson dressed as a man and went by the name *Robert Shurtleff* to fight in the Revolutionary War.) The Boston terrier is the official bowser, the tabby is the official state cat, Boston cream pie (which is actually a cake) is the official dessert, and the black-capped chickadee is the official state bird. And, in case you were wondering, the ladybug became the state insect in 1974 after intense lobbying of the legislature by second-graders from Franklin, Massachusetts.

★ ★

Syn(thetic) City, USA

Leominster

Fifteen years before Dustin Hoffman received unsolicited career advice in the 1967 movie *The Graduate,* Brownie Wise was cleaning up in plastics. Brownie Wise was a marketing genius who built an empire out of bowls that burped. Wise teamed up with Earl Silas Tupper, the inventor of the bowls that bear his name, and their work earned them a place in plastics history. Today a Tupperware party is held somewhere in the world every two and a half seconds, and 90 percent of American homes own at least one piece of the flexible containers.

The story of Tupperware is just one of the plastic fantastic tales told at the National Plastics Center and Museum in Leominster. From bulletproof "glass" and Styrofoam cups to Saran wrap and soda bottles, the past, present, and future of plastics is presented at the museum.

The museum that pays homage to plastics and polymers is aptly placed. In Leominster nearly half the companies are involved in the plastics industry. You could say the pioneering plastic city got its roots as the comb capital of the world. In 1770 Obidiah Hill moved to Leominster and began making combs by hand out of natural materials. By 1885 there were twenty-five comb companies in the city. As the demand increased and the supply of horn, tortoise shell, and ivory became scarce, the hunt for a replacement material began. A hundred years later, when celluloid (the first semi-synthetic material) was developed, one of its first uses was in making combs. Unfortunately, celluloid was highly flammable. For the next thirty years it caused many a bad hair day, until a safer plastic was invented.

Among those honored in the museum's Plastic Hall of Fame are John Wesley Hyatt, "the grandfather of plastics," and Roy Plunkett, the inventor of Teflon. But you won't find Dustin Hoffman among the notables, even though he has made his career in celluloid. Inexplicably, another notable exclusion to the Plastic Hall of Fame is Don Featherstone, creator of the pink plastic flamingo.

The National Plastics Center and Museum is located on Derwin Street off Route 117. For the museum's hours of operation, call (978) 537-9529 or visit www.plasticsmuseum.org/museum.html.

Ironically, they only accept cash at the museum—no plastic.

A Towering Accomplishment, in a Roundabout Way
Milford

We've heard of keeping those native traditions when you travel, but this seems extreme. Ireland has round towers scattered about, erected at the time that the Vikings—the Scandinavian raiders, not the fancy kitchen stoves—were looting the coast of western Europe. To the Irish, the Vikings were technical wizards, with fast ships and tempered-steel swords, who also had an advantage with a degree of organization not available to the separate European tribes. They were also wizards at pillaging and burning. The latter was particularly problematic when what went into the fire were priceless illuminated manuscripts, often the only copy of works of learning. Dealing with the Dark Ages was bad enough, and no one likes to start over, especially when the job takes months, so the Irish monks responsible for the manuscripts began to build round towers, nearing 100 feet in height, with doors some 15 feet off the ground. When the Vikings came a-callin', they had a hard time a-knockin': The community would climb a rope ladder into the tower to seek refuge, then pull the ladder up behind them. A lookout floor at the tower's top allowed them to see when things were clear and they could leave. It was frustrating for the invading hordes and a relief to the monks, who must have figured that the privations of the early monastic life were ample hardship.

Of the original one hundred towers, sixty-five still survive in Ireland. And a single one remains in North America, at St. Mary of the Assumption Cemetery (27 Pearl Street, Milford). It's shorter than

its native brethren, rising only 65 feet. The cemetery, one of the
first Catholic burial grounds in Massachusetts, was built around the
turn of the twentieth century by Irish immigrant stone workers who
decided to re-create one of the structures from their motherland.
They must have had a tough time leaving work at the office. Did
anyone tell them that while the Vikings did come to America, it was
eight hundred or nine hundred years earlier?

Nowheresville, USA
Podunk

Yes, Virginia, there is a Podunk. The place, whose name is usually
analogous with Nowheresville, is an unincorporated town of about
6 square miles located in East Brookfield, about 15 miles west of
Worcester. About a hundred families live there. *Podunk* is the Indian
word for bog or swamp. And this town is podunky.

The town includes the Podunk Gift Barn and the Podunk Cemetery. To visit Podunk, permanently or otherwise, from Route 9/West
Main Street in East Brookfield (hey, we said it was Nowheresville),
travel south on Philip Quinn Memorial Highway. The road turns
into Podunk Pike. Where the Pike intersects Adams Street and
Adams Road, just before the cemetery, a sign welcomes you to
Podunk.

A Guy Walks into a Bar
Southbridge

The bar has become a standard fixture in jokedom. Who knows
how many priests, nuns, rabbis, ministers, salespeople, and average
Joes and Janes—to say nothing of all the monkeys, penguins, talking dogs, and parrots—have sidled up to take their parts in people's
attempts to bring some lightness into the world. When you can find
regular bars, juice bars, and oxygen bars in the world, it was only a
matter of time before someone created the Joke Bar. And you can
find it at Four Eyes Joke Shop.

For years, Four Eyes advertised itself as New England's largest joke shop, and it still does. But in 2006 they had to close the retail operation. They still sell big on the Internet, but everyone missed the Joke Bar. It was about 15 feet long, with big springs with cushions on them, originally used in amphibious assault vehicles, as the bar stools. Local people would drop by, but so would others from around the country and around the globe. The patrons would come in, hang out, and swap jokes. Some would tell the things they had done to each other or to family members. Owner Valerie Pontbriand remembers one regular. "[He] put a fake security camera in his bathroom, and people wouldn't notice until it started moving in on them while they were doing their business, and they'd be very surprised," she says.

Like an advanced research center, the Joke Bar was a place where those who wanted to have a laugh or play a prank could pick up ideas. The bar was stocked with gag items, like the nickel nailed into the bar that suckered many who tried to pick it up. There was the electric shock pen, or the "bagel surprise": a realistic bagel sitting on an even more realistic cockroach. When you picked up the bagel, a bit of fishing line made the bug look like it was running. It's all family fun, even if not necessarily clean, in the pest sense.

People missed the bar, so Valerie decided to bring it back every now and then. To get the schedule, or a whoopee cushion, head to www.foureyesjokeshop.com, or call (877) 565-3746.

The One and Only Ewe
Sterling and Sudbury

For the past two centuries, the towns of Sterling, Massachusetts, and Newport, New Hampshire, have been locking horns over a critical civic matter. Did Mary really have a little lamb, or are she and her mutton just a myth? At stake in the historic debate is a claim to fame, if not fortune.

Sterling says that in 1815, when Mary Sawyer Tyler lived in the town, she had a little lamb named Nathaniel and it did indeed follow her to school one day. A visitor from Harvard University reportedly witnessed the entire event and penned the poem.

Supporting Sterling's version of things are reports that seventy-three years later Ms. Tyler announced that she was *the* Mary. She used her fame to solicit donations to restore Boston's Old South Meeting House by selling wool from unraveled socks made from *the* lamb's fleece.

Photo by Bruce Gellerman

The lamb statue in Sterling.

You can find a statue of the scholarly Nathaniel in the Sterling town square. There is also an entire room in the town's historical society dedicated to his memorable trip to school. Descendants of Ms. Mary Sawyer Tyler still dress up as Mary, and her lamb dutifully follows in the town's annual parade.

Folks 70 miles away in Newport, New Hampshire, say they have evidence that makes mincemeat out of Sterling's claim to Mary's fame. They say there was no Mary, no lamb, and no school. It seems that Newport poet and abolitionist Mary Hale made up the catchy little ditty and published it in 1830. Newport's claim is supported by the *Oxford Book of Nursery Rhymes,* which lists Hale as the author but notes the historical controversy.

To complicate the lamb's tale, the little red schoolhouse to which Mary allegedly went is in Sudbury, Massachusetts, not Sterling.

Reportedly, Henry Ford discovered a barn built out of wood from the original school in Sterling, had it disassembled, and then rebuilt the one-room schoolhouse in Sudbury. Ewe figure it out.

A statue of Nathaniel, the lamb whose fleece was white as snow, can be found in Sterling's town square on Route 62.

The Little Red School House in Sudbury is located on Wayside Inn Road off Route 20 South on the grounds of the Wayside Inn. It's open from May 15 to October 15, Wednesday through Sunday, 11:30 a.m. to 5:00 p.m. But to make sure school is in session and you're not tardy, call (978) 443-1776.

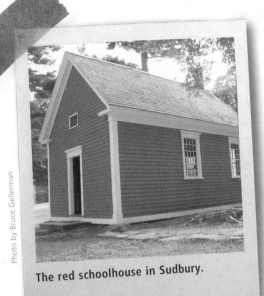

photo by Bruce Gellerman

The red schoolhouse in Sudbury.

Play Ball—Carefully

Southborough

The catcher's mask is a protector of youthful good looks, good or not, among those who take that position in baseball. And they can thank an unnamed 1875 student at St. Mark's School, a feeder school for Harvard at the time. A broken nose kept the lad worried about the pain that might be involved in having his face become the default backstop for any ball heading his way. The young man, obviously inventive as well as wary, took a fencer's mask and modified it so he could see and still get protection for his proboscis.

★ ★

That might have been the last we heard of this, except that the team was playing Harvard in this game. A player for the university, Fred Thayer, noted the invention and went away with more than he came with. By 1878 he had obtained a patent for the idea, thus demonstrating that the robber baron instinct can start early on.

The patent would have run out before the turn of the century, and there's no word whether Thayer made a penny on his ill-gotten game gain. But the catcher's mask is still around, as is St. Mark's at 25 Marlborough Road. Abner Doubleday would have been proud.

Yes, Hell Does Freeze Over
Sutton

Purgatory Chasm State Reservation, in the southeastern part of central Massachusetts, is an immense, unique, and perplexing place. The chasm is nearly half a mile long and 50 feet wide, with perpendicular walls that rise 70 feet in some places. Scientists are at a loss to explain how the chasm was formed. Some believe it was created 14,000 years ago when an earth dam holding back melted glacial ice suddenly burst and eroded the granite rock. Others suggest it was formed only a few hundred years ago by an earthquake.

Whatever the cause, the area now offers a lot of hiking trails, places to climb, and caves, along with a number of interesting rock formations bearing quirky names such as the Coffin, Lover's Leap, and Fat Man's Misery.

Purgatory Chasm is open year-round, and good hiking shoes are a must, especially in the winter. Purgatory freezes over and the rocks are very slippery. For more information call Purgatory Chasm State Reservation at (508) 234-3733 or go to www.mass.gov/dcr/parks/central/purg.htm.

From the Mass Pike (Interstate 90), take exit 10A to Route 146 South and follow the signs to Purgatory Road.

★ ★

His Name Is Danger—At Least, We Think It Is
Wales

There is a category of words called *aptronyms*—that's when people's names convey their occupations, such as Dr. Cutter, the surgeon, or a fisherman named Baiter. We don't know if Doug Danger is the name this daredevil was born with, but if the shoe fits, throw it over dozens of cars. Danger did this literally, all the while keeping his foot in the shoe. In 1990 he sent his motorcycle soaring and cleared either forty-two cars, parked side by side, for a total of 251 feet, or thirty-eight cars, depending on who is recounting the record. Either way, that's longer than the efforts of the more famous Evel Knievel.

You might think that a modicum of fame would satisfy someone, but apparently *danger* in some language translates to "insane under-taking." Some riders have actually died trying to break this record. Danger is still alive, but that is due only to luck and competent medi-cal care. The year after setting the record, he missed an eleven-car jump and crashed, breaking seventeen bones and winding up in a month-long coma.

For most people that would have been a sign to hang up the leather chaps. But unfortunately for Danger, he had complete mem-ory loss as a result of an accompanying head injury, so even if he had learned a lesson, he forgot it. The man actually returned to jumping motorcycles, even though, as his own Web site (www.dougdanger .net) states, he had little memory of anything, including how to jump a motorcycle. Danger is a fast learner, though, because he has since managed to jump seventeen semi-trucks as well as an L-1011 jumbo jet, wingtip to wingtip. Hopefully it was on the ground at the time. You can read more about him, or even book his one-hour jump and stunt show, at www.endeavorentertainment.com/Thrill_Shows/ doug_danger.htm.

★ ★

You Say It Your Way, I'll Say It Mine
Webster

Webster Lake, in the town of Webster, is also known as Lake Chargoggagoggmanchauggagoggchaubunagungamaugg. And contrary to popular opinion, the lake with the longest name in the United States does not mean "You fish on your side, I fish on my side, nobody fishes in the middle." The real meaning of the elongated word is derived from the local Indian name that means "Englishmen at Manchaug at the fishing place at the boundary." The Englishman in this particular instance was one Samuel Slater, who built a mill near the lake, near the village where the Monuhchogok Indians lived.

Lake Chargoggagoggmanchauggagoggchaubunagungamaugg is more than 1,400 acres in size and composed of three lakes joined by narrow channels. You'll probably find large-mouth bass there. Very large-mouth bass.

A Fly-by-Weekend Museum
Winchendon

The Top Fun Aviation Toy Museum is all about the Wright stuff. It is the only museum in the world devoted to aviation-related toys. Its mission is to "give children's dreams the Wright wings." Here, on the first floor of the Old Murdock School, kids will find noteworthy (if not airworthy) toys, from hot-air balloons to spacecraft. There are flying toys from around the world made with metal, plastic, and wood. There are cast-iron statues of Bugs Bunny in his plane, and Olive Oyl soars in a die-cast model. A helicopter and an airplane made by children in Burkina Faso were fashioned from Dutch milk tins. Covering the entire wall of one room is an "On-the-Wall Airport" offering a pilot's-eye view of the ground and the feeling that you're flying overhead.

The museum encourages kids to take flights of fantasy and test-fly their balsa and paper creations in the large, high-ceiling activity room. The Top Fun Aviation Toy Museum is at 22 Murdock Avenue, about an hour west of Boston as the crow flies. If you feel like wing-ing it, the closest airport is in Gardner. For hours and directions call (978) 297-4337 or visit www.topfunaviation.com/default.htm. Check ahead, as the museum is currently looking for new digs. Or would that be hangars?

Watch It with That Fork, Buster!
Worcester

In August, business is slow at the Sole Proprietor in Worcester. To pump up the volume, the proprietor of the seafood restaurant calls upon Buster the Crab, the world's largest inflatable crab. Buster has a 75-foot claw span, and if he were real, he'd feed 200,000 people. Of course, according to his owners, that would require 35,116 pounds of butter, 45,447 lemons, and who knows how many moist towelettes. The Sole Proprietor is at 118 Highland Avenue, (508) 798-FISH, www.thesole.com. Tell 'em Buster sent you.

Photo by Bruce Gellerman

Buster the Crab presides over his favorite Worcester restaurant every August.

★ ★

The Poop on Indoor Plumbing

Worcester

The curators of the American Sanitary Plumbing Museum have been the butt of countless jokes, so don't even try to pull their chain. Despite the obvious potty humor that goes along with the subject matter, the institution is a serious effort to pay tribute to the devices that made cities livable and prevented countless deaths from disease. On display in the museum's two floors are toilets dating to the nineteenth century, along with sinks, bathtubs, and tools of the toilet trade.

The museum also puts to rest many myths about sanitary plumbing. For example, you'll be relieved to know that Sir Thomas Crapper did not invent the toilet. (He did have a hand in making some of the innards of the tank.) As his name graced many a toilet, it became equated with its function.

When you've just gotta go, you'll find the museum at 39 Piedmont Street. You can take the toilet tour Tuesday and Thursday from 10:00 a.m. to 2:00 p.m. The museum is closed in July and August.

World Smile Day

Worcester

Commercial artist Harvey Ball believed that when you smile, the whole world smiles with you. He wanted to spread the message far and wide, and he succeeded beyond his wildest imagination. Today his Smiley design is one of the most recognized faces in the world and a universal symbol of good cheer.

In 1963 Ball, a native of Worcester, was asked by a local insurance company to design something to boost worker morale. The company had just merged with another firm, and employees were unhappy with the move. Ball created Smiley, a face that was turned into pins and given to employees and clients. Since then the face has been featured on everything from underwear to yo-yos, stamps to T-shirts.

Photo courtesy of Harvey Ball World Smile Corporation

On October 4, 2002, more than 750 people gathered on Worcester City Hall Plaza to create the world's largest living smiley face, honoring both Harvey Ball and World Smile Day IV.

Although Harvey Ball was paid just $45 for his design, he was proud that his creation became the international symbol of goodwill. In 1999, when he felt his original message had become lost in the commercialization of Smiley, he created World Smile Day to restore the meaning of the symbol.

On the first Friday in October each year, World Smile Day is dedicated to good works and good cheer. The catch phrase for the day is, "Do an act of kindness. Help one person smile."

Second Firsts

In the 1970s Worcester residents affectionately began calling their city "Wormtown" because it was, well, lifeless, and it spoofed Boston's "Beantown." More recently local boosters have started calling Worcester "the Paris of the 00s." While we wouldn't necessarily go that far, being the second-largest city in Massachusetts (and in New England) does not mean that Worcester is an also-ran. Far from it.

According to administrators at the Hampton Inn in downtown Worcester, "the city is the center of the known universe." Notwithstanding Beantown's claim to that title, each of the hotel's five stories is a unique tribute to the second city's many firsts, featuring books, memorabilia, and photographs. The hotel employees have also been schooled in Worcester lore and are brimming with facts and figures.

Consider these noteworthy Worcester claims to fame:

- WORC–AM disc jockey Dick "the Derby" Smith was the first DJ to play a Beatles song in the United States. The grateful Fab Four gave him a gold record of "She Loves You" and signed it, "To the first true believer."

- America's first Nobel Prize went to Albert A. Michelson of Clark University (in 1902, for his measurement of light).

- In 1952 Frank A. Firoillo was the first to market a pizza pie mix; five years earlier he had the first pizza stand in Worcester.

- The monkey wrench was invented in Worcester in 1840 by Loring and Aury Coes of the Coes Knife Company.

- Albert Tolman of Worcester built a "man-drawn lorry" for a missionary heading to South America in 1846. The rickshaw was an instant hit in Asia.

- Worcester was once "the shredded wheat capital of the world." Henry Perky of Worcester created the flaky breakfast biscuit in his Jackson Street factory.

- In 1833 Worcester State Hospital became the nation's first publicly financed insane asylum. That same year the Boston and West Worcester Rail Road became the first in the country to charge commuter fares.

- The typewriter and ballpoint pen were both invented in Worcester.

- Last but not least, Worcester was the second city to celebrate First Night. (Boston was the first.)

★ ★

Surely We Joust
Worcester

Fair maidens in *amour* and their knights in shining armor will feel right at home at the Higgins Armory Museum in Worcester, Massachusetts. The museum is the only institution in the Western Hemisphere dedicated solely to arms and armor, and it is available for wedding receptions as well as birthday party "OverKnights," when kids can suit up and really wreak havoc. It's all in good joust, of course.

Those who really want to take in the knight life can take lessons in medieval combat at the Higgins Armory Sword Guild. We're told it is the only organization of its kind in the world, and since they're armed and we're not, who are we to argue with them?

Courtesy of the Higgins Armory Museum, Worcester, Massachusetts

Hunting dogs were sometimes outfitted with body armor to protect them from antlers and tusks of stag and boar.

Perfect Pitch

Back in 1880 baseball was a different game from the one we know today. Eight balls were a walk, the batter got to determine the strike zone, and the pitcher stood just 45 feet from the plate. And forget about eating sushi at the concession stands.

Still, whatever the differences, the record books show that on June 12, 1880, John Lee Richmond of the Worcester Ruby Legs (sometimes called the Brown Stockings) pitched the first perfect game in major league baseball. He beat the Cleveland Blues 1–0, in what by all accounts was a nail-biter, delayed by rain in the ninth inning.

What makes Richmond's historic feat even more remarkable is that his perfect game in Worcester was actually the second game of two Richmond pitched that day . . . in two different states.

At the time Richmond was a senior at Brown University in Rhode Island and just four days from graduation. As was the tradition of the time, he had been up all night celebrating and had taken part in the traditional senior class baseball game. It's said that at 5:00 in the morning, Richmond took to the mound with a bottle of champagne in hand; he finished that game at 6:30 a.m., took the 11:30 train to Worcester, and commenced to pitch his perfect game.

Just five days later the second official perfect game was pitched, but it took nearly twenty-five years for it to happen again. (Cy Young did it for the Boston Americans on May 5, 1904. Note: In 1907 the Americans became known as the Boston Red Sox.) Historians also generally credit Richmond, a southpaw, with throwing the first curveball. Known as a pitcher of "cunning and control," he earned his keep. He finished the 1880 season with a 31–32 record, pitching 590.2 innings.

A stone monument on Sever Street marks the spot where Richmond threw the first perfect game in baseball history.

★ ★

Receptions are held in the Great Hall of the museum, which is lined with scores of knights in armor and their steel-plated steeds, some dating back to ancient Rome. The collection of more than 4,000 artifacts includes swords, lances, maces, and various other instruments of Asian and medieval mayhem. There's even a hunting dog decked out in armor.

The Higgins collection also includes a real chastity belt, but it is not considered appropriate to display and is locked away.

The Armory Museum began once upon a time (1929 to be exact) when one of Worcester's leading industrialists, John Woodman Higgins, a man of steel (he owned a steel mill) built a four-story Gothic castle to house his personal collection of arms and armor. The art deco building is one of the earliest in the nation to have an exterior constructed exclusively of steel and glass. It is on the National Register of Historic Places.

The Higgins Armory Museum is located at 100 Barber Avenue. For directions call (508) 853-6015 or log on to www.higgins.org.

6

Western Massachusetts, the Connecticut River Valley, and the Berkshires

They think big in western Massachusetts. In Cheshire you'll find a concrete cheese press that memorializes the 1,235-pound cheese sent by its good citizens to Washington, D.C., to celebrate the election of Thomas Jefferson to the presidency in 1800. Other larger-than-life figures include the 20-foot Tin Man at the Good Time Stove Company in Goshen.

If you're in a more artistic frame of mind, in Colrain there's the 28-by-16-foot neon American flag designed by artist Pacifico (Tony) Palumbo as a memorial to the World Trade Center tragedy. Called Glowing Glory, it's located off Coombs Hill Road. The largest American museum devoted to contemporary art, the Massachusetts Museum of Contemporary Art—Mass MoCA—is located in North Adams. Besides an impressive permanent collection, the museum hosts special exhibits, performance art, and Bang on a Can, its summer music festival.

Amherst is home to the Eric Carle Museum of Picture Book Art, 40,000 square feet devoted to kids' picture books and picture book art. Springfield celebrates the work of its own Dr. Seuss with the Dr. Seuss Memorial Sculpture Garden at the Quadrangle, featuring bronze statues of Seuss's beloved childrens' book characters.

And if you're anywhere near Washington in early September, don't miss the Northeast Squeeze-In festival celebrating all things accordion. It'll be music to your ears!

Western Massachusetts, the Connecticut River Valley, and the Berkshires

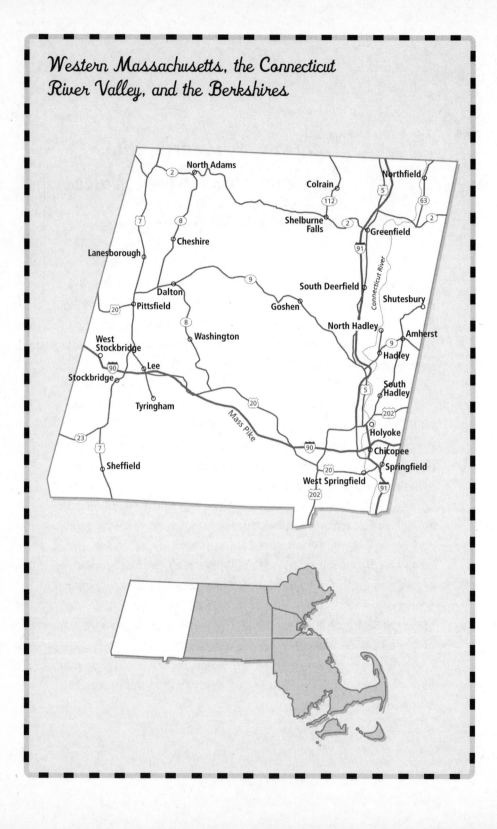

★ ★

Picture Perfect

Amherst

Some of us look at the latest bulging bestsellers and wish for simpler times, when men were men, women were women, and books were illustrated. Before moving on to Dostoyevsky, most people start their exposure to reading with picture books. These graphically evocative, deceptively simple tales pair a minimum of narration with engaging illustrations to help kids understand that, in the end, books are all about telling stories.

If you have a longing for less literature and more looking, then stop by the Eric Carle Museum of Picture Book Art. This is the first large museum—40,000 square feet, to be precise—devoted to kids' picture books. Carle's name may sound familiar if you've had young children in the last thirty years or so. He is a famous children's book illustrator, with such credits as *The Very Hungry Caterpillar* and *The Grouchy Ladybug*. (We wonder if, when in grade school, Carle submitted sheaves of drawings in lieu of book reports.) While there are Carle originals on display—what good is it if you can't exhibit at your own museum?—you can also take in the work of other noted American and international illustrators. The entrance fee is low, but don't plan to bring in food, drink, or pens and markers. (What, your parents never told you that you shouldn't scribble on the pictures?)

The museum is open year-round and even has free parking, a feature that is almost worth the trip in and of itself. For more information call (413) 658-1100 or visit www.picturebookart.org. The museum is located at 125 West Bay Road.

Oy Vey

Amherst

If you had to name a major center of Jewish culture outside the Middle East, what would you pick? If you said, "New York City," you would at least be in the right country. Given the subject of this book,

★ ★

Photo courtesy of Ned Gray

The National Yiddish Book Center hosts lectures, films, concerts, and live performances.

you should certainly guess some place in Massachusetts. But the honor doesn't go to Boston or even Brockton or Sharon, all of which have a tradition of Jewish community. Instead, it goes to Amherst. What locked down the designation in 1997 was the opening of the 37,000-square-foot home for the National Yiddish Book Center.

The center has become a big destination for Jewish tourists and claims to be visitor-friendly. No, the signs are not in Yiddish and English. Oy, our heads hurt from the thought. Maybe you don't know Yiddish (nor the Hebrew letters typically used for spelling), but it's worth some acquaintance. The sounds are really intriguing. Yiddish is a language once shared by Jews all over Europe; it is derived from German, Hebrew, Aramaic, and several different Slavic and Romance languages. It is a language for schmoozing, a definite mishmash—a linguistic jumble. Yiddish is also probably the world's best language for cursing and lamenting the indignities of life.

The center is free (certain events within do have a charge), open to the public, and offers gardens, exhibitions, and even an English-language bookstore. The center also has research facilities.

To enjoy the National Yiddish Book Center, schlep over to Hampshire College at 893 West Street and ask for directions. To check whether you're trying to arrive on a Jewish holiday, or if you're *farblonzhet* (lost), call (413) 256-4900. You can get more information—in English, even—at www.yiddishbookcenter.org.

The Cheese Whizzes

Cheshire

Cheshire was established by the first non-Puritans in the area—the founders were descended from followers of Roger Williams, who had headed off to Rhode Island in the mid-1600s in search of religious freedom. Perhaps they inherited his rebellious streak, for when a young United States of America voted for its third president, in 1800, Cheshire was the only town in that part of the state that sided unanimously with Thomas Jefferson. Driven on by Elder John Ireland, the local preacher, the dissidents for once managed to align themselves with the winning party, and they wanted to celebrate. Fun back then wasn't quite the same as our current concept. The dissidents lived in dairy country, and someone had the bright idea of creating a giant wheel of cheese—Cheshire, to be precise. The town worked hard, gathering curds from every resident farmer and pressing them into a wheel totaling 4 feet across, 1½ feet thick, and 1,235 pounds in weight. It took six horses pulling a sled to bring the slab to a ship on the Hudson River, which then brought it to Washington, D.C. (Maybe the town fathers hoped to have their whey with the president.)

★ ★

It took a few months for the appetizer to reach Jefferson. The president was duly impressed and put it on display in the East Room of the White House in January 1802, with Supreme Court justices, foreign diplomats, and Congress looking on. Federalist critics of Jefferson tried to make fun of the cheese as a trivial interest and not worthy of the country's attention. In doing so, they compared the big cheese to the recent unearthing of mastodon bones in New York. (The excavation, which had taken place with aid from the Jefferson administration, was another unworthy endeavor in the eyes of the critics.) These writers called the wheel the "mammoth cheese," giving rise to a new adjective. (Never underestimate the power of cheese.) Jefferson, unfazed, responded to the town with a personal letter.

In the twentieth century, town residents decided to commemorate their earlier commemoration. In 1940 they created a monument, a concrete cheese press, in memory of "the big Cheshire cheese." You can see it for yourself near the intersection of School and Church Streets.

Ruling the Roost
Cheshire

Herbert Hoover promised Americans a chicken in every pot. Today the people of Cheshire would be hard-pressed to find a pot that was big enough. Apparently the people in this town, who also have that memorial to a giant cheese, have an affinity for big food. Sitting atop the town's former Country Charm restaurant is a statue of a rooster standing about 10 feet tall. Over the years many small businesses have had the idea that creating some sort of unusual decoration would help attract business. What hatched this particular bird was the Chicken Stop, a restaurant that had previously occupied the premises.

The rooster stood proudly on the grass in front of the Chicken Stop and then the Country Charm until college students abducted the mascot in the mid-1990s. Perhaps the whole lot of them were trying to fly the coop. But sanity—and the rooster—returned, the latter being relegated to the roof, where a casual acquaintance could not easily turn into a pickup. You can still see the proud poultry atop the site of the former Country Charm on Route 8. Maybe the restaurant laid a business egg, but the rooster didn't.

Championship Chilling
Chicopee

Know that saying, "Save room for dessert"? Here's one treat that would have required, oh, about fifty-odd years of judicious eating. Many people have done some extreme and downright crazy things for an entry into the *Guinness Book of Records.* On July 1, 1999, owners of the Dairy Queen in Chicopee decided that it would only be natural to try for the title of largest blended dessert. This frozen feat was a mass of vanilla ice cream (or whatever it is that Dairy Queens serve) with a copious amount of crushed Oreo cookies. The sweet treat topped out at a walloping 5,316.6 pounds. And you thought that a brownie sundae at the local family restaurant was a challenge. Undoubtedly Jenny Craig is still having psychically induced nightmares from it.

Actually, "largest blended dessert" sounds a bit dull. We think that *Guinness* missed the banana-split boat by ignoring a more apt title: biggest brain freeze. The post-entrée entry was too large to host at the shop, so it made its debut at the nearby Riverside Amusement Park in Agawam, now part of the local Six Flags theme park. You can still see the shop that created the confection at 1535 Memorial Drive, or call (413) 535-3005. Don't be surprised, however, if service is slow; we are sure that some of the staff is still recovering.

The Big Man
Chicopee

What does Uncle Sam do when he retires? Why, wear white and wave at people. The Big Man—or, we supposed, the Plantation

Man—stands in front of the Plantation Inn, visible as you leave the Massachusetts Turnpike tollbooth at the Route 291 exit. It may seem odd for such a figure to be in front of a hotel, but a talk with the owners made things clear.

Originally, the Big Man was a Pizza Man in Framingham, Massachusetts. His upraised hand held a slice of pie and he was painted white, with a flat hat, like a chef. For years he stood guard at the pizza parlor, until his services were no longer needed. The owners of the inn bought him in 1960 and moved him in front of the Mutual Ford auto dealership in Chicopee, where he stood for the next twenty-eight years. Instead of white, he was painted red, white, and blue, the pizza slice disappeared, and the hat turned into a top hat. Now Uncle Sam reigned over the dealership, with a slogan of Buy American. The dealership closed in 1988, however, as foreign cars really took hold. The owners leased the space to a used-car dealership, which didn't need the Big Man, who became the Reclining Man in storage.

Now the big guy's owners had some hotels, called Plantation Inns, in Louisiana and bought their current property here. People from the area kept asking about old Uncle Sam; some had grown up with the figure. So the inn's owners decided to resurrect him. Back he went into white and up in front of the inn. Inside the inn is an all-white statue of Jack Daniels, because the owners also have a package store. But don't be fooled: We know the big guy out front, and he is no Jack Daniels. To see him head to 295 Burnett Road. For more information you can call (413) 592-8200 or go to www.plantation-inn.com.

Bridge Over Troubled Waters
Colrain

Few bridges jump around the way the Arthur B. Smith covered bridge has. The peripatetic pathway started its history in the 1800s in one location. Then a reconfiguration of some roads made it unnecessary. Transportation's discard was the boon of farmer Arthur Smith, who had been driving his cows across an open bridge to pasturelands. But that structure had collapsed, giving his cattle what was probably their first and only bath.

The existing covered bridge was moved to aid Smith and served him well. Years later, when Smith was no longer in the agriculture business, a major local employer—a cider mill—needed a bridge to move its product across the river. Again the covered bridge was moved, taking Smith's name with it. (Are you feeling dislocated yet?)

The bridge enjoyed a relatively long period of stability until 1981, although it did suffer some deterioration. No surprise, as any of us would have worn down a bit after 150 years. Now on the National Register of Historic Places, the bridge could not simply be disassembled and turned into firewood. The Colrain Historical Society involved itself, and the town worked hard, supporting an effort to raise $40,000 to repair and move the bridge yet again, this time to a cornfield. A local logger donated his efforts, and the state offered lumber from a nearby forest.

It had been an example of civic efficiency—until the wood was obtained. Then one delay after another occurred. Some residents claim that someone misappropriated a portion of the raised funds. The historical society opposed suggestions to make the structure a footbridge and insisted that the bridge be used for vehicle travel only. During all the arguing, the replacement wood, sitting under a tarp next to the bridge, eventually rotted.

But eventually things worked out: New wood was had, construction started and finished, and now there is a pleasant covered footbridge going nowhere in a hurry. You can usually see the bridge from Route 112, but if the corn is high, go to the end of Lydonville Road.

Long May It Glow
Colrain

Neon artist Pacifico (Tony) Palumbo moved to Colrain with his partner, Michael Collins, in 1994. As electrically charged art is not a major industry in this part of Massachusetts, the two opened a well-received upscale restaurant, the Green Emporium. But you know what they say about neon—it's in the blood, or tubes. No matter; Palumbo couldn't keep away from bending the light. So he kept producing art, with a number of galleries exhibiting his work. Fast forward to September 19, 2001, right after the attacks on the World Trade Center. Local farmer Kenny Shearer stopped to talk with Palumbo, and the conversation turned to the recent tragic event. Palumbo, a native New Yorker, was feeling badly, and Shearer said that he had thought of erecting a large flag on his own property. Suddenly the switch flipped on for Palumbo, who asked, "Why not neon?"

The two got to work, getting permission from town selectmen and obtaining a building permit. Shearer drew to scale what he had envisioned. Turns out that when he thinks, he thinks *big*. The flag he had envisioned was to be 28 feet wide and 16 feet high. More people got involved. Shearer enlisted his friends and family, and an electrician neighbor donated his time to do all the electrical wiring. Palumbo's assistant, Scott Hoffman, joined in. Neon tubing came from Palumbo's studio in Brooklyn, and he trucked the 350 feet of powdered tubing himself. The local electrical utility, WMECO, helped by donating the power cable, while E. W. Martin Electric dug the trench. Obviously the Colrain crew was charged up over the project. You might think that art, when political, is usually hypercritical, but this is one time when it was deeply moved by current events.

Palumbo's installation, *Glowing Glory,* was officially lighted on November 25, 2001. You can see the flag online at www.glowing glory.com. For the real thing, use Palumbo's directions: From exit 26 off Interstate 91, take Route 2 west for 3.5 miles, turn right (north) onto Colrain/Shelburne Road, drive 2 miles to the Colrain/Shelburne line, then look left at Coombs Hill Road. Keep your head up and you can't miss it.

★ ★

Rags to Riches

Dalton

There are people who dream of wading through piles of money. We can relate, but short of either being employed by the U.S. Mint or being adopted by the likes of Bill Gates, the closest you might get is the Crane Museum of Papermaking. While you won't see the finished product, you can learn a great deal about the paper that our money is printed on. Crane sold paper to Paul Revere in 1775, who printed the first paper money in what was then the colonies, and it has regularly provided stock for American currency since 1842. In 1844 Crane

Photo courtesy of Crane & Co. Inc.

The Crane Museum of Papermaking traces the history of American papermaking from rags to riches.

developed a technique for weaving silk threads in banknotes to help deter counterfeiters; more recently it has patented the technique of putting in those identifying security threads. Even though the company knows where the money is, Crane also produces stationery and paper for digital printing.

Instead of using wood pulp like most mills, Crane continues to produce papers with high rag content for strength and beauty. And you thought cotton was just for blue jeans. You can learn about how the company has historically made paper and see old paper molds and other educational displays at the museum in Crane's Old Stone Mill, built in 1844 on 30 South Street. It's open early June to mid-October; call (413) 684-6481, or go to www.crane.com/navcontent .aspx?name=museum. Oh, and as for that banknote paper—sorry, but no samples.

Tin Giant
Goshen

The Good Time Stove Company has been in business for over thirty years, renovating and selling antique stoves. If it's old, metal, and burns stuff to make heat, these people are interested. In fact, not only do they have a showroom, but they have a museum of antique stoves, and admission is free. You may be scratching your head and trying to reconcile a stove museum with the title of this entry. That's because while the stoves are the main attraction, what caught our eyes was the giant tin man standing in front of the showroom.

Maybe proprietor Richard Richardson had too much time, and metal, on his hands. We think he was hoping the creature would come to life. Think a moving woodstove is easy? Actually, the Tin Man of Goshen, who has become a landmark, had his business start in 1955 when he advertised a fuel company. When Richardson first visited the area in 1971 in a Model T Ford, he knew he had found where he should be. By 1973 he was back to start the stove company.

Killer Beavers

Beavers are known as the engineers of the animal world, not as predatory killers. At least that's their reputation until you get out to parts of western Massachusetts where Indian legends tell a different story. According to the Pocumtuck tribe of Deerfield, a giant beaver lived in a lake, now long gone, that was once in the area. Apparently the buck-toothed wonder, tired of wearing down its incisors chewing wood, would from time to time venture into the surrounding area and eat people.

This was not a habit to endear the creature to the Pocumtuck. According to their legends, the people requested the aid of another giant—the spirit Hobomock, who hunted the beaver and killed it. The beaver sank back into the lake, transforming from animal into rock. After the lake drained, over time, the carcass was left exposed. There are legends from some other nearby tribes that mirror the basic story, varying some details, such as what Hobomock used to smite the amphibious rodent.

These days, the beaver's body is what we call the Pocumtuck Range and the head is Mount Sugarloaf, now a popular ski resort.

But the 20-foot-tall Tin Man, wielding a large hammer, didn't join the enterprise yet. He was put up for auction, bought by a farmer who couldn't *give* the sculpture away to the local historical society, and so was put out in the fields to act as a scarecrow. Eventually the farmer and Richardson did a swap—stove parts for the man, sans head, which had gone missing. And he sat for years, worse for his long wear.

Eventually Richardson got a local vocational school to do a restoration and, on his way there, ran into the farmer, who had found the head. Now he stands again, with a heart set into place by the shop students, and hopefully a place he can warm up during the cold winter nights.

To see the Tin Man and showroom/museum, it's easiest to check the company Web site at www.goodtimestove.com/directions.html, because the directions vary greatly, depending on where you're coming from. If you want more information, call (413) 268-3677.

Tunnel to Nowhere
Goshen

Unexplained natural structures may be mysterious, but they are at least understandable in some remote, prehistoric way. It's when something unnatural is more recent, when you would think that there must be some record of the effort involved, that the unknown can be plain annoying. In those terms the Goshen Tunnel is extremely irritating and confusing.

In the nineteenth century, some hunters came upon a big hole in the ground, more than 3 feet in diameter. The opening runs straight down about 15 feet. At the bottom, two tunnels, about 2 feet tall, run parallel to the surface in two different directions. One of them is another 15 feet or so in length, while the other extends five times as far. Both end at cave-ins. It's a tidy hole, lined with rock and flagstones, so obviously someone spent considerable time and energy creating it.

But why? On that point, there is only conjecture. Recently people have started calling it the counterfeiter's den, because authorities once apprehended some practitioners of that art a few miles away. However, it is hard to imagine a counterfeiter creating such an elaborate hideaway with no light and little room to run a printing press. Others hypothesize that some settler in the area was trying to raise silkworms, or that someone in the Underground Railroad took the term too seriously. However, some research indicates that parts of the tunnels were dug about 10,000 years ago and that the stone ceiling was put into place around 3,000 b.c. Given the age, we think that the tunnels were actually an early relic of the Big Dig, the project that depressed the central artery of Boston underground—and depressed everyone who had to put up with the delays. Any century now, the link between there and Goshen is bound to open up. In the meantime, to view the site (the entrance is usually blocked for safety), take a trip to the Goshen Cemetery off Williams Drive between Cape Street and Route 9.

Grave Rubbers

Greenfield

Does history leave you cold? Not as cold as the subjects of this organization's focus. The Association for Gravestone Studies thinks that much of history is written in stone—headstones, to be specific. They see important information— from genealogy and religious history to changing fashions in art and literature—locked into the letters at the tops of burial sites.

This organization hopes to rub you the right way.

Photo by Robert Posson/Courtesy of the Association for Gravestone Studies

Any of the association's over 1,200 members can check with the central registry to get information on gravestone subjects. The association has a lending library of reference volumes and an online store with instructions on how to do research on the occupant of a particular grave. The association also offers cemetery guides, calendars, note cards with images of gravestones in the snow (be careful whom you send these to), and even software for recording details of gravestones. Information kits give you the practical instructions on how to do everything from making gravestone rubbings to understanding symbols on the stones to learning techniques for analyzing cemetery data.

For more information call (413) 772-0836 or go to www.grave stonestudies.org. The organization's headquarters are at 278 Main Street, Suite 207.

What Comes Down Must Go Up
Greenfield

Isn't it nice to know that some things don't change? For example, the trusty law of gravity is bound to bring things to their lowest point. Well, it will, *most* of the time. If you're the type who likes to know about exceptions to the rule, head over to Greenfield and take the exit off Interstate 91 for Gravity Hill. According to legend, a horrible accident happened there, involving a bus full of children going off the overpass, killing all the occupants. As the story goes, if you stop a car beneath the overpass and take it out of gear, the phantom children's hands will push the vehicle down the road a bit so that you won't get hurt.

Okay, so the story might seem a bit hard to believe. But many people who've tried it have found that their cars rolled at least a good 20 feet in a direction that seemed to be uphill. If you are interested in seeing where people have sworn that gravity bends to someone else's will, take I-91 to exit 26. But be careful: this is a rotary, so if you aren't careful, you could end up dizzy, if not floating.

Spiked!
Holyoke

In 1895 William G. Morgan, who directed the YMCA in Holyoke, had an idea for a new sport based on the game of badminton, with elements of tennis and handball thrown in. A tall net stood in the middle of a court, but instead of swinging at a shuttlecock, as many players as a team could fit would whack a ball back and forth with

Supernatural Citizens

For some reason Hadley seems to have attracted the worst and the best of the supernatural. We have all heard someone describe a woman as a "witch" when what they are really thinking involves a simple substitute of the initial letter. We wonder whether that might be what provoked the denunciation of Mary Webster, the Witch of Hadley. She reputedly had an unpleasant temper under the best of conditions. After a life of poverty and social shunning, she had a tongue ready to attack those who drew her displeasure.

Some of Webster's neighbors decided that she must be a witch. They blamed her for scaring cattle and children, among other things. At a time when accusations were almost as good as proof, she was brought before a local court, sent on to Boston, and held over for further trial. Yet ultimately she was found not guilty by a jury. (Perhaps they thought they would be safer were she back from whence she came.)

Back in Hadley, Webster's neighbors disagreed with the judgment. A group of young men dragged her from her house, attempted to hang her, then tossed her in the snow. Being a tough old bird, she lived another eleven years and died of old age at around seventy. If they thought she was a witch before, we'd hate to see what she was like after.

Hadley also had an angel—William Goffe. He was one of the fifty-nine judges who signed the death warrant of Charles I of England, endearing none of them to Charles II. Both Goffe and fellow judge Edward Whaley had to flee to the New World in 1660 and go into hiding.

After a few years of moving about, the two were hidden by Rev. John Russell for sixteen years. It is said that once, when a group of Indians were attacking the colonists, an aged man, unknown to any of the group of fifty or so families, took charge. He repelled the braves and then vanished. The people said that it was an angel sent to protect them, but the legend claims that it was Goffe, who had left his hiding place to lend aid and then disappeared as soon as the fight was over. Unfortunately, later scholarship disputes that Indian forces ever approached the town and suggests that the "angel of Hadley" story started in the eighteenth century. We consider it a case of miraculous conscription.

★ ★

the team on the other side. Drop the ball, and the other side won a point, much as might happen in badminton. It seemed like just the thing for older members of the Y who didn't like the roughhousing that went on during basketball games. The first recorded game of mintonette took place on July 7, 1896, in Springfield. Thank heavens someone came along and refined the idea. Instead of an unlimited number of players, there was a limit, first of nine, and then of six. And the name mintonette, which sounded more like a cut of beef and a workout, had to go. Devising the replacement was Alfred Halstead, who noticed just how much volleying the match involved. Thus people came to know mintonette as volleyball.

The YMCA these days is in a different location, but you can find the Volleyball Hall of Fame in Holyoke at 444 Dwight Street. It's open from Tuesday through Sunday, noon to 4:30 p.m. For more information call (413) 536-0926 or go to www.volleyhall.org.

On Balance
Lanesborough

Keeping on your toes will be easy after a visit to Balance Rock. This massive piece of limestone, 25 feet by 15 feet by 10 feet and weighing some 165 tons, perches delicately on another rock 3 feet above the ground. You'd think it was a shaky position, and it is—touch the rock and it shivers—but it hasn't come down yet.

This wasn't some invention by a tipsy architect, but rather a natural result of glacial action. That might explain why stories about the boulder go back centuries. In the 1800s it was owned by the Hubert family, who welcomed those who came to gawk. Then a traveling band of rascals who asked to see the rock promptly set up shop and tried to charge others a dime each for the view. Grove Hubert, the family member in charge at the time, was angry enough to try to rock the rock. Luckily, he learned that oxen do little when it comes to moving large chunks of mineral.

Eventually the state purchased the property and planted tens of thousands of trees to make it an inviting park. There are some other interesting rocks here, too: a rock that looks like a whale, one with a series of cracks that look like a cross, and a pair of twin rocks.

On balance, we know it's only a rock that doesn't roll, but we like it. See the stone at Balance Rock State Park on Balance Rock Road in the northwest corner of Pittsfield State Forest. For more information visit www.mass.gov/dcr/parks/western/pitt.htm.

Face Facts
Lanesborough

Ever had that funny feeling that someone is watching you? That is what happened to residents in northwest Massachusetts from May 10 through May 14, 1990. Heavy rains throughout that time finally sent earth, granite, and everything else tumbling down the side of nearby Mount Greylock, revealing the image of a face on the slope of this tallest peak in the state. In sort of a reverse face lift, the rough visage of an Indian appeared, staring down. People started calling the figure Chief Greylock, after a Waronoke Indian who spent a good part of his time in the early 1700s harassing English soldiers from a secret cave in the mountain. At one point he had half his foot amputated after a run-in with an animal trap; little wonder that he gained the nickname "the frowning chief of the Waronokes." But apparently that didn't slow him down. He sided with the French during the French and Indian Wars and was never caught or defeated, although he did manage to humiliate English forces time and again.

You can find the Mount Greylock State Reservation on Rockwell Road in Lanesborough. The road through the reservation is closed, but the trails are open. However, it's easier to go to Route 8 in Adams and look over—it's visible.

This Is the Church, This Is the Steeple

Lee

Record-tall buildings are usually the province of corporations. But for some reason, the First Congregational Church in Lee has come out on top in the area of timber frame construction—that's where the skeleton of the building is a series of large posts and beams that interlock. It's a beautiful style of building to see because the frame is exposed on the interior, adding not only great strength but also aesthetic pleasure.

For the First Congregation Church building, the timber construction is in the 105-foot-tall spire. It is the highest structure in the country using this method of construction. But remember, we're talking about the steeple—the very top of the church, a needle point rising even above the church bells, which are above the four-faced clock (itself a curiosity because it is wound by hand and runs for seven days before needing another winding). Sitting atop the rest of the church, the steeple reaches 192 feet high. In other words, this is a part of the church that rarely receives visitors.

However, some people have had a look. Built in 1857, the steeple had been struck by lightning and by 1987 needed some repair. (What kind of makeover do you think *you* might need at the age of 150?) Besides other bits of maintenance, it seems that the tower was tilting a couple of feet. Over a period of two weeks, Dalton-based Hill Engineers, Architects, Planners, Inc. used hydraulic jacks to move some columns up an eighth of an inch a day. Presumably, they wanted to avoid moving too quickly and causing a need to yell "timberrrrrrrr." To see the no-longer-tipping tower, head to 25 Park Place.

The Big Show

North Adams

Where would you go for contemporary art? New York? L.A.? Chicago? San Francisco? How about an old textile town in northwest

★ ★

Massachusetts with a population hovering around 15,000? North Adams is home to the Massachusetts Museum of Contemporary Art, or Mass MoCA—the largest American museum devoted to the genre.

How such an institution found itself in an economically depressed region of the commonwealth is an interesting story that starts in 1988, when then-governor Michael Dukakis earmarked funds for the project. The idea was to provide an economic transfusion to the region. Then "the Duke" had his picture taken while wearing a helmet and sitting in a tank, and not long after, he lost his presidential bid. The Massachusetts economic "miracle" turned out to be a

Photo by Doug Bartow/Courtesy of Mass MoCA

Natalie Jeremijenko's *Tree Logic* greets visitors to Mass MoCA.

temporary turn of events, money became tight, and gubernatorial successor William Weld froze the funds. But in 1995 he finally approved a large sum of money to begin converting old textile mills into galleries and theaters. These days, Mass MoCA sprawls among twenty-six nineteenth-century factory buildings on a thirteen-acre campus and covers not only the visual arts, but electronic media and the performing arts as well. Included amid the 110,000 square feet of exhibition space is a single gallery that is as long as a football field; undoubtedly, some artist will bring in two eleven-man teams and make the project interactive by selling beer and hot dogs.

It seems equivalent to finding a major league baseball stadium in the middle of a wheat field. But Mass MoCA seems to be thriving on the concept that "if you build it, they will come." With theaters, outdoor cinemas, workshops, and even companies subletting office and retail space, this is almost a mall-as-art project. You can see plays, hear music, dine at restaurants, and even bring the kids to a family gallery and studio space called Kidspace at Mass MoCA. You can probably even get lost and organize your own rescue expedition. Check the days and hours for Kidspace at www.massmoca.org/kidspace or at (413) 662-2111. You can get information on the parent organization by calling the same phone number or by visiting www.massmoca.org. To tour the main galleries, head to 87 Marshall Street; Kidspace is at 1032 Mass MoCA Way. Bring your own football helmet.

Lost Its Marble
North Adams

If you can take slang literally, then North Adams must be one of the craziest places in Massachusetts, having lost a lot of its marble. No, not *marbles*—we're talking about white marble, the stuff used in hearthstones and fireplace mantels and cemeteries. For more than a century, the area now called Natural Bridge State Park was the leading source for the material used throughout Massachusetts.

The famous author Nathaniel Hawthorne wrote in 1838 that parts of North Adams seemed gloomy and stern to him. Well, of course, Nat; we're talking the essence of fancy headstones here. The marble owes its quality in part to its chemical makeup: 98 percent calcium carbonate, otherwise known as limestone or natural chalk (or the antacid pills you might pop into your mouth after a bad burrito). Not only is the material beautiful and suited for building, but the dust and chips left after slicing slabs were also put into toothpaste, putty, and soap. How versatile: You can get your hands dirty cutting it, then wash with it afterward.

From 1837 to 1947 the mill literally ground out all these products, eventually shipping 400,000 pounds of stone a day. Then came a fire, putting the mill out of business and leaving the place as quiet as a mausoleum. A man by the name of Edward Elder purchased the upscale rock pit from the company that had owned it, and he ran it as a tourist attraction until his death in the mid-1980s. Shortly afterwards, his widow sold the site to the Massachusetts Department of Environmental Management, which turned it into a park.

One of the interesting features is a natural marble bridge. (Hence the name.) For more information see www.mass.gov/dcr/parks/western/nbdg.htm, or call either (413) 663-6392 (May to October) or (413) 663-6312 (November to April). To cross to Natural Bridge State Park, drive north on Route 8 half a mile from downtown North Adams.

Getting Kidded

Northfield

Ahoy, matey. *Ahhhrrrr,* you'd think that a pirate's story would take place on the ocean. Last map we checked, this part of Massachusetts is some 90 miles from the Atlantic. So why would anyone associate raiders of the high seas with Northfield? The legend goes that Captain Kidd actually sailed here up the Connecticut River, trying to find a hiding place for his loot. After all, even in the early eighteenth century, it was difficult to walk into a bank with chests of stolen goods to make a deposit.

So Kidd and some compatriots supposedly buried a chest of gold somewhere on Northfield's Clark's Island. That alone might sound suspicious, as the Connecticut River is often too shallow in spots for any boat, let alone one carrying a chest of gold coins.

According to the stories from Temple and Sheldon's *History of Northfield, MA, 150 Years,* Kidd and a few of his crew managed to make their way to Clark's Island at a part called Pine Meadow. They supposedly buried a treasure chest and left. After the hangman's noose snagged Kidd, the treasure was left to be found. A legend grew that the only way to find the gold was to have three people dig soundlessly under a full moon that was directly overhead. In the 1800s a trio of men reportedly was digging about under these conditions, not even swatting the mosquitoes that were munching them (for fear of making noise), when they spotted a chest. Someone spoke in elation, at which point the money sank out of reach, never to be found again.

Feel the need to dig into the legend more? Maybe you will be the one who finds the treasure. At some point cartographers took the legend seriously enough to rechristen Clark's Island as Kidd's Island. It's roughly in the middle of the river alongside a spot about half a mile down from the northern start of Pine Meadow Road. Bring your own boat—and be very quiet. You're hunting treasure.

Derby Day
Pittsfield

Traditional 4-H fairs are a staple of rural areas, including much of western Massachusetts. Youths compete by exhibiting vegetables, flowers, and even livestock they have raised. But while the Berkshire County *4-H Fair Handbook for 2004* states how much cleanliness—both of animals and the areas in which they are kept—contributes to scores awarded by judges, there is a delicate lack of mention of the annual dung drop derby.

The derby is an annual fund-raiser. Fair organizers and workers divide a field into a large grid. People purchase a square for $5, much as they might buy a raffle ticket. A cow is turned loose in the field, where it is welcome to stroll around, chew its cud . . . and drop a cow patty. The person who wagered on that square is the winner. It's not clear what happens if the deposit drops on the border between two grids.

Unfortunately, there have been times when the cow simply wouldn't cooperate, at which point another is brought in. It might seem udderly silly to you, but we have it on good authority that locals anticipate the event. To find the next derby, check the Massachusetts listings of youth agricultural fairs at www.mafa.org/youth.htm and look for the Berkshire County 4-H Fair. You can also call (413) 448-8285 for more information. The fair itself runs one day, usually the third Saturday in August, and can be found at Utility Drive, which is off Holmes Road.

Sing, Sing, Sing
Sheffield

Do inveterate shower singers make you wish that the ring around the tub was a wringing of a neck? If you want to K-O people who start bellowing, "O-K-L-A-H-O-M-A . . . Oklahoma!" then by all means be wary of Sheffield in the summer, when it hosts the Berkshire Choral Festival. Started in 1982 and running on the campus of the Berkshire School, the festival attracts 1,600 people from all over the world who have an insatiable desire to burst into song and want to spend a week doing nothing but that. They call it "the week that lasts a lifetime," and we have a funny feeling that we would agree with them. So many people want to participate in song that would-be choristers must enter a drawing by February to get a spot on the roster. Warning: This event is not over in seven days. Professional conductors switch off to provide a season that lasts for about five weeks.

If you'd like to sing classical works in intensive rehearsal periods under accomplished conductors, this place might be for you. Just make sure you are vocally in shape. The choral music is moderately difficult, and if you don't know how to keep to your part—whether soprano, alto, tenor, baritone, or bass—the music lovers around you may cease to be lovable. You have to study tapes and written music ahead of time, and if management thinks that your singing is not up to snuff, they reserve the right to kick you out on your andante. If you like singing but have a voice that depresses even the tone deaf, you can still attend . . . as a member of the audience. For more information call (413) 229-8526 or visit www.chorus.org.

Bridge over Troubled Lilacs
Shelburne Falls

There are people who will turn *anything* into a planter, but most are amateurs compared to the folks in Shelburne Falls. These gardening gurus took an old trolley bridge and transformed it into a garden. And this isn't some little stone structure adorned by a few gladioluses and petunias. The Bridge of Flowers runs some 400 feet, with 500 varieties of flowers that start blooming in April and end in October in a floral last hurrah of chrysanthemums. Originally built in 1908, this piece of civil engineering was as staid as any waterworks or highway overpass. It was the property of the Shelburne Falls and Colrain Street Railway and part of the route of the freight trolley that operated between this town and the mills in nearby Colrain.

But progress reared its ugly head as the automobile made way for its big brother, the truck. Suddenly it was cheaper and easier to make runs between the towns with individual vehicles and not maintain an entire train system; the rail company went out of business in 1928. Sure, there was no problem taking the cars off the tracks, pretending that the entire venture never existed, but a bridge is a hard thing to hide, especially when water mains run across it. To keep from being high and dry, the town bought the bridge in 1929. Some locals thought that there was no reason that something so utilitarian had to look seedy. If water was going to run over the bridge, they reasoned, they might as well sprinkle some *on* it. That year, the town raised money to transform the bridge into a public garden. (Undoubtedly, this was before the great stock market crash, which left few people with a pot to plant in.) Since then, donations and a largely volunteer effort have kept the bridge in bloom and the weeds at bay. Today the Shelburne Falls Women's Club does much of the work, along with a hired gardener. Just travel to the intersection of Water and Bridge Streets—how appropriate—to see the floral frenzy.

Prehistoric Potholes

Shelburne Falls

If you've ever made pothole jokes like, "Oh, this one is so big that it almost swallowed my car," take time to visit Shelburne Falls and see what real potholes are like. These aren't the measly little pits that dot pavements after a cold snap. The biggest of them ranks as the world's largest pothole, 39 feet across. Not only could you literally lose your car in this mother of all potholes, you could probably say goodbye to a good-size truck.

Luckily for the residents, the potholes are not on the streets but down near a hydroelectric dam. It seems that during the time of the last glaciers melting, the region's level of high water was quite impressive and the Connecticut River greatly expanded its reach. Stones, trapped in a riverbed, were shaken about by the flow of water and acted as drills. They created the potholes near the dam.

You might think it strange for a town to look at a collection of old holes in the ground and consider it a tourist attraction. Even stranger is that people actually *do* come by to see the potholes. Residents have even given them a name: the Glacial Potholes. (Better that than the Pits.) Go to the end of Deerfield Street and you will find an observation deck overlooking the potholes, as well as some local falls. Just get there before some zealous department of public works makes a pilgrimage and leaves a mass of asphalt.

Simple or Simple-Minded?
Shutesbury

Eugenics is the dubious pursuit of using genetics to argue for the supposed superiority of groups of people. Although it turned into a horror in World War II, before that it actually had proponents in the United States. And the evidence they waved about was actually garnered from Shutesbury, a sleepy town of under 2,000 that hasn't any stores. As explained in an interesting story in *Boston Magazine* (www.bostonmagazine.com/special1/eugenics_1202.shtml), the Shutesbury Study of 1928 was a deceptive inquiry into the personal, medical, and educational histories of the residents. It was used as evidence for the necessity of culling society's undesirables. Getting shameful support from leading academics from such schools as Harvard as well as others less "qualified" (the man who arranged the study, Leon Whitney, was actually a dog breeder), the movement gained attention for its views at the time. Much of the evidence came from field studies where people were supposedly trained to detect human character by appearance. One of the proponents, Walter Fernald, was the first resident superintendent of the Massachusetts School for the Feeble-Minded, an institution that would eventually take his name and go on to greater fame by feeding radioactive cereal to children in the 1950s as part of another experiment.

Yet Shutesbury seems to have survived it all. People still live there, the air is clean, the traffic is insignificant, and the surroundings are beautiful. When you come from a congested urban locale, it makes you wonder who the simple-minded people are after all.

Wax Job

South Deerfield

Need a candle? Two? Two hundred? Is that all? Any normal candle shop could probably handle even that, but we're not talking ordinary. Yankee Candle is to candles what the New York Public Library is to a bookmobile. We've seen people walk into the place and drop their jaws practically to the ground, and for good reason. There is room after room, many with particular themes, such as the Bavarian Christmas Village and its 25-foot-tall Christmas tree, the medieval Nutcracker Castle, the Black Forest and snow that falls year round, and Santa's Enchanted Toy Works. Although it's not all candles—there are knickknacks, toys, 16,000 square feet of housewares alone, and an animatronic country band—you have to be into the wax. Stop by the candle-making museum, with demonstrations of nineteenth-century candle making, and try not to be assaulted by the 160 different candle scents. This is an outing, and if you need to restore your strength, there is a restaurant, plus a baker, café, and fudge stand. Yankee Candle hosts special events and group tours. We're waiting for the company to have done with it and just install bunks for the truly devoted. Open daily from 9:30 a.m. to 6 p.m., the store is closed on Thanksgiving and Christmas and closes at 5 p.m. on Christmas Eve. For more information call (877) 636-7707.

Fee, Fie, Foe, Foot

South Hadley

Many youngsters are interested in dinosaurs, and for a few, the fascination never ends. In the case of the Nash family, you might say that dinosaurs became an obsession that turned into a vocation. The business used to be called Nash Dino Land, but when the founder, Carlton Nash, died a few years ago, his son, Kornell, changed the name to the Nash Dinosaur Track Quarry.

★ ★

Dinosaur tracks go back a long time in the area. (Okay, okay, they go back a long time *everywhere*.) But it was in 1802 that people found the first prehistoric footprints in the South Hadley area. For some reason, during the Jurassic period the roaming lizards were ill-bred, walking through the local mud flats and never wiping their feet. Such is the way of the world that one man's messy ground can be another man's living. Growing up in the area, Carlton Nash was fascinated with dinosaurs. Right after high school he began prowling through the local woods, hoping to unearth a cache of footprints. He found one in 1933, but it took him six years to save enough money to buy the property.

The elder Nash began working his track mine. It must have felt as though he was on a treadmill: At first he cut Christmas trees in the fall, worked for the electric company in the spring, and sold dinosaur prints in the summer. By 1950 he was able to make dinosaurs his business. His son eventually joined him, and now Kornell spends his time trying to update displays that are showing their ages. (Though after the first million years, who notices a decade or two?) Much of Kornell's living comes from selling two groups of actual fossil prints: one about 4 to 7 inches, and the other about 12 to 20 inches. Prices start at $50 and go to roughly $1,000, depending on the size of the track and the condition. It must be said that he prices by the foot.

Nash Dinosaur Track Quarry is at Route 116, 39 Aldrich Street in South Hadley; call (413) 467-9566.

Seuss I Am
Springfield

That Dr. Seuss, that Dr. Seuss, you cannot fault that Dr. Seuss. Could he, would he illustrate? Books for kids would seem his fate. And his words were always pat. He could write about a cat. He could top the cat with a hat from the desk at which he sat. Kids would laugh and that was that.

Dr. Seuss and the Cat in the Hat sculpture.

Before he found his kids' book fame, young Ted Geisel's job was tame, marketing a corporate name. After this came work more rare, magazines requiring care: *Judge* and *Life* and *Vanity Fair.* Then he got to draw and write; publishers had seen his light, work that was a pure delight. Raves from critics it did woo: Emmys, Oscars, Pulitzer, too.

When he died, his hometown thought, "Celebrate," and so they sought something fun, not overwrought. Artist Lark Grey Dimond-Cates was called in, to craft bronze statues thick and thin. These show Dr. Seuss, cat in tow, Yertle Turtle, Grinch, and Max, Horton's Who and the Lorax. The author had watched the sculptress grow; he was her step-dad, you should know. So drive to State and Chestnut Streets to see some art that can't be beat.

Dunking Do-Its
Springfield

If you think a New England winter is cold, imagine December 1891, when central heating was hardly ubiquitous. Spending time in the outdoors generally meant a coat and hurrying from one location to another. But a body needs exercise, so Dr. Luther H. Gulick decided that the young men at the Springfield YMCA needed some whole-some indoor recreation. He asked the Canadian physician and cler-gyman James Naismith, who worked for him, to see what he could devise. The answer was a cross between football, soccer, and hockey. Peach baskets went up on the walls, and teams of nine men vied to get a soccer ball into one of them.

Naismith had invented basketball, and the sporting world—and social standing of extremely tall people—would never be the same. The game spread like a fast break, and during World War II the U.S. military introduced it throughout the world. The first pro league actu-ally started in 1898 to look after players' interests and promote a gentler game. Who would have thought that the current professional version with its roughhousing would be the outcome?

The Y of those days is now part of Springfield College, a private institution, founded in 1885 to train people to run YMCAs; it's at 263 Alden Street. But if you really want a basketball fix, head over to the Naismith Memorial Basketball Hall of Fame at 1150 West Colum-bus Avenue. For more information go to www.hoophall.com or call (413) 781-6500.

★ ★

Extra-Large Stack
Springfield

Most of the breakfast-going world divides into two camps: short and full stacks. Where you come down on the question is a matter of devotion and capacity because, let's face it, instead of soaring, those doughy flying saucers can pin you to the floor as efficiently as a professional wrestler. For some people, a mass of pancakes is something to avoid, while for others, it means a bigger sponge for sopping up the syrup. Do you find yourself asking, "May I have more?" If so, the answer is that you may—in May. Every May the city of Springfield hosts what it has come to call the world's largest pancake breakfast, in celebration of its anniversary. Forget any church or charity breakfast you have seen. This is the morning's first meal on a scale frightening to behold. The event takes place outside (there is no indoor venue that will do) along Main Street, from State to Bridge.

In the past few years, about 70,000 people have shown up for this feast each year, which is a huge jump from the estimated 40,000 in 1999. We are talking enough flapjacks to make a stack that is literally miles high. The Library of Congress has deemed this May-munching-madness a Local Legacy Event. Undoubtedly it happens only once a year so that the volunteers have a chance to wash all the dishes and pans in time for the next observance. If you want more information, call (413) 733-3800.

Statuesque
Stockbridge

We thought that artists were supposed to be perpetually hungry and ensconced in garrets. After learning about Chesterwood, we've come to the conclusion that such stories are nothing but aggressive public relations to induce tax authorities and debt collectors to forgo phone calls and write off any owed money as unobtainable. This 122-acre estate was not even the main residence of sculptor Daniel Chester

★ ★

French, but rather the man's summer home and studio. Oh, well, he was in his seventies when he acquired the property, so some allowance can be made for financial endurance.

While French's name may not be immediately familiar, his work is bound to be. It includes such memorials as the seated president in the Lincoln Memorial and the Minute Man statue in Concord. There are literally dozens of his statues tucked away in various parts of Massachusetts. At Chesterwood you can see models of some of French's works, as well as paintings that he created and others that he collected, his tools, and even exhibitions of other artists' sculpture. Enjoy

Photo by Ron Blunt/Courtesy of Chesterwood

The 1920s summer home of Daniel Chester French is open from May through October.

the spacious Italian gardens May through October, and remember, it was a summer residence, so don't expect to wander the grounds in the off-season (although there are special programs at Christmas). For more information call (413) 298-3579 or visit www.chesterwood.org. To reach Chesterwood go to the west end of Main Street and follow the signs to the location on Williamsville Road.

No Wicked Witch Here

Tyringham

Most of us grew up with fairy tales, including the story of Hansel and Gretel, who were enticed by the gingerbread house. They had troubles, but nothing that putting a little heat on the situation couldn't cure. Those visiting Tyringham, however, can feel as cool as a cucumber while visiting the gingerbread house of Sir Henry Kitson. The edifice, which he called Santarella, was his art studio. It featured a whimsical design that made visitors feel like they were in the middle of a storybook. But whimsy can be deceptive. The studio's wavy thatched roof is actually a carefully constructed sculpture, formed from sliced dyed asphalt roof shingles set in stacks more than 1½ feet thick. Heavy chestnut beams hold the estimated eighty tons of weight.

There is a certain degree of irony that Sir Henry, a Brit, was the sculptor of the Puritan Maid in Plymouth. He was also responsible for the Minute Man statue in Lexington, commemorating a war in which, to put it nicely, our side whooped his. (The statue is not to be confused with the Minute Man in Concord, created by Daniel Chester French, whose former house is now a museum in Stockbridge.) Some of Kitson's other works include statues of Robert E. Lee and Jefferson Davis, so his subjects weren't always on the winning side.

Like French, Kitson built his getaway when he hit his seventies. Perhaps on a small scale, Kitson struck one for Britain, taking the money he made in statues of the political elite and in memorials and hiring workers from the United Kingdom to build his roof. But he was reputedly an incredibly difficult man to work for, so we wonder how many came to wish that the project's roof would just cave in.

Santarella is open from Memorial Day through the end of October and is at 75 Main Road. Not only can you visit the museum and gardens, but there are even overnight guest rooms to rent here—just make sure you have easy access to the oven. Call (413) 243-3260 or go to www.santarella.us for more information.

The Big Squeeze

Washington

If you have a taste for French cafes, Cajun two-stepping, Italian weddings, or just a lively polka band, we have an event for you. Something that all four have in common is the accordion—or squeeze box, to use the more down-home and eclectic title. The instrument has been the butt of humor for years, whether called a concertina or a button box. Yet to its devotees, there is nothing more endearing than the reedy, wheezy sound produced by this family of miniature, portable, wind-driven pianos. In Amherst there is a shop that specializes in the sales and repairs of accordions and concertinas. Obviously the management has a soft spot in their hearts (and, those who don't like the sound would say, in their heads) for the instruments and those who love them.

And so, to promote camaraderie (and presumably sales) the store, called the Button Box, began to organize and sponsor the Northeast Squeeze-In Festival in Washington. Every September it sports what is undoubtedly the largest collection of players who gather to do nothing but to press their own buttons, if not each other's. The gathering takes place at Bucksteep Manor, an estate on Washington Mountain Road. For more information call (413) 665-7793 or visit www.button box.com.

Forward into the Past

West Springfield

Have your kids seen any of the television programs in which modern families live in the setting of some earlier era—whether Edwardian, frontier time, or Pilgrim? They can actually have a taste of it themselves at Storrowton Village, a re-creation of a nineteenth-century New England community, complete with town green. Kids can spend a day or even a week dressed in period clothing, trying their hand at such crafts as candle dipping and tile mosaics, milking a cow, and spinning wool and weaving. If they are going for the day, the kids bring their own lunch. (What, there was a time without Big Macs?) For longer visits, meals are provided.

We bet that no matter how good the program, your children won't return ready to haul the water or feed the pigs. But at least you'll have a few days of relative quiet. For more information call (413) 205-5115 or visit www.thebige.com/storrowton.html to check programs and events.

A Nose for Business

West Stockbridge

When things go well, most businesspeople would not say that they smell. But a heavy aroma is a good sign at Charles H. Baldwin and Sons, a shop established in 1888 and dedicated to the proposition that not all vanillas are created equal. The store is a major source of upscale vanilla extract—a distillation of the fruit of tropical orchids. And here the dismissive phrase "plain vanilla" is a euphemism for "unbelievably expensive." Baldwin's uses only Madagascar Bourbon vanilla beans distilled in a copper apparatus that is over sixty-five years old. They then age it in hundred-year-old oak barrels to add to the flavoring and color. When Charles Baldwin started his business, he went by horse and buggy from door to door. Today orders come in from chefs and demanding amateur cooks from around the world over the Web site (www.baldwinextracts.com). But as good as vanilla is, the current owners, the Moffatt family, have branched out to such flavors as lemon, almond, and peppermint. They also have a Worcestershire sauce and a maple syrup with walnuts and (what else?) vanilla, both from old recipes the Moffatts found in the store.

Years ago many women used a dab of vanilla instead of perfume. Men who might feel a bit uncomfortable doing the same can pick up a bottle of Baldwin's bay rum. Accept no substitutes, as you'll "nose" the difference. The shop is at 1 Center Street, (413) 232-7785, or you can save a drive and go to www.baldwinextracts.com.

index

index

index

index

index

index

index

index

index

index

Orlando has greatly helped me focus on the adaptation issue.

13. Tim Krabbe, *The Vanishing*, (New York: Random House, 1993), p. 42.

14. Richard Kohl, 'The lady vanishes', *Time Out Amsterdam*, October 1993, pp. 10–11.

15. See Carol C. Clover, 'Her body, himself: gender in the slasher film', in James Donald (ed.), *Fantasy and the Cinema* (London: BFI, 1989), pp. 91–133 (originally in *Representations* 20 [1987]). Clover's argument is extended in her *Men, Women and Chainsaws* (London: BFI, 1992).

16. Jean-François Lyotard, *The Inhuman* (Oxford: Polity Press, 1991). 'Passibility as the possibility of experiencing (*pathos*) presupposes a donation. If we are in a state of passibility, it's that something is happening to us, and when this passibility has a fundamental status, the donation itself is something fundamental, originary. What happens to us is not at all something we have first controlled, programmed, grasped by a concept [*Begriff*]. Or else, if what we are passible to has first been plotted conceptually, how can it *seize us*?' (pp. 110–11). See also the crucial paragraph on pp. 116–17: 'About the confusion between passible and passive ... [Once,] when you painted, you did not ask for "interventions" from the one who looked, you claimed there was a community. The aim nowadays is not that sentimentality you still find in the slightest sketch by a Cézanne or a Degas, it is rather that the one who receives should not receive, it is that s/he does not let him/herself be put out ... let him/her reconstitute himself immediately and identify himself or herself as someone who intervenes. What we live by and judge by is exactly this will to action ... [This] implies the retreat of the passibility by which alone we are fit to receive and, as a result, to modify and do, and perhaps even to enjoy.'

17. André Bazin, 'The ontology of the photographic image', in *What Is Cinema?*, vol. 1 (Berkeley: University of California Press, 1967), pp. 9–16. Another Bazinian text in the same collection which is highly pertinent to the concerns of this paper is 'In defense of mixed cinema', pp. 53–75.

18. The uses of still photography within both the film versions
    of *The Vanishing* would sustain analysis. For instance,
    contrast the photographic reminder to Raymond of his
    first *acte gratuite*, which gives him the idea of looking
    vulnerable by (re)placing his arm in a sling (photography
    as aid to planning), with the ultra-Bazinian, and quite
    useless, photo of Saskia which is Rex's final visual record
    of her. A hidden photographic 'shrine', along with a
    disguised computer file (what would Bazin have made of
    computer files?) brings home to Rita, very painfully, Jeff's
    continuing obsession with the lost Diane. And what
    vanishes last in the original *Vanishing* are Saskia's and Rex's
    photographic images, first appearing in a newspaper
    account of the mysterious doubling of the one disap-
    pearance by the other, then visually held while the
    newspaper text disappears, in simple oval (old-fashioned
    portrait? *egg*?) framing. A more daring critical move would
    be to see Rex's death as a 'hyper-photograph' of Saskia's
    death (with Raymond as the 'camera'). Bazin's argument
    about photography as the technological fulfilment of the
    ambition behind mummification or the modelling of
    death-masks would then find here an appropriately
    macabre extension.

2

The Vampire Writes Back: Anne Rice and the (Re)Turn of the Author in the Field of Cultural Production

Ken Gelder

This chapter will look at the fortunes of a particular author in relation to the filming of one of her novels: Anne Rice's *Interview with the Vampire* (1975; released as a film at the end of 1994). I want to use Anne Rice as a case study, to look at how the author might function in relation to what can be called – following Pierre Bourdieu – 'the field of cultural production', a phrase which is suitably non-specific since what is involved here is not just the relationship between novelist and film, but also media which negotiate that relationship and which themselves constitute and produce that 'field'. My suggestion here is that, following the traumatic announcement by Roland Barthes of the 'death of the author' in the late 1960s, nevertheless the author is still *not quite* dead. Indeed, the author – and the image is obviously appropriate for an author of vampire novels in particular – may well be 'undead' in the sense that she may be able to be reanimated when her work is reproduced elsewhere in the field of cultural production. The notion of the 'death of the author' has two kinds of uses: firstly, it refers to the author's disappearance in the very act of writing, which enables often indeterminate meanings beyond the intentions of the author; and secondly (although this owes more to Walter Benjamin than Roland Barthes), it refers to the author's disappearance at the moment of 'mechanical reproduction' (e.g. through the film-of-the-novel), where the author's intentions may be only one contributing factor amongst many others. But during the filming of *Interview with the Vampire,* Anne Rice did *not* disappear. She returned to the scene of reproduction – and this is why I've broken this word in two in my title – by throwing a *turn*, a tantrum. She made the film an occasion for the author of the novel-on-which-it-was-based to 'have a turn', in both senses of that phrase. And in this way, she hasn't exactly *re*turned – but she hasn't exactly disappeared, either. By 'writing back' to the film of her novel, she unsettled the equilibrium of the field; she effected this primarily by becoming an author who did not behave like an author, an author who did not know her place (in the field of cultural production).

I have found Pierre Bourdieu's book, *The Field of Cultural Production* (1993), useful for this essay because it helps to organise our sense of how cultural production – and reproduction – operates. In relation to the artist – the author – the cultural field is structured by what he calls 'the distribution of available positions'.[1] The field gains its dynamics through 'position-takings' – one artist may take a position in relation to positions already occupied by artists he or she may wish to be identified with, or distinguished from, and so on. The point is, however, that this is not so much a struggle between or amongst artists-as-individuals, as a struggle built around those 'available positions', and the 'orientation of practice' an artist adopts in relation to them.[2] One chooses to become a popular novelist, for example; but even here, one can occupy an 'available position' in relation to conceptions of popularity (which is not a homogeneous thing) – conceptions which are *already* available in that field. Those available positions have values attached to them; they are located in culture in a certain way; and they locate the artist in a certain way, attributing to the artist certain effects in culture.

These available positions are often seen as variants on a binary opposition which can be expressed simply in terms of the difference between producing cultural goods for money (economic capital) and producing cultural goods for a less tangible kind of prestige (symbolic capital). This kind of difference is often invoked when we think about films on the one hand, and writing on the other: films, obviously, are a form of 'large-scale' production, while writing (novels, poetry in particular) is a form of 'restricted' production. Our conception of the 'author' is generally tied to this latter form: large-scale production, on the other hand, seems to do away with this concept. (Howard Becker's influential book *Art Worlds* [1982] is precisely about how social *groups* produce film; it describes how the intentions of an individual count for very little in the large-scale, incorporated world of film production.) But in fact, the relationship between large-scale production and restricted production is often unclear, especially in the realm of popular writing. The novelist Fay Weldon has given what seems like a belated account of the modern writer, when she claimed not long ago. 'The writer, like the scientist, is no longer pure. He/she works and creates, ultimately, for the profit of others. The scientist has to please the funding body; the writer, increasingly, has the publisher and script editor to please, else his/her work does not see the light of day.'[3] In the realm of the 'popular' in particular, this account has probably always been true – although it is worth thinking about why it is under renewal today (following middlebrow author Martin Amis's contract with HarperCollins for half-a-million pounds – to write a novel precisely about the writer's 'available positions' in relation to popular fiction – we can think of Amis himself as a highly constrained novelist in this respect, with only a limited number of available positions, partly because of his own genealogy).

Even a popular novelist can be 'returned' to the field of restricted production, however. After the release of the film of *Interview with the Vampire*, John Ezard wrote an article for The *Guardian* which took us back to the novel-upon-which-it-was-based, characterising that novel – even though it had sold over four million copies – as a text with a limited circulation:

I spent, or misspent, part of the seventies trying to find someone to talk to about a story called *Interview With The Vampire*. I chanced on a copy 17 years ago in the small paperback section of a now long-shut Co-op furniture shop. The blurb said it was 'the most seductive evocation of evil ever written … a strikingly original work of the imagination.'

For once a blurb turned out to be right. Nothing since has shaken my belief that the novel is not only the best, strangest story of the supernatural ever written – head and shoulders

above Mary Shelley's *Frankenstein* or Bram Stoker's *Dracula*
– but the first work of art to emerge from horror fiction.[4]

This passage clearly works to lift this popular novel out of
circulation: it was discovered 'by chance' rather than because
of corporate publicity; it was found not in a multinational-
owned mega-bookstore but in a Co-op furniture shop which
has now closed down. Ezard relocates this novel in a field of
restricted production precisely in order to claim it as 'art' ('the
first work of art to emerge from the horror genre') – as opposed
to business, or large-scale production – and in turn, to retrieve
the concept of an author from the film-of-the-novel, which
would seem to have no particular need for that concept. In
spite of this, however, Ezard seems to *like* the film, which he
claims 'is a remarkably faithful, highly animated version of the
original'. The earlier distinction between the private or restricted
field of the novel and the public or large-scale field of the film
becomes problematic at this point: exactly what *is* being lost
when a novel is turned into a film? Ezard's closing paragraph
at last comes to the point of the article:

> But there is one wretched difference [between the novel and
> the film]. The worst of the horror – Lestat toying with a half-
> drained, terrified prostitute, dancing crudely with the corpse
> of the plague child's mother – is played as a game for the
> audience; and the audience at my preview joined in. What
> I found just about artistically acceptable on the page I
> watched with a sense of appalled collective degradation in
> the cinema. It made me long for the years when the tale was
> little known.[5]

I have already suggested that there never was a time when this
particular 'tale' was 'little known': it was always a bestseller.
So this paragraph (and much of the article) is more ideological
than real in its outline of the 'wretched difference' between
novel and film. What it turns on is the suggestion that pleasures
derived from a restricted field of production (private pleasures)
may be 'artistically acceptable', whereas pleasures derived
from a large-scale field of production (public pleasures) are
'degrading' – *even when those pleasures are the same* (since the

film is 'remarkably faithful' to the novel). In other words, the same kinds of pleasure produce different effects, depending on whether the form of cultural production is restricted or large-scale. But this view of pleasure simply reproduces the nature of the field of cultural production in its ideological view. Ezard's strangely nostalgic argument seems to be: when pleasure itself is restricted, it can be sanctioned and, more importantly, it can be author-ised, since the author is a concept which is built around a notion of restriction. But when pleasure is *not* restricted (when it reaches a wider audience), it can no longer be sanctioned because a certain loss of author-ity has taken place. The structure of Ezard's relation to the text itself changes radically here: whereas he had identifed the novel through the author, now he identifies the film through the *audience* ('I watched with a sense of appalled collective degradation ... '). The audience here has quite literally done away with the 'author' in the signifying chain: they themselves enable 'the death of the author' to come about. And in fact Ezard's article works very much as a kind of epitaph, mourning the loss of 'Anne Rice' – which also amounts to mourning the loss of one's privacy, a loss attributed here to nothing less than the film-of-the-novel.

But in the actual case of the filming of *Interview with the Vampire*, Anne Rice, as I have said, emerges as an author who simply will not go away. In fact, she had spent over fifteen years negotiating in Hollywood for the film production rights for her novel. One of her particular interests was in who might be cast as Lestat, her 'favourite' vampire: she had suggested Rutger Hauer (whom she had liked in *Bladerunner)*, and later Daniel Day-Lewis, who turned it down. When the film was given to Irish director Neil Jordan, working with producer David Geffen, the role of Lestat was given to Tom Cruise. Anne Rice thought that this was a disastrous choice and she said so somewhat bluntly in an interview with the *Los Angeles Times*: 'Cruise is no more my vampire Lestat than Edward G. Robinson is Rhett Butler.'[6] Now this is not the comment of a novelist who expects to see her novel end up on the shelf of a Co-op furniture shop. The author here 'writes back' to the film, and she does so firstly by moving into the field of large-scale production (the newspaper), and secondly by aligning the film of her own novel with the American popular film epic *Gone with the Wind* – that is, her rejection of Tom Cruise is articulated through a monumentalisation of the film-to-be of her novel, as if this scale of reproduction was its inevitable outcome. (In fact, the film of *Interview with the Vampire* became in its opening week the fourth-highest earning film in the US.) So Anne Rice is an author who does not sit quietly in the field of restricted production. In *People* magazine, Rice went on to say about Cruise: 'I don't want somebody "less clean cut" to play the vampire Lestat. I wanted a great actor of appropriate voice and height who would carry the part – Malkovich, Daniel Day-Lewis, Jeremy Irons. It's a different league. Do any of you actually read? When you're talking Lestat, you're talking Captain Ahab, Custer, Peter the Great.'[7] What I like about these comments is the way they confuse distinctions between popular and high culture – and, for that matter, distinctions between canonised textual heroes such as Ahab and canonised non-textual heroes such as Custer. The complaint 'Do any of you actually read?' may thus have little to do with literature; it precisely responds to her tendency *not* to operate in a restricted field of production.

When the film of *Interview with the Vampire* appeared, Tom Cruise was himself interviewed in a number of populist venues – from *OK! Magazine* (February 1995) to popular film magazines such as *Film Review*, *Premiere* and *Empire*. These venues all work to 'produce' Tom Cruise, to shape him in relation to readers and viewers of the film. In every interview I have read, the article stresses Cruise's 'diplomatic' position on Anne Rice: the actor never stoops to criticise the author. *Empire* called Cruise 'politely diplomatic' when he said of Rice, 'She was opposed to me being Lestat based on other characters that I've played … She had created Lestat and feels great affinity for this character because of her family, her daughter and what occurred. It was very important to her – but it hurt me.'[8] The author's personal relations to her character are stressed here (the novel was supposed to have been written by Rice in part as a response to the death of her five-year-old daughter from leukemia). But at least the actor is 'hurt' by the author: she has a certain unsettling effect. In the interview in *Film Review*, Cruise noted, 'As an actor I had a great time playing Lestat, but it certainly was unusual to start a movie with someone not wanting you to do it'.[9] So there is a sense here of the actor remaining 'un-authorised' by Anne Rice even as the filming gets underway. This lack of authorisation carries over into Cruise's commentary about the film. In *Premiere* magazine, Rachel Abramowitz asks Cruise about the erotic aspects of his performance as Lestat: '"You're going to have to see for yourself", becomes his standard answer to questions,' she says, 'until he finally gets frustrated: "It doesn't matter what I think about a movie".'[10] What is interesting about this kind of response – a not untypical one for actors – is that it de-authorises the actor's position in relation to the film. The actor is not an author: it 'doesn't matter' what he thinks about his role, although it may matter (to him) what an *author* thinks of his role. What we have with Anne Rice and Tom Cruise in relation to this film, then, is an opposing structure. Whereas Anne Rice intervenes in the filming of her novel by asserting her authorial rights, Tom Cruise withdraws from commentary. In other words, whereas the author uses the film as a means of *refusing* the restricted field of literary production – by occupying more 'available positions' than she might otherwise have occupied as a novelist, by becoming transgressive in this sense – the actor uses the film in order to *maintain* a set of restrictions, sitting 'diplomatically' or conservatively within the frame of an 'available position' defined by his role *as* an actor. The actor is in place as an actor; this means, in short, that he is not an author.

It probably seems like an obvious thing to say: an actor is not an author. But in relation to film, the actor may well carry an 'authorial' role simply by virtue of the fact of his or her visibility on the screen and in screen-oriented media. Actors imprint their own 'signature' on a film, and this signature may be complete enough to erase other kinds of authorial signatures, including the signature of the author of the novel-on-which-the-film-might-have-been-based and, even, the signature of the director (who I shall discuss in a moment). The problem is that the actor's signature in a film is split between the actor himself and the character he plays. Because the actor is engaged (increasingly) in promoting his or her image outside the film itself, he or she is less likely to be taken as the character *in* the film and nothing more. Celia Lury, in her somewhat neglected book *Cultural Rights: Technology, Legality, and Personality* (1993), goes on to note one outcome of this split, where the actor in fact can never be the character precisely because the image marketed outside of film collapses back into the film itself.[11] In a specific sense, the actor can no longer act, meaning that he or she can no longer be anything other than their image outside of the film which casts them in a given role (which may be chosen anyway because of their image). In this way, Tom Cruise can never be anything other than Tom Cruise, as Anne Rice had suggested (although she had also suggested that other actors *could* be the character Lestat). Celia Lury turns to Bruce King's article 'Articulating stardom' (1985) to clarify this point, that acting these days is valued less in terms of impersonation (where the actor disappears into the role) and more in terms of personification (where the role is subordinate to the actor's persona).[12] And yet, when Cruise finally did take up his role as the vampire Lestat, Rice herself enacted an about-face: she claimed that she liked Tom Cruise in the role precisely because, as it unfolded, his acting did in fact privilege impersonation over personification. Notoriously, she took out a two-page, $3,450.00 advertisement in *Variety* (Autumn 1994), in which she stated: 'I was honoured to discover how faithful this film was to the spirit, the content and the ambience of the novel *Interview with the Vampire* ... The charm, the humour and invincible innocence which I cherish in my beloved Lestat are all alive in Tom Cruise's courageous performance.'[13] She is quite specific about what she now values in Tom Cruise: 'I was swept away ... The high point was to see Cruise in the blond hair speaking with the voice of my Lestat. He makes you forget the boyish image of his past films. He is that mysterious and immortal character. I found it an uncompromising movie: I was kind of sick before it came, and I'm cured.'[14] In terms of authorial rights – cultural rights – the point to notice here is not so much the way Rice has revised her earlier claim by suggesting now that Tom Cruise *can* successfully impersonate her character Lestat (to the extent of totally subordinating his own persona), but rather the rhetorical claim she makes *herself* on her character: 'my Lestat'. The actor is subordinated to the character because the novelist says so: it is simply a strategic response to the 'loss' of her character, and the loss of control over her character, at the point of the novel's reproduction as film. Her character Lestat, in other words, is powerful enough to reach beyond the restricted field of the novel – powerful enough to make us 'forget' Tom Cruise.

In fact, Anne Rice was commissioned by producer David Geffen to write the script for the film of *Interview with the Vampire*. She also endorsed Geffen's choice of director, the Irishman Neil Jordan. But Jordan decided to rewrite Anne Rice's script, opening up the distinction between author and scriptwriter (even though the film continued to credit Rice with the screenplay). Jordan claims to have developed the role of Louis, and built up the family relationships between the vampires in the film: 'It's something I had made more central to it than Anne had done.'[15] He also contributed to the screenplay 'a streak of black humour' which, he had said, 'is totally absent from Rice's own work'; and he invested the film with an Irish-Catholic aura.[16] Interestingly, while changing the novel in these and no doubt other ways, Jordan also claimed that he had rewritten Rice's script because 'she wasn't faithful to her own book ... What I had to do was reintroduce aspects of her own novel into the screenplay.'[17] So here, the director is more 'faithful' to the novel than the author: it is one way of authorising his own involvement with the re-directed screenplay. But there was apparently a more banal, institutional reason why Rice continued to be credited with the screenplay, as Jordan 'grumbles' to his interviewer in *Empire*: 'It was put into arbitration with the Writers' Guild and they have rules that if you're a director *and* a writer, you have to prove that you've written 50 per cent of the original stuff to get the credit ... In the case of this, it was impossible because the way in which I changed the screenplay was by taking bits from her novel.'[18] Jordan is more 'faithful' to the original novel than Anne Rice, but he is unable to transgress a clear point of distinction: the director (of a film) is not the author (of a novel). In fact, Adam Mars-Jones, in his review of the film, even de-authorises Jordan's direction: 'Neil Jordan's direction', he says, 'is highly accomplished, without bearing a strong signature.'[19] I would only go on to note that, in quite another sense, Jordan *is* an author: his own novel, *Sunrise with Sea*

Monster, was released at the same time as the film of *Interview with the Vampire*. But there is no overlap between the restricted field of this novel and the large-scale field of the film: they remain distinct, with probably no cross-over audience interest. Rice, however, was publicising her own new novel *Lasher* during the release of *Interview with the Vampire*, and the large-scale publicity she achieved in relation to the film no doubt directly fed into that novel's fortunes.

What I have wanted to suggest in this chapter is that one's relations to the popular are located in the relationship one *already occupies* in, or in relation to, the field of cultural production. One speaks for or against the popular from an 'available position' in that field – a position which enables (or disables) a particular kind of discourse *about* the popular. Obviously, writing an academic chapter with a restricted circulation, I myself am similarly 'positioned' within the field. The academic bears a particular relationship to popular forms of cultural production, usually negotiating a process of enjoyment alongside a process of analysis, the latter in particular depending upon a restricted set of genealogies (one writes an article citing other academics such as Bourdieu, Becker, Lury, etc.) which may have little to do with those popular forms and which may well go unrecognised or unnoticed by them – or if they *are* noticed, those popular forms may, in the sense that Andrew Ross has used this term, have 'no respect' for them. An academic may at best impact upon popular forms just enough to be located in turn by those forms as, precisely, a restricted field of cultural production. I should like to close this chapter by giving as an example a citation from my book *Reading the Vampire* (1994) by the Bristol-based popular film listings magazine *Venue*. This magazine's article on the film of *Interview with the Vampire* has two subsections which are distinguished from the article proper. The first is a selection from Anne Rice's various commentaries on the casting of Tom Cruise and on the film of her novel, entitled 'That Anne Rice volte-face in full'. The second is a column with the more provocative title, 'Cor! So what's it all about then, eh?' This column gives the following advice: 'Impress your chums by memorising these pearls of academic wisdom to regurgitate with suitable intensity after 15 bottles of expensive foreign lager in your local arts centre bar.'[20] It goes on to quote two short passages from *Reading the Vampire* about Anne Rice's novel, and it ends by citing me as the author of that book and an academic at De Montfort University. It can be an unsettling experience for an academic to be located in this way – with what seemed (and still seems) to me to be an instance of Andrew Ross's 'no respect'. Not to be respected, however, is not the same as not being noticed: the column ironically locates or identifies the academic field (the arts centre bar, the foreign lager, the tendency to want to 'impress' others), but it also quotes me accurately and at some length, in a bold type face which is left standing without subsequent comment. Moreover, I have the feeling that the two passages from my chapter on Anne Rice were selected not at random, but carefully and with a certain level of investment in the points being made – which in fact concern the way Rice builds a 'personal' relationship with a fan audience into the structure of the fiction itself (a relationship which John Ezard simply reproduces in his *Guardian* article). In other words, there is both 'no respect' and *some* respect for the academic in this feature on the film of *Interview with the Vampire*: the academic is both distinguished or segregated from the interests of the magazine and *included*; authorisation is both withdrawn and given. The mutuality of this arrangement (where the extract is included, only to be ironised, distanced, etc.) works to produce the academic response *as* a restricted field of cultural production (the production of one kind of knowledge about a text). And yet even this mode of location is not quite watertight. The view – at least in the popular magazines looked at here – of Anne Rice's various publicity-seeking statements on the film of her novel is that she is not 'hysterical' (which might have been the nineteenth-century diagnosis) so much as *histrionic*. The word comes from the Latin word for 'actor': the author is an actor. She gains attention in a theatrical way, in order to impress others. What I enjoy about *Venue*'s use of my book is that, tongue-in-cheek, it gives me a similar kind of function: 'Impress your chums by memorising these pearls of academic wisdom ...'. Histrionics for Rice quite literally contribute to that author's fortunes by relocating her in a field of large-scale cultural production, making her transgressive in this sense: she is an author who is out of place because she is making theatrical claims, because she is making the business of acting *her* business. Histrionics, as it is attributed to me, is far less enabling, and it is certainly not tied to (the making of a) fortune. But at least I am given a role to play, minor and comical as it might be, both in *Venue*'s 'arts centre bar' and, more importantly for me at least (since academics value their impact upon the popular, no matter how restricted it might be), in the 'production' of the film of Anne Rice's novel.

Notes

1. Pierre Bourdieu, *The Field of Cultural Production: Essays on Art and Literature*, trans. and ed. Randal Johnson (Oxford: Polity Press, 1993), p. 17.
2. Ibid., p. 17.
3. Fay Weldon, 'Not quite as mad as we are', *Independent on Sunday*, 19 March 1995, p. 27.
4. John Ezard, 'Rice of passage', *Guardian*, 12 January 1995, Screen 14. *Premiere: The Movie Magazine*, February 1995, p. 70.
5. Ibid., Screen 14.
6. Cited in Rachel Abramowitz, 'The vampire chronicles', *Premiere: The Movie Magazine*, February 1995, p. 70.
7. Ibid., p. 71.
8. Jeff Dawson, 'Bloody hell!', *Empire*, February 1995, p. 68.
9. Roald Rynning, 'The vampire interviews', *Film Review*, February 1995, p. 35.
10. Abramowitz, 'Vampire chronicles', p. 71.
11. Celia Lury, *Cultural Rights: Technology, Legality, and Personality* (London: Routledge, 1993), pp. 71–2.
12. Ibid., p. 72; see also Bruce King, 'Articulating stardom', *Screen* 26, 5 (1985), pp. 27–50.
13. Cited in Robin Askew, 'Bestial bloodletting', *Venue*, 20 January–3 February 1995, p. 24.
14. Cited in Abramowitz, 'Vampire chronicles', p. 71.
15. Dawson, 'Bloody hell!', p. 67.
16. Askew, 'Bestial bloodletting', p. 24.
17. Ibid., p. 24.

18. Dawson, 'Bloody hell!', p. 67.
19. Adam Mars-Jones, 'Deathless, ruthless and bloodless', *Independent*, 19 January 1995, p. 25.
20. Askew, 'Bestial bloodletting', p. 23.

3

Is s/he or isn't s/he?: Screening *Orlando*

Nicola Shaughnessy

> All the famous novels of the world, with their well-known characters and their famous scenes, only asked, it seemed, to be put on the films. What could be easier and simpler? The cinema fell upon its prey with immense rapacity, and to the moment largely subsists upon the body of its unfortunate victim. But the results are disastrous to both. The alliance is unnatural.[1]

In her 1926 essay on the cinema, Virginia Woolf characterises film as a parasitic, scavenging monster, devouring the body of the text. She presents the novel as a passive, weaker entity. The terms are implicitly gendered: film is the male aggressor, and the literary text its helpless, feminised subject. Despite the imagery, however, this is not nature red in tooth and claw, as Woolf deems film's predatory activity to be unnatural. The cinema's consumption of the novel is presented as a monstrous, vampire-like activity. Woolf then shifts associatively from the relationship between literature and film to that between the spectator and the cinematic text: 'Eye and brain are torn asunder ruthlessly as they try vainly to work in couples.'[2] The conflict that she perceives between visual apprehension and comprehension is central to Sally Potter's 1992 film adaptation of Woolf's novel *Orlando*. It underpins the opening shot of the film, which reveals Tilda Swinton dressed as an Elizabethan courtier, reclining languidly under an oak tree. In voice-over, Swinton quotes the first sentence of the novel: 'there can be no doubt about his sex', but the disjunction between eye and brain, as we see a male character, whilst knowing that it is a woman cross-dressed, establishes from the outset that gender

43

identity is to be viewed sceptically, as a not altogether convincing masquerade. As the omniscient narrative voice continues, 'but when he', Orlando intervenes with a direct address to the camera 'that is, I', thereby reinforcing self-reflexively the sense that his/her gender is a performance.

Given Woolf's strong reservations about the medium, I felt rather treacherous when my first response to Potter's adaptation was an exhilarated celebration of the film text. Several subsequent viewings have done nothing to temper my enthusiasm for it. Contrary to Woolf's concerns, what I perceive in *Orlando* is not an assault upon literature by film but a form of mutual sexual exchange between the primary source and its cinematic other, and between masculinity and femininity in both texts. I would suggest that Sally Potter has brought a maternal perspective to *Orlando*, in an intervention into the fraught relationship between literature and film. Rather than beating the novel into submission and denying its primary source, and in psychoanalytic terms transferring its allegiance from the maternal body (the literary text) to the phallocentric order of film, Potter's version acknowledges and foregrounds its primary source through postmodern, self-reflexive strategies. Thus it gives birth to a new text which is an offspring of its original, but, like Orlando's daughter, looks to its (m)other as she moves into the literary-cinematic future. In this chapter I want to examine three questions: first, the relationship between the literary and the cinematic in *Orlando*; second, the representation of gender in the film text; and, finally, the gendering of the implied spectator.

Running through Potter's *Orlando* is a commentary upon the relations between film and literature. The novel's metafictional musings upon the history of English literature, and upon its own mechanisms of composition, are transposed into a metacinematic framework. At first viewing *Orlando* seems to belong loosely within the genre of costume drama, presenting a synoptic view of English history; on closer inspection, it appears to be more about the mediation of Englishness within literary, cinematic and art history. Woolf's novel is a compendium of literary styles and allusions, and, at one level, Orlando's travels through history trace the trajectory of English literature itself; Potter's version amplifies and extends this intertextual quality through a density and breadth of reference which is characteristically postmodern. The consciously painterly style of the film, the ostentatious artifice of the visual texture, its elegantly symmetrical and formalised compositions, its baroque opulence and occasionally surreal detail, provide obvious parallels with the work of Derek Jarman (especially *Jubilee*, *The Tempest* and *Carvaggio*) and Peter Greenaway (from *The Draughtsman's Contract* to *Prospero's Books*). The echoes of Greenaway's work are strengthened by Potter's conspicuously Michael Nymanesque score, but the range of cinematic reference is far wider than this. Potter acknowledges Michael Powell in the end credits, and has admitted that she 'unconsciously stole from his film *Gone to Earth*: the scene where she's running in the garden in her dress'.[3] But there are also hints of Ingmar Bergman in the moody, icy love scenes with Sasha, of *Lawrence of Arabia* in the desert sequences, *Brief Encounter* in the parting with Shelmerdine, and even, perhaps, of *The Great Escape* and *Easy Rider* in the penultimate scene showing Orlando on a motorbike. However, the film is also stuffed with literary allusions and references, far too numerous to catalogue. The opening section abounds in references to Renaissance poetry, Shakespeare, and Elizabethan and Jacobean drama. When Queen Elizabeth first appears it is on a barge which invokes both *Antony and Cleopatra* and *The Wasteland*, and when Orlando meets her he quotes Spenser's *Faerie Queene*. Orlando's relationship with the old Queen (played, of course, by Quentin Crisp), who makes him a favourite and an object of her desire, invokes the homoerotics of Marlowe's *Edward II*. The love affair between Orlando and Sasha proceeds along the lines of an Elizabethan sonnet sequence, progressing through infatuation with the unobtainable to jealousy and inevitable betrayal. Having been abandoned by Sasha, Orlando writes poetry in his mansion retreat, and is similarly betrayed (in satirical verse) by the impecunious Robert Greene, who is played by the real-life poet and dramatist Heathcote Williams (more Jarman intertextuality). The self-referentiality of this performance is also evident in the casting of the wit and raconteur Ned Sherrin as himself among the eighteenth-century wits, and in the use of singer and gay rights activist Jimmy Sommerville to serenade 'fair Eliza' in the opening moments ('The idea is Jimmy Sommerville parodying Quentin Crisp'[4]): at such moments, the illusion of historical verisimilitude surrenders to a consciousness of its constructed status in the here-and-now.

The interplay between fiction and cinema reaches its culmination in the final sequence, 'Birth', which is linked to the earlier 'Poetry' by the doubling of Heathcote Williams as poet and publisher. Orlando presents her manuscript (the script of *Orlando*, possibly) to a much-spruced up Williams in his docklands office, and he advises her to 'increase the love interest. Give it a happy ending.' This metacinematic touch is part of the overall commentary upon the demise of literature and the ascendancy of cinema. The great house represents the novel, and indeed the heritage of English literature. Even the trees on the drive are covered with dust sheets. The literary echoes throughout the film are like fossils. Literature, for Woolf, is a living entity, but in the film of *Orlando* it is an archaic remnant. Orlando's poetry, and Heathcote Williams's poet, are the subjects of comedy, while the self-conscious posturings of the literary cast of characters, ranging from the three sisters to the Heathcliff/Rochester-like Shelmerdine, present literary history as a picture-book which is quaint but sadly out of date – a branch of the heritage industry. When Orlando's daughter takes the camera in the final sequence, the future of film supersedes the literary past. The film is born out of the novel and transcends it. The last shots of the film, through the viewfinder of a video camera, are shakily managed by Orlando's daughter. Film itself is surpassed by video. The point of view, finally, is that of the next generation.

Amid this promiscuous proliferation of signs, Orlando him/herself can hardly be seen as 'character' in the conventional sense. Both before and after the transformation, Orlando is ill-at-ease in the situation in which s/he is placed, not as a result of personal idiosyncrasy, but as a function of the contradictions within subjectivity that s/he embodies. In the first half of the film this is obviously signalled through the disparity between the genders of the performer and the role, and by Orlando's looks-to-camera (to which I return below), which propel him/her out of the illusionist cinematic space. In such moments, Orlando occupies the position of the voyeur, the commentator or the visitor, rather than that of the participant in history. In the second half, Orlando's alienation is more evidently gendered, readable at the most obvious level, as one reviewer put it, as 'a straightforward parable about a young man who has a rattling good time' which 'turns into a woman who doesn't have such a good time'.[5] In my view, it is not so clear-cut: the female Orlando is for the most part less a 'real' woman than a focus for conflicting ideas of woman, as dictated by the contexts within which 'she' is situated, ranging from the epi-grammatic misogynies of the wits to the claustrophobia of the Victorian era. The figure of Orlando is a series of shifting, conflicting and discontinuous roles, a series of masculine and feminine subject-positions which are successively unable to sustain the burden of signification imposed upon them by the context of the *mise-en-scène*.

In the penultimate sequence, Orlando stands in the midst of tourists in the hall of the great house, looking at a portrait of herself as a young man. This has been preceded by a voice-over which echoes the opening lines of the novel and film: 'she – for there can be no doubt about her sex – is visiting the house she finally lost for the first time in over a hundred years'. This is a reprise of the opening sequence, but in different terms. Orlando is a woman, rather than a man, and a mother. The portrait she studies positions him/her in the historical picture-book frame. The pose is reminiscent of Vita Sackville-West's photographic portraits when she modelled as Orlando for the first edition of the novel. Orlando is thus identified with the past, and with death, which returns us cyclically to the theme and title of the first section.

In this respect, the film is structured around female life rhythms, and thus can be read in terms of Kristeva's notion of 'women's time', whereby 'female subjectivity would seem to provide a specific measure that essentially retains repetition and eternity from among the multiple modalities of time known through the history of civilisations.[6] The episodic structure of the film reinforces this, in spite of the chronological order derived from the novel. This is not 'time as project, teleology, linear and prospective unfolding; time as departure, progression and arrival', which Kristeva identifies with masculine structures.[7] There are two modalities of time operating in *Orlando*: historical time and cyclical time, with the former subordinate to the latter. During the episode entitled 'Politics', the monarch changes – almost imperceptibly. Orlando presents himself to the Khan as 'a representative of His Majesty's government'. When the Archduke Harry arrives, several minutes and several short scenes later, he announces himself as an 'emissary from Her Majesty'. The gender of the monarch has switched, just as the gender of Orlando switches towards the end of this section. 'Repetition' and 'eternity', through which Kristeva characterises female temporality, are thematic and structural features of both film and novel. However, the novel *Orlando*, as a (mock) biography of Vita Sackville-West, betrays an anxiety which is central to the novel's form and subject. As Clare Hanson points out:

> To textualise a person is to fix them, to appropriate them, in a manner which might well trouble Woolf. Yet beneath this level of concern over appropriation, there is a deeper sense of unease evidenced in the text which might relate to Kristeva's notion of 'abjection'. To write a person into a text is to translate them into a medium which is neither living nor dead and thus perhaps to transgress or unsettle the fixed boundary between life and death and evoke the experience of abjection.[8]

Vita's name means life, and in writing *Orlando*, Woolf was perhaps endeavouring to make her subject eternal through her textual life. I find it interesting that, in the novel, birth and death seem to be avoided, but in the film version these are the terms which frame the entire narrative. In the final sequence, critically, Orlando could be dying, and this was certainly my interpretation when I first saw the film. According to Potter, the intended effect was more ambiguous:

> It seemed to me that *Orlando* was, at its heart, a celebration of impermanence. Through the vehicle of Orlando's apparent immortality, we experience the mutability of all things and relationships ... the film ends on a similar metaphysical note to the book, with Orlando caught somewhere between

heaven and earth, in a place of ecstatic communion with the present.[9]

This temporal and spatial ambiguity is, however, part of the underlying concern with gender identity. The figure of the angel hovering in the sky is poised literally between heaven and earth. The angel is Jimmy Sommerville, the falsetto who sang earlier in the film for Queen Elizabeth as she travelled up the river, supposedly four hundred years previously.

This gender-bending, as a male actor sings with a feminine voice, is, of course, central to the shifting subjectivities of the film. Potter explains:

> the longer I lived with Orlando and tried to write a character who was both male and female, the more ludicrous maleness and femaleness became, and the more the notion of the essential human being – that a man and woman both are – predominated.[10]

Ludicrous is an interesting term, as this is precisely the word I would use to describe my discomfort with the image of the angel in gold who disrupts the final scene in an obviously postmodern metacinematic device which foregrounds the artifice of the film's methods. The gaudy amateur theatricality of this device is like a ludicrous last-night joke, lifted from Potter's live performance work. (It also refers to the 'stormy weather' sequence of Jarman's *The Tempest*.) Is it a comment on the impossibility of filming Woolf's text? It certainly prevents a sense of closure at the end of the film; narrative, like the angel, is left suspended. Faced with Orlando's unblinking stare at the end of the film, I felt no sense of the ecstatic dissolution of difference that Potter proposes. Nor is it an androgynous site of sexual communion, despite Sommerville's shrill assurances that 'I am coming'. Potter writes that 'at the moment of change, Orlando turns and says to the audience "Same person ... different sex." It is as simple as that.'[11] It is certainly not as simple as that.

'Is s/he or isn't s/he?' is a central question throughout the film, in a complex interplay between cross-dressed male and female actors. Early in the film, Tilda Swinton and Quentin

Crisp are involved in a dressing-room scene of intense theatricality and queasy voyeurism. Orlando watches the Queen
undressing; his eyes are averted, looking away from the Queen
and, initially, from the gaze of the camera, indicating his
discomfort with the spectacle. Orlando's unease with his role
as voyeur is shared by the spectator. Playing upon our consciousness of the male body beneath the Queen's clothes, the
editing of this scene plays games with what can and cannot
be seen whilst sustaining the cross-dressing convention. As she
starts to disrobe, the camera shifts us discreetly outside the
bedchamber: we watch Orlando looking (and not looking) at
the off-screen spectacle. When Orlando returns our gaze, it is
a mute appeal, as if he has seen, or is about to see, something
forbidden, even monstrous (the body of the mother?). In the
bedchamber scene that follows, the gender relations between
the aged Queen and the youthful courtier are dynamically
altered by the transvestitism: Crisp as Elizabeth simultaneously
embodies both patriarchal and matriarchal power, while
Orlando's fictive masculinity is repositioned in terms of
sexualised subjection to the Queen. Remembering that the title
of this section is 'Death', the contrast between Elizabeth's
ghastly pallor and Orlando's clear skin and flushed cheeks is
especially striking in this scene: we are presented with a dis-
concertingly ambiguous picture of sexual (and political) power,
exploitation and subordination.

The direct address to the camera, used in this scene, is a device
which is deployed repeatedly to transgress gender norms. The
jealousy of Orlando's fiancee Euphrosyne when she witnesses
his/her attentions to Sasha causes her to throw her ring at
Orlando and proclaim 'the treachery of men'. Orlando, as the
published script has it, *'turns to camera with a slightly guilty
expression, which changes to one of light bravado'*,[12] and in a direct
address declares 'it would never have worked. A man must
follow his heart'. We are made conscious of Orlando's
performance of masculinity. The look to camera is traditionally a male preserve: from Oliver Hardy to Michael Caine (in
Alfie), it is a gesture of complicity towards a spectator who is
presumed to be male. Here, the duplicity of the aside draws
attention to the woman playing a man. We are conscious of
the *double entendre* in Orlando's statement, but the irony desta-

bilises the precarious sense of gender identity that Tilda
Swinton as Orlando inhabits.

The irony is compounded by the fact that Swinton returns
the gaze of the spectator whenever there are doubts about
gender identity. During his courtship of Sasha, Orlando
witnesses a performance of *Othello* on a makeshift stage on the
frozen Thames. At the close of this performance, the actor
playing Othello kisses the boy actor playing Desdemona and,
falling on the bed, dramatically 'dies'. Orlando pauses, then
turns to the camera to whisper 'Terrific play'. A terrific play
on sexual identity it is. In the subsequent scene, we observe
Orlando's despair when he is abandoned by Sasha. Again, he
looks at the camera to declare 'the treachery of women'. The
Sasha episode plays on desire and eroticism in the sexual
encounter between two female performers. The spectator is
presented with close-ups of Orlando caressing Sasha. The
directions in the script are explicit: *'Orlando lifts his head and
moves his mouth across her cheek to her mouth. They kiss slowly
and sensually.'*[13] The ostensibly heterosexual encounter clearly
has a lesbian subtext. However, this duality does not quite
match the hermaphroditic fantasy of Woolf's text. Woolf
presents Sasha in the following terms:

> The person, whatever the name or sex, was about middle
> height, very slenderly fashioned, and dressed entirely in
> oyster-coloured velvet ... But these details were obscured by
> the extraordinary seductiveness which issued from the
> whole person ... Legs, hands, carriage, were a boy's, but no
> boy ever had a mouth like that; no boy had those breasts;
> no boy had eyes which looked as if they had been fished
> from the bottom of the sea.[14]

In Potter's script, she is introduced as *'a dark slender figure
dressed in furs'*.[15] But there is nothing particularly boyish about
Charlotte Valandrey's Sasha, who during her first conversation with Orlando is rendered in soft focus and becomingly
lit by candles; if anything, her femininity is emphasised in order
to make explicit the interplay between female heterosexual-
ity and lesbian eroticism.

I find Orlando most convincing as a man in a wig. In the 'Politics' section, where he is in ambassadorial costume, Orlando becomes a comic figure whose clumsy posturings ridicule the behavioural codes of nation, class and gender. Orlando betrays his/her vulnerability as, staggering, he drinks to 'manly virtues' and 'brotherly love'. In this section masculinity is explicitly connected with arrogance and violence. Orlando's compassion for the dying man, and regret when he hears the crying babies, trigger his transformation into a woman. For Potter, this transformation 'is a result of his having reached a crisis point – a crisis of masculine identity'.[16]

Orlando is equally uncomfortable in the female costume she is forced into after her metamorphosis. In a reprise of the scene of Queen Elizabeth's undressing we see Orlando being straitlaced into corsets, confining her body and fixing her into a conventional feminine identity. Her escape into marriage is transformed by Potter into a love affair with an American, 'the voice of the new world – the romantic and revolutionary view of the beginning of the American dream'.[17] Potter cast Billy Zane as Shelmerdine because he combined the looks and presence of a matinee idol ('He's very Errol Flynn') with 'slightly androgynous beauty'.[18] Even in the most heterosexual part of the film, sexual identity is still in flux. This is reflected in the camerawork. During their conversation, there is a shift from the conventional male–female, shot-reverse-shot formula to fluid panning between the two speakers. As desire and gender ambiguities become the subject of the dialogue, the position of the spectator itself oscillates (a similar effect is seen in Orlando and the Khan's toasting scene, which is infused by an implicit homoeroticism). The scene then shifts to Orlando and Shelmerdine in bed, and the camera surveys a body, the identity of which is uncertain, moving slowly over the flesh until it rests upon an eye which returns the gaze of the spectator. Although this is Orlando's eye, it is interesting to note that when I first watched the film I thought it was Shelmerdine who was looking at me at this point. The male friend I was with, however, identified the eye as Orlando's immediately.

This brings me, finally, to the question of how the reader is gendered by this film text. What is the identity of the implied spectator and whose 'pleasure' does it cater to/for? To address these questions I want to return finally to the pivotal moment of both literary and cinematic texts – the transformation of Orlando. This is effected through a sleeping beauty scene, where Orlando wakes up after seven days sleep, takes off his wig, and reveals her long woman's hair. After two short, sensual shots of Orlando washing, she surveys herself in a long, keyhole-shaped mirror (echoes of Botticelli's *Birth of Venus*). We share her own full-frontal view of her body. Thus, whereas in the novel, Orlando's metamorphosis is achieved through a grammatically and logically 'impossible' sentence – 'He was a woman' – it is in the film effected through the disclosure in a mirror of the female body. 'Same person. No difference at all', says Orlando, and then turns to the camera with a change of voice: 'Just a different sex.'

How are we to read this moment? At one level, the exposure of Orlando via the spectacle of the female body seems to endorse Laura Mulvey's well-known theorisation of the dominant cinematic apparatus in terms of 'woman as image, man as bearer of the look'.[19] At such a moment, female subjectivity is coterminous with the sexualised body. As the *Sight and Sound* reviewer, Lizzie Francke, noted: 'Orlando is never seen naked in his male incarnation – he is never authenticated as a man, rather he remains effeminately boyish.'[20] Practical considerations aside, the point is, of course, that within the terms of conventional filmic representation, Orlando is not authenticated in this manner because he does not have to be: the female Orlando *is* her body in a way that the male Orlando is presumed not. And yet the effect of this pivotal moment is more ambiguously subversive than this, not least because we are positioned with Orlando as she confronts her own mirror-image. Importantly, the shot of the naked Orlando is actually very brief, and it is both preceded and followed by sustained close-ups of Orlando looking at her mirror-image. Quite clearly and emphatically, it is the female subject who has ownership of the gaze at this crucial moment: a point which is underlined by her triumphant look to camera that ends the sequence. It is this calm, confident act of looking that re-appropriates the image from the domain of male sexual fantasy and offers the possibility of an empowering, pleasurable and non-masochistic identification for the female spectator.

Notes

1. Virginia Woolf, 'The cinema' (1926), *Collected Essays*, vol. 2 (London: The Hogarth Press, 1966), p. 269.
2. Ibid., p. 269.
3. Sally Potter quoted in David Ehrenstein, 'Out of the wilderness: an interview with Sally Potter', *Film Quarterly* 47, 1 (1993), p. 4.
4. Ibid., p. 6.
5. Jonathan Romney, 'Baroque and role-reversal', *New Statesman and Society*, 12 March 1993.
6. Julia Kristeva, 'Women's time', in *The Kristeva Reader*, ed. Toril Moi (Oxford: Basil Blackwell, 1986), p. 191.
7. Ibid., p. 192.
8. Clare Hanson, *Virginia Woolf* (Basingstoke: Macmillan, 1994), p. 96.
9. Sally Potter, *Orlando* (London: Faber and Faber, 1994), p. xiv.
10. Ibid., p. xiv.
11. Ibid., p. xv.
12. Ibid., p. 16.
13. Ibid., p. 17.
14. Virginia Woolf, *Orlando: A Biography* (1928; London: Granada, 1977), pp. 23–4.
15. Potter, *Orlando*, p. 12.
16. Ibid., p. xi. B. Ruby Rich makes a similar point in a discussion which interestingly contrasts *Orlando* with the recent cinematic preoccupation with violent masculinity (as evidenced in *Reservoir Dogs*): 'Orlando's mythic transformation from man to woman occurs at the exact moment in which he is required to enter into battle and kill' ('Art house killers', *Sight and Sound*, December 1992).
17. Potter, *Orlando*, p. xii.
18. Potter, quoted in Ehrenstein, 'Out of the wilderness', p. 5.

19. Laura Mulvey, 'Visual pleasure and narrative cinema', *Screen* 16, 3 (1975), reprinted in Gerald Mast, Marshall Cohen and Leo Braudy (eds), *Film Theory and Criticism: Introductory Readings*, 4th edn (Oxford: Oxford University Press, 1992), pp. 750ff.
20. Lizzie Francke, 'Orlando', *Sight and Sound*, March 1993.

4

Feminist Sympathies Versus Masculine Backlash: Kenneth Branagh's *Mary Shelley's Frankenstein*

Heidi Kaye

In *Mary Shelley's Frankenstein*, Kenneth Branagh attempts to create a *Frankenstein* for the 1990s. On one thematic level, the film offers a feminist interpretation of the text by stressing the issues surrounding motherhood and women's roles, which follows two decades of such readings of the novel. Yet on another level, Branagh's version recreates the gendered polarities which feminist readings of the novel argue are undermined by Shelley. Instead of critiquing the way Victor's act of creation symbolically kills off the female, Branagh's film can be seen to recapitulate Victor's 'crime' by emphasising male/male relationships over male/female ones, reinforcing women's role as token of exchange in essentially homosocial relationships.[1] This chapter will consider both the inter- and extra-filmic aspects of these competing themes.

First of all, I'd like to consider some of the main changes Branagh's *Frankenstein* makes to Mary Shelley's story in order to investigate the significance of his different emphases. Most noticeably, he expands the role of Elizabeth and makes explicit the importance of motherhood. The other important changes lie in the main male characters surrounding Victor: his father, Waldman, and the Creature. While the changes involving the female characters serve to stress the feminist elements in the story, those involving the male characters bring out the theme of father/son relationships. Branagh develops the feminist reading of *Frankenstein* by reading into the story Mary Shelley's own life. As various feminist critics have done (notably

57

Ellen Moers, Mary Poovey, Sandra Gilbert and Susan Gubar, Margaret Homans, and Anne Mellor),[2] although rather less subtly, Branagh produces a semi-biographical interpretation informed by feminist readings of the text. The death of Shelley's own mother, Mary Wollstonecraft, in childbirth becomes in the film Victor's mother's death giving birth to his brother William; this in turn gives rise to Victor's desire to create life from death. In the novel, Victor's mother dies of scarlet fever after nursing Elizabeth through the disease. Shelley's own experience of losing her first child within two weeks of its birth (compounded later by the death of another of her children) and her horrific dream of its revival ('Dream that my little baby came to life again; that it had only been cold and that we rubbed it before the fire, and it lived. Awake and find no baby. I think about the little thing all day. Not in good spirits.'[3]) have been read into the novel's concerns for non-reproductive creation and/or reanimation of the dead. Branagh's film shows him using amniotic fluid and a semi-sexual mechanism (to which I shall return) to bring life to the dead Creature.

In addition, Mary Wollstonecraft's Enlightenment feminism is brought into the film through the expanded role of Elizabeth. In the novel, she plays a very minor part, acting only as a love interest and, even worse, is viewed by Victor as a possession. She is presented as a 'pretty present' from his mother as a child:

> I, with childish seriousness, interpreted her words literally and looked upon Elizabeth as mine – mine to protect, love, and cherish. All praises bestowed on her I received as made to a possession of my own ... my more than sister, since till death she was to be mine only.[4]

Elizabeth as played by Helena Bonham-Carter is represented as an equal to Victor, intelligent, passionate, with a sense of humour and a strong will. This was a key decision for Branagh, as he states:

> It was important to me to have a very strong woman's role in a film of this size ... and I wanted Elizabeth and Victor to be two equal partners, utterly entwined from the beginning. These two people were absolutely meant to be together.[5]

Bonham-Carter's Elizabeth is Mary Shelley and Mary Wollstonecraft rolled into one: rational, emotional, independent,
expressive. She seeks out Victor in Ingolstadt to convince him
to come home; when he refuses because he must complete his
work, she boldly offers to help him. Nowhere is her strong will
and independent mind more clearly portrayed than in the final
sequences of the film. On their wedding night, Elizabeth is
equally as lustful as Victor, rather than 'the purest creature of
earth' (III, 6, 189), and when Victor reanimates her using parts
of Justine's body, Elizabeth refuses to be a party to her objec-
tification and sets herself on fire with the kerosene lamp.

I'd like to look at this scene in a bit more detail. Victor, after
removing the reborn Elizabeth from the sarcophagus, dresses
her in her wedding dress, complete with ring on the hand that
was Justine's, and sits her down on a crate like a limp rag doll.
He kneels before her, imploring her to remember him: 'Say my
name. Please, you must remember. Elizabeth ... Elizabeth.' The
screenplay stage directions state: *'She lifts her head to look at
him. A flicker in her eyes? His saying "Elizabeth" seems to have
triggered some memory.'*[6] He helps her to stand, encouraging her
to remember, and then begins what the screenplay calls *'the
most sweepingly romantic and hair-raisingly demented image of the
film'* (*MSF*, p. 131) when Victor dances with the Creatures
Elizabeth, while the camera swirls crazily around them and the
waltz theme madly plays in Victor's head. At the peak of the
action, it crashes to a halt as the Creature appears in a flash
of lightning.

A showdown between the two men over the woman is
inevitable. The Creature says 'She's beautiful' and Victor replies
'She's not for you'. The Creature beckons to Elizabeth, who is
drawn to him, while Victor calls out 'Elizabeth? ... say my name
...'. The Creature calls 'Elizabeth' and tells her 'You're beautiful',
whereas Victor keeps desperately asking her to 'Say my name'
(*MSF*, p. 132). It is not surprising that it is to the Creature that
she goes in this scene. It is he who has been calling her name
and telling her she's beautiful, whereas Victor has been self-
centredly asking her to remember him, not herself. If she
remembers who she is, or who she is supposed to be, she may
well reject what he has fashioned her into. When the scene
turns into a literal tug of war, where the viewer may well

expect that the two men will tear an arm or hand off the patchwork woman, Elizabeth finally comes to a recognition of the situation, cries out and breaks free of them both. After a mime of attributing blame to Victor for recreating her as a monster, she snatches up the lamp and crushes it between her hands, throwing flaming kerosene all over herself. She wants no part in these men's games with life and death, and she refuses to be possessed by either of them; she creates her own destiny.

The film emphasises, as the novel does, the gendered split between the public and private realms, the university and the home. Branagh's film uses strong contrasts of colour to portray the Frankenstein home as harmonious and happy, with bright blues and pinks, wide open spaces such as the ballroom and the Alps, and plenty of natural light. The domestic world is safe and comfortable, innocent and cheerful. In direct opposition is Ingolstadt, portrayed in shades of umber and grey, with miserable, starving peasants and enclosed spaces such as the circular lecture theatre and Waldman's secret laboratory. The only vast space, Victor's attic workshop, is dark and crowded with looming equipment, like some nightmare factory. The domestic sphere is the realm of the family, gendered female by Elizabeth's dominating presence as receiver of Victor's ever-scarcer letters home. The university is dominated by men, students and professors, and is the site from which Victor rejects his home and family for his scientific work. Although we lose the parallel with Waldman's situation as explorer of the unknown outside world, since he does not write letters to his sister in England (as in Shelley's text), he does make clear the opposition at the end when asked by his first mate which direction they should go and he replies 'Home' (*MSF*, p. 139). Elizabeth stands out as she runs through the streets of Ingolstadt in her red clothes; she does not belong in this world barren of colour and domestic affection. The red obviously symbolises blood: menstrual, from birth, and also from death; she will be carried home a corpse in a flowing red shawl. Red and blood are therefore female, and life and death are connected in this way with femininity; but this is a power that Victor wants to claim for himself, without the intervention of women.

The other major emphasis in Branagh's film is on the father/son relationships. In contrast to the feminist reading of Elizabeth and the will to recreate motherhood, through the father/son dynamic Branagh recreates a world of male/male relationships that are primary and which exclude or threaten the female, just as Victor does in Mary Shelley's story. There are three relationships on which I want to focus here: Victor and his father, Victor and Professor Waldman, and Victor and the Creature. Unlike in the novel, where he is a bourgeois gentleman, Victor's father in the film is a doctor. This establishes a goal for Victor to follow in his father's footsteps, even to exceed his father's success: 'You'll become an even greater doctor than your father', says his mother (*MSF*, p. 42). His father kills his mother during childbirth; Victor resurrects his own wife. Or another way to look at it is that his father's child kills his wife; Victor's 'child' kills his own. Both women are, in either case, tokens to be saved or killed to represent something about their men. Victor's mother is self-sacrificing – 'Cut me. Save the baby' (*MSF*, p. 43) – and Elizabeth kills herself – her biggest self-assertion is in self-annihilation.

Even more important is the relationship Victor has with Professor Waldman. Other Frankenstein films have also increased the role of scientific mentor figures, most notably James Whale's *Frankenstein* (1931) in which the mad scientist is called Dr Pretorius, who returns in *Bride of Frankenstein* (1935) to blackmail Henry Frankenstein into creating another Creature. In both of these films, Frankenstein is presented as less guilty because of the power of the older scientist who leads him into the unhallowed experiments. Whereas in the novel, Victor is obsessed and alone in his studies, with even Henry Clerval left back in Geneva since his merchant father will not allow him to attend the university, in the films Victor almost always seems to need an assistant, which helps lessen his sole responsibility for the Creature and its deeds. Shelley's character isolates himself from his family and friends, and even from the university authorities, to conduct his research, and comes up with the answer by himself. Branagh's character learns from Waldman some of the arcane knowledge, eventually stealing his secret research journal to discover how far he got in creating life and adapt his methods. He tries to involve Clerval in his research, but he refuses, raising the moral grounds that are brought out by the hindsight narrative in the novel: 'Even if it were possible, and even if you had the right, which you don't, to make this decision for us – can you imagine for one second that there wouldn't be a terrible price to pay?' *(MSF,* p. 69).

Waldman, with his flowing grey hair and intense, sinister mien, makes for a dangerously seductive mentor. From the moment they lay eyes on each other, the two men seem mutually fascinated. As his coach drives away after Victor's first lecture and confrontation with Professor Krempe over the purposes of medical study, Waldman stares out of the window at Victor; Victor returns his look, full of curiosity: 'Who was that?' *(MSF,* p. 59). When Waldman invites Victor and Henry into his private laboratory, the professor is impressed at Victor's ability to rescue Henry from the out-of-control monkey's arm. Victor offers to help Waldman in his research; the two men exchange intense looks, and Waldman seals their private bond with 'You shall, of course, tell no one' *(MSF,* p. 65).[7] Victor is distraught when his mentor is killed, so preserves his great mind by transplanting his brain into the body of his murderer. This not only adds to the link between Victor and Waldman and intensifies that between Creature and Creator, but also spreads the responsibility for the Creature's actions to Waldman. Unlike in *Young Frankenstein* (1974) and some other versions, the Creature's brain cannot be excused as 'abnormal'; instead, it is a highly superior model, intelligent and humane, with a sense of moral responsibility since Waldman had abandoned his experiments in reanimation. The Creature is both victim and killer, intellectual and peasant, related to both Victor and Waldman as spiritual and physical fathers.

An even more tangled father/son dichotomy occurs between the Creature and his Creator in this film, partly because of the age difference between De Niro and Branagh; the Creature states after Victor's death, 'He was my father' *(MSF,* p. 137). Certainly, Victor stands in the father's position in this relationship, which is underlined by the creation sequence in which the two men scrabble about amidst the amniotic fluid, with Victor trying to help his Creature to stand. Yet even in this scene, the size of the Creature and the slipperiness of the floor are such that it appears that both are having equal difficulty in gaining their feet and each is essentially helping to support or drag down the other as they alternately rise and fall again.

This potential for a reversal of roles is made manifest in the ice cave scene. Here, when Victor is confronted by an eloquent (despite the Bronx accent) and sensitive Creature, we see what might appear to be a father/son discussion, but this time the Creature seems to have taken the father's role. The Creature has dragged Victor out of the pool and when he awakes he finds a fire lit and the Creature inviting him over for a chat. The Creature presents his case rationally and effectively dresses down young Victor for his irresponsible behaviour:

> You gave me these emotions, but you didn't tell me how to use them. Now two people are dead. Because of us. Did you ever consider the consequences of your actions? (*beat*) You gave me life, and then left me to die. (*beat*) Who am I? (*MSF*, 115–16)

In this scene, the only shot of the two characters in the same frame is the establishing one, showing them at opposite ends of the cave. Once Victor comes up to the fire, the shot switches to alternate close-ups of one character then the other. This emphasises the distance in their relationship at this stage, with Victor rejecting his child and the two in conflict after the Creature has killed William. The older actor adds authority to the role of the Creature, making him able to lecture Victor in this way and convince him to create a mate for him. The young Victor asks his Creature simply, 'What can I do?', and accepts, despite his immediate horror, his responsibility: 'If it is possible to right this wrong ... (*beat*) ... then I will do it' (*MSF*, pp. 116–17).

Outside the film, the choice of De Niro to play the Creature creates a similar father/son dynamic. Once again, there are multiple father/son combinations in the film's production. The chapter on 'The filmmakers and their creations' in *MSF* notes this father/son, American/British relationship, without irony: 'TriStar Pictures soon added its considerable weight as the *parent* studio' (*MSF*, p. 145, my italics). Francis Ford Coppola, fresh from his own *Bram Stoker's Dracula* (1993), produced the film, adding Hollywood clout and money and his own theatrical style to the picture. A director/producer father figure for Branagh, Coppola is an older film-making mentor as well as an attractive bet for American audiences, backed by a major Hollywood studio. Although in his interview with *Empire*, Branagh claims that it was he who sought De Niro to play the Creature, *MSF* states that it was the producer (Coppola, along with a string of production executives) who were 'pursuing' De Niro in order 'to land' him for the part, as well as seeking Branagh as director since Coppola chose not to direct this project (*MSF*, p. 145). Thus the creative hierarchy is rather more complex: is Branagh seeking a father/mentor or is Coppola seeking a son/heir to hand this project on to him? Coppola claims to have 'discovered a kindred spirit in Branagh: "... I recognized in him some of the same kind of energy and competence to do whatever it takes that I fancied I had myself, also coming out of the theater"' (Coppola, quoted in *MSF*, p. 147). Branagh takes up his role equally: 'For his part, Branagh was appreciative of the older film-maker's "supportive presence" on the set and behind the scenes, saying, "I'm grateful for the opportunity to have a genius looking over my shoulder"' (*MSF*, p. 147).

De Niro is an acting mentor of the same generation as Coppola, from a different tradition than Branagh's, who offers a certain amount of artistic seriousness and American pulling power to his film. Branagh says of him in his publicity material that he needed 'an actor of great courage and brilliance'; De Niro returns the compliment by saying of Branagh in his fatherly role of director, 'Ken understands how actors like to work and how they talk'.[8] Branagh admits to being excited and somewhat starstruck by both men before and after making the picture: 'It was a trip. (*Long pause.*) It was a *trip*. Coppola, I just wanted to soak up all his stories ... So to meet De Niro in the same day was too much, frankly.'[9] These American filmic father-figures help legitimise Branagh's project and enable it to be produced on such a large scale and high budget. Yet the film is presented as 'A Kenneth Branagh film' or as 'Kenneth Branagh's *Mary Shelley's Frankenstein*', just as we had 'Francis Ford Coppola's *Bram Stoker's Dracula*'; it is assigned as the creation of patriarch Branagh even over its original female author.[10]

These father/son relationships both inside and outside the film compete directly with the motherhood and strong woman themes. It is not surprising that the locket which William carries and which leads to his death at the Creature's hands is now a portrait of Victor, rather than one of his mother, as it is in the novel. Victor as father/brother has replaced the importance of the mother. The enormous sack containing the electric eels that get injected into the sarcophagus of amniotic fluid at the moment of recreation looks like a gigantic scrotum. The screenplay itself describes it as 'a huge bollock-shaped container' (*MSF*, p. 78). The sexual imagery is therefore explicitly male: the sperm-like eels are ejaculated down the glass tube from the bollock-shaped container into the waiting sarcophagus to bring to life the Creature. The human-sized fish kettle is called a sarcophagus and is certainly not womb-shaped, rather it is likened to a coffin, which indicates the death-dealing aspect of this motherless method. Victor's deadly asexual reproduction method has short-circuited the system, eliminating the need for the female principle; hence the film prioritises male/male relationships even over the main male/female one between Victor and Elizabeth. Derek Malcolm in the *Guardian* accurately writes, 'The film seems to think Frankenstein's love for Elizabeth carries the same weight [as the Creature's relationship with Victor]. It doesn't.'[11] The two men, Victor and Creature, compete for power as alternate father and son, just as they fight over the body of Elizabeth/Justine. The women are, despite the attempt to retain independence, merely ciphers, who can act as replacement parts for each other.

Victor's journal is a posthumous present from his mother, expected 'to be filled with the deeds of a noble life' (*MSF*, p. 50). It is filled with Victor's experimental notes and inherited by his 'son', the Creature, who finds it in the pocket of Victor's greatcoat. From it, the Creature learns of his 'accursed origins' (II, 7, 126) and discovers where to find his lost 'father', in Geneva. The mother is once again written out of the story, since the Creator/Creature link is much stronger than the mother/son one, despite the fact that it is supposedly his mother's death that spurs Victor's research in the first place.

Mary Shelley's book is similarly 'written out' of the film's story, despite its title. Although some of the film's publicity claims that the title *Mary Shelley's Frankenstein* was chosen to indicate the film's intention to return to a more 'faithful' adaptation of the novel, in reality the title was a necessity, since Universal still own the copyright of the title *Frankenstein* used in the 1931 James Whale version. The same was true for *Bram Stoker's Dracula*. Branagh's film brought along with it the expected literary tie-ins, including a Macmillan edition with De Niro and Bonham-Carter on the cover. In addition, the takeover of Mary Shelley's novel continued with a 'novelisation' of the film, written by Leonore Fleischer and called *Mary Shelley's Frankenstein*. Finally, there is the text to which I have been referring throughout, *Mary Shelley's Frankenstein: The Classic Tale of Terror Reborn on Film*, with Branagh credited as author of the book, which includes the screenplay by Steph Lady and Frank Darabont, a director's note, a biographical note on Mary Shelley, Branagh's introduction to the screenplay, information on the film-makers, an afterword on the Creature, and a rather brief *Frankenstein* filmography (describing a mere 17 of the more than 110 film versions of the story). Kenneth Branagh's name appears above, albeit in smaller letters than Mary Shelley's, but that is mainly because the title of book and film are *Mary Shelley's Frankenstein*, so it is the book's title that is larger than Branagh's name, not Shelley's name standing as itself. Information on the philosophy of the production abound, overshadowing the film script itself; thus once again Branagh as director takes precedence over Shelley's tale. Nevertheless, as some of the above discussion has shown, Branagh does seem to reassert more of the original themes of the novel, as well as introducing elements from its author's biography. The publicity material and most of the newspaper coverage stress Shelley's life and the circumstances of the novel's creation, including the story of her dream of the monstrous creation which she tells in her 1831 preface. In emphasising this, Branagh is again seeking authority in his film; it is to be much closer to the 'real' story and 'real life', not just another horror film, but a 'serious' adaptation of a literary work for the

1990s. Shelley herself told the tale of the events leading to her creation of the story in the preface to the revised edition of 1831 in order, as Christopher Frayling claims,

> to turn them into a cliffhanger, to reinterpret her own novel which had proved controversial in religiously orthodox terms, and to provide a suitably melodramatic curtain-raiser to a story which had already acquired a reputation as a piece of theatrical blood and thunder. The preface was, most likely, a canny piece of marketing.[12]

Marilyn Butler, in her preface to the recent edition of the 1818 text for Pickering and Chatto, argues that Shelley's preface as well as her changes to the novel were designed 'to fend off possible charges of materialism or blasphemy' by making it 'a substantially different and less contentious novel'.[13] This mixture of titillation and conservatism in Shelley's revision can be seen in the combination of feminist and masculinist concerns in Branagh's version.

Branagh himself is described in several articles on the film as an obsessive and driven director, not unlike his character, Victor Frankenstein. Helen Hawkins and George Perry in the *Sunday Times* criticised his 'semi-hysterical direction', and Geoff Brown in the *Independent* described him as 'equally wild-eyed as director and Victor Frankenstein'.[14] Certainly the director offers a kind of god-like power over the actors, as Branagh said appreciatively of De Niro: '"He would do what I asked and put himself into my hands"' (*MSF*, p. 151). Several critics could not resist the chance to remark along the lines of 'Branagh has created a monster'.[15] Some comment was caused by the creation sequence, in which Branagh appears stripped to the waist, his newly acquired pectorals oiled and gleaming (his personal trainer gets a credit, as does De Niro's). David Thomas in the *Sunday Times* half-seriously asks whether Branagh, despite his superior acting talent, was trying to compete with the likes of Mel Gibson and Keanu Reeves in the body department: 'Did we really need to see those newfound muscles, that hard-earned torso, that suggestive patch of stomach hair?' He sees it as a sign of the universal attention-seeking ego of actors.[16] This is a rather more significant issue, since Branagh's muscle-bound scene reinforces the male bonding/competition themes in the film, rather than the romance theme. Competing with the action heroes in physical attributes, Branagh's semi-nakedness is not represented as heterosexual. He is showing off for the boys, not the girls. Since this scene ends up in a semi-nude struggle with the Creature, it recalls the naked wrestling match in Ken Russell's *Women In Love* (1969), with all of its homosexual connotations. Julie Burchill writes, 'Branagh claims he intentionally made [it] homoerotic'.[17] Whether or not this is true, Victor's naked chest is on display in this scene, and simply emphasises his muscular masculinity at the moment of his creative act. Both the text and Victor are masculinised by this expectation of male bonding and male viewing.

Shelley's novel has been seen as a book born of other books, responding to Milton, her parents', Percy Shelley's, and other works crucial to the Romantics and her own literary interests. Childbirth and writing are both creative processes linked by Mary Shelley in the novel. Branagh continues in the same vein as he appropriates the novel for his own creative purposes. The description of his turning the novel into a film echoes Victor's desire to probe the hidden secrets of nature in his search for the secret of life: 'As Branagh thought his way into the story, *discovering more and more of its unexplored dimensions*, it became clear to him that certain themes needed to come out in the screenplay' (*MSF*, p. 146, my italics). Are these dimensions unexplored by Victor, by Shelley, by previous film-makers? What enables Branagh to discover them, when others have not? He, like Victor, seeks to uncover what is hidden and thereby display his genius, even more than Shelley's. The crucial addition of a scene where Victor reanimates Elizabeth builds up her role only to force her into self-immolation. Ironically, in his male egotism/hero-worship as director and actor and in his emphasis on homosocial relations over heterosexual or mother/child relations, Branagh seems to recreate, at least to some extent, the 'abomination' abhorred by Shelley through the character of Victor, recapitulating the (virtual) elimination of the female from representation in the patriarchal order.

Notes

1. In this way, the film can be read via Eve Kosofsky Sedgwick's theories about homosocial bonding and male-male-female triangles. See *Between Men: English Literature and Male Homosocial Desire* (New York: Columbia University Press, 1985).
2. It is a vast oversimplification of the work of these critics to say that they encourage a semi-autobiographical reading. However, in that they do interpret the text as representing female experience, especially that of Mary Shelley, such a broad generalisation will serve for this comparison. See Ellen Moers, *Literary Women* (New York: Doubleday, 1977); Kate Ellis, 'Monsters in the garden: Mary Shelley and the bourgeois family', *The Endurance of Frankenstein*, ed. George Levine and U.C. Knoepflmacher (Berkeley: University of California Press, 1979), pp. 123–42; Mary Poovey, *The Proper Lady and the Woman Writer: Ideology as Style in the Works of Mary Wollstonecraft, Mary Shelley, and Jane Austen* (Chicago: University of Chicago Press, 1984); Sandra Gilbert and Susan Gubar, *The Madwoman in the Attic: The Woman Writer and the Nineteenth-Century Literary Imagination* (New Haven: Yale University Press, 1979); Margaret Homans, *Bearing the Word: Language and Female Experience in Nineteenth-Century Women's Writing* (Chicago: University of Chicago Press, 1986); Anne Mellor, *Mary Shelley: Her Life, Her Fiction, Her Monsters* (London: Methuen, 1988).
3. Mary Shelley's journal, 19 March 1815, quoted in Moers, *Literary Women*, p. 147.
4. Mary Shelley, *Frankenstein* (Harmondsworth: Penguin, 1985), based on the 1831 edition, I, 1, p. 35. All further references will be included in the text.
5. Kenneth Branagh, quoted in 'Mary Shelley's Frankenstein: Production Information', 1994, p. 6.
6. Kenneth Branagh, *Mary Shelley's Frankenstein: The Classic Tale of Terror Reborn on Film*, with the screenplay by Steph Lady and Frank Darabont (London: Pan, 1994), p. 130. All further references will be included in the text as *MSF*. Darabont is described in the text as 'a great fan of the

Shelley novel', which supposedly gives him the right credentials 'to make a film that was truer to Mary Shelley, both in letter and spirit, than any preceding version, but that spoke directly to today's audiences', *MSF*, p. 145. Although often considered as a canonical 'literary' text, *Frankenstein* has 'fans', which might make it seem more like a popular novel. See Ken Gelder's discussion, in this volume, of the idea of the fan in relation to the author.

7. See also Julie Burchill, 'Charge of the fright brigade,' *Sunday Times*, 6 November 1994, section 10, p. 6, who sees this as a 'sexy' relationship.

8. Kenneth Branagh and Robert De Niro, quoted in 'Mary Shelley's Frankenstein: Production Information', 1994, pp. 5–6.

9. Barry McIlheney, 'Mission accomplished?', *Empire*, December 1994, p. 103.

10. Lizzie Francke also notes this search for 'respectability' and 'legitimacy', 'Creatures great and tall', *Guardian*, 27 October 1994, G/2, pp. 8–9. Barry McIlheney goes to the extreme of this parental authorisation nomenclature by referring to the film as *'Francis Ford Coppola's Kenneth Branagh's Mary Shelley's Frankenstein*, to give it its full, wonderful title', p. 100.

11. Derek Malcolm, 'Stitched up and let loose', *Guardian*, 3 November 1994, G/2, p. 12.

12. Christopher Frayling, 'Monstrous regiment', *Sunday Times*, 10 April 1994, section 7, p. 1.

13. Marilyn Butler, 'The first *Frankenstein* and radical science', *Times Literary Supplement*, 9 April 1993, p. 12.

14. Helen Hawkins and George Perry, 'Film check', *Sunday Times*, 27 November 1994, section 10, p. 54; Geoff Brown, 'Coffin and spluttering', *Independent*, 3 November 1994, p. 37.

15. *Variety* is amongst these: 'Branagh has indeed created a monster, but not the kind he originally intended'; Hugo Davenport writes, 'Brankenstein's monster may thus be a hybrid in more than the intended sense, bringing bits of himself from the far side of the Atlantic', 'Branagh Hatches a Patchy Monster', *Telegraph*, 4 November 1994; slightly more original, the *Evening Standard* writes,

'Branagh's new film adds up to considerably less than the parts' (quoted in Giles Whittell and Dalya Alberge, 'Film Critics Savage Branagh as Prince Woos Tinseltown', *The Times*, 3 November 1994, p. 3).

16. David Thomas, 'Spare us the parts', *Sunday Times*, 4 December 1994, section 9, p. 21.
17. Burchill, 'Charge of the fright brigade', section 10, p. 6. In contrast, Suzi Feay sees this scene as simply 'a moment of parent-child bonding', 'Mother to the Monster: With Kenneth Branagh's New Film, Frankenstein Walks Again', *Independent on Sunday*, 6 November 1994, Books.

5

The *Henry V* Flashback: Kenneth Branagh's Shakespeare

Deborah Cartmell

Kenneth Branagh, dubbed in *The Times* on the day before *Henry V*'s release in 1989 as 'the young pretender', claimed that the play needed 'to be reclaimed from jingoism and World War Two associations'.[1] Without doubt, Branagh's film pays homage to Laurence Olivier's film of 1945 while seemingly rewriting the history for a 1980s audience. As Graham Holderness has argued, Olivier's *Henry V*, sponsored by the Ministry of Information, was designed as a morale-boosting exercise, in keeping with the dominant Shakespeare criticism of the period. Holderness has illustrated how in the 1940s Wilson Knight's *Olive and the Sword* and E.M.W. Tillyard's *Shakespeare's History Plays* view Shakespeare as a spokesman of national unity.[2] In the words of Wilson Knight, writing in 1943, 'we need expect no Messiah, but we might, at this hour, turn to Shakespeare, a national prophet if ever there was one, concerned deeply with the royal soul of England'.[3] In this chapter, I will examine how Branagh's film blends popular culture with academic nostalgia and succeeds in reaching, to use Branagh's own words, 'a large group of potential Shakespeare lovers'.[4]

In his production of *Henry V*, Kenneth Branagh reverses many of the editorial decisions of Olivier; most notably, not to appear anti-Europe, he turns the French into worthy opponents and even makes the Dauphin a likeable figure. As with all film versions of Shakespeare, speeches have to be reduced in order to make the plays filmic – the long speeches freeze the action and can be boring to watch. As in the Olivier version, Branagh's Chorus is fragmented so that a few lines punctuate the action rather than suspend it. On the rare occasions when speech does suspend action, it has a shock effect on the audience. Such is the case of Judi Dench's rendering of Mistress Quickly's account of Falstaff's death and Michael Williams's delivery of his namesake Michael Williams's rebuke to the king, suggesting that Henry's cause is unjust and his word untrustworthy. Here we have close-ups, concentrating on the suffering of the individual and hanging a question mark over the ethical position of the King. Henry himself achieves this intense visual scrutiny in his desperate prayer to the god of battles on the eve of Agincourt. Initially it would seem that the close-ups are used by Branagh to question rather than approve the King's actions. Certainly, unlike Olivier's production, Branagh's film is striking for its *inclusions* rather than its exclusions.[5]

Perhaps the most notable of these inclusions are the sentencing of the conspirators and the hanging of Bardolph (which Branagh shows rather than simply has reported). Branagh also includes flashbacks to the *Henry IV* plays, depicting Falstaff and crew in the tavern, ostensibly to suggest Henry's betrayal of his comrades. The flashbacks are used again with the hanging of Bardolph and in the final moments of the film. Flashbacks function in Branagh's film by abruptly offering new connotations to the narrative, the process which Roland Barthes calls the 'semic code'.[6] Initially these flashbacks seem to function to discredit or call into question Henry's imperialist ideology.

The film begins with Henry presented as ruthless, distrustful and potentially evil. He tricks the conspirators and the atmosphere is one of tension – there are spies everywhere and the King can only maintain his position through subterfuge. The archbishops, unlike the ineffectual jokey figures of Olivier, are conspiring together, hardly holy figures, but shrewd and corrupt politicians. The King enters the film literally cloaked in darkness, forecasting the disguised King on the eve of the Battle of Agincourt. For a 1980s audience, the inhuman black masked figure inevitably recalls Darth Vader in *Star Wars* (1977), and thus the audience is invited to regard the King – as does Michael Williams in the later scene – with the utmost suspicion. Like the Olivier film, Branagh takes the image of doors opening to visually connect different scenes. (The dark figure of Henry (seen from behind) framed by a door is used in the publicity posters for the film.) Branagh underlines the fact that this is a Henry capable of opening doors, in the Machiavellian sense of using his position of power to seize every opportunity. As if by magic, the doors open for the King at the beginning of the film (preparing us for the opening of the gates of Harfleur), and they close on Scroop and his fellow conspirators in Southampton. While Renee Asherson in Olivier's film is confined within doors and like a damsel in distress is liberated from the effete French by the heroic Olivier, Emma Thompson's Catherine opens the door to discover a gloomy and desperate world of her care-worn father (played by Paul Schofield whose French King visually recalls his portrayal in Peter Brook's *Lear*).

This dark side of Henry is in direct contrast to Olivier's Christian warrior king and is undoubtedly the product of the influential revisionist readings of the mid 1980s, most notably Stephen Greenblatt's 'Invisible bullets' and Jonathan Dollimore and Alan Sinfield's 'History and ideology: the instance of *Henry V*'. The picture of Branagh's Henry at the beginning of the film is in keeping with Stephen Greenblatt's account of a Henry who 'deftly registers every nuance of royal hypocrisy, ruthlessness and bad faith – testing, in effect, the proposition that successful rule depends not upon sacredness but upon demonic violence'.[7] Branagh seems to do to Olivier what Dollimore and Sinfield do to E.M.W. Tillyard in attacking the notion of a natural hierarchical order in Shakespeare. Dollimore and Sinfield consider *Henry V*'s strategies of power and its representations in which the human cost of imperial ambition is revealed through Henry's own ideological justifications.[8] This is most apparent in the play text in Henry's exchange with Michael Williams when Henry tries to rid himself of the responsibility of war; although the disguised Henry insists that the King will keep his word, he later fails to keep his word to Williams – the glove is returned without the promised fight, subtly confirming Williams's assertion that Henry, because he *is* a king, will not be true to his word. Henry, in this respect resembles Machiavelli's ideal prince; and this episode is very close to Machiavelli's chapter on why a prince should (not) keep his word.[9] Fluellen's historicising of Henry's war (the continual comparison of his prince to ancient predecessors suggests Machiavelli's own method of analysis) results in an unintentional truth: Fluellen notes that Alexander 'did in his ales and his angers, look you, kill his best friend' (IV, vii, 34–5).[10] Although the comparison stops here for Gower – 'Our king is not like him in that. He never killed any of his friends' (IV, viii, 36–7) – in denying the likeness he affirms it. Inevitably the comparison recalls Henry's sentencing of Scroop ('that knew'st the very bottom of [Henry's] soul') and of course Falstaff (who the 'king hath run bad humours on').[11]

The chiaroscuro effects of the dark beginning of Branagh's *Henry V* hark back to Orson Welles's *Chimes At Midnight* (1967) in which Welles's Falstaff is incrementally reduced and brutalised by a self-aware and self-serving Prince Hal. Branagh's throned Henry visually recalls John Gielgud's cold and isolated Henry IV, the Darth Vader (or dark father) of Welles's film. Through a series of intertextual references – flashbacks to other plays and films – the film initially seems to build a picture of Henry who is hostile and repellent. The close-up and flashback, however, rather than questioning his motives, ultimately soften and humanise the figure. When Bardolph is being hanged, Branagh has Henry recall through flashback the ribald days of the tavern while the close-up reveals his eyes to be moist – the tears blending with the rain. After the prayer to the god of battles in which Henry acknowledges his father's guilt in taking Richard's crown, there are definite tears in the King's eyes, and in his union with Fluellen after victory he's clearly weeping. The vulnerability of the King in this scene is contrasted with and compared to the slaughtered boys. As David Robinson notes on the eve of the film's UK release: 'Branagh's Henry is strictly according to the Geneva Convention'.[12] The image of the King carrying the dead boy – a former companion of his 'wild Hal' days and a victim of his dubious war[13] – provides the emblem of the film, used in many of the publicity pictures: it visualises the ambivalence of this production which simultaneously glorifies and condemns Henry's war. Youth has been sacrificed; the King emerges at the end of the film as a 'real man'.

The film doesn't inspire feelings of nationalism, as in the Olivier film, but rather, as Graham Holderness remarks, Branagh's film conveys the *emotions of patriotism*.[14] But these emotions grip you unaware. The first third of the film is markedly anti-war and anti-patriotic; but by the end, the audience should be cheering the King alongside his rebel ranks (like the opportunistic and corrupt Pistol and Nym who can't help but feel inspired by the St Crispen Day speech).

It is often noted that the film, made in the late 1980s and following the lead of Adrian Noble's 1984 production (in which Branagh played the title role), is a post-Falklands, anti-war production. The realism of the piece is in direct contrast to the painted scenery of Olivier's version (with the exception of the fanciful scene depicting the English coast behind the Chorus: Derek Jacobi looks as if he's literally standing on a map of Great Britain).[15] Branagh imitates and pays tribute to Olivier, following in his footsteps by commencing his film career, like Olivier's, by directing and starring in *Henry V*, a play which appropriately dramatises a young man's rite of passage. The St Crispen's day speech offers a clear visual flashback to Olivier – Branagh uses a cart, like Olivier, as a humble platform for his rousing words. Likewise, Branagh imitates or rivals Olivier in the hail of arrows fired in unison by the British footsoldiers at the beginning of the battle sequence.

The film, however, also pays tribute to contemporary Vietnam war films which present a simultaneous fascination and contempt for war.[16] Chris Fitter has argued that through the rhetoric of class transcendence, Branagh's film conveys the double message that war is hell but it also heroises.[17] Unlike Olivier's *Henry V*, Branagh's film was not paid for by the government but was made in spite of reduced subsidies. Branagh's own company, Renaissance Films plc, shows how success can be achieved, like Henry's war, against all the odds. It gained a BAFTA and Academy Award and made money (approximately seven and a half million pounds). Quick on the heels of the film's critical success, Japan's giant Sony Corporation made an investment in Renaissance Films.[18] Branagh's Henry V, unlike the aristocratic characterisation of Olivier, reveals throughout his working-class Belfast origins; he is the epitome of the self-made man who rises from the common ranks through sheer entrepreneurialism. In his auto-biography, *Beginning*, Branagh underlines the similarities between himself and Shakespeare's king when he first undertook the role at Stratford: 'Henry was a young man, and so was I. He was faced with an enormous responsibility. I didn't have to run the country and invade France, but I did have to control Brian Blessed and open the Stratford season.'[19] During the filming of *Henry V*, Branagh was inevitably prone to making comparisons between his and Henry's predicament. In fact, his diary of the shooting reads like a rewriting of Shakespeare's play, climaxing in Branagh cutting his Harfleur wall-shaped birthday cake. Henry-like, he continually underlines the risks he was taking in embarking upon the project: 'As the nights wore on there were less people available, and the shooting schedule had to be planned so that we covered as much large-scale action as possible early in the week, before it really was a case of we few, we very, very few.'[20] On returning home after the filming of the battle sequence, Branagh writes 'I felt as if I had come back from the war'.[21] Branagh's identification is with a king who has more in common with Richard Branson than Winston Churchill – he seems to have grown out of an age of football hooliganism and the conquest of privatisation. Eventually Henry is transformed into the ideal 1980s man: rugged, yet a lover of children, confident yet self-mocking. Clearly, this Henry struck a chord: contemporary reviews are full of praise for the inspirational tone of the production. Allegedly Prince Charles – Patron of Branagh's company – cried.

The Chorus – a seemingly inappropriate figure for a film – is retained by Branagh, as he was by Olivier, to manipulate our reactions and engage us with the action. In the play text, Shakespeare's Chorus calls attention to the inadequacies of theatre, continually reminding us that we are watching a play. Branagh's Chorus, played by Derek Jacobi, dressed in a modern replica of a First World War trench coat, introduces the play on the film set as if he were the director. Initially he seems cynical and detached. As the action develops, his emotional involvement builds – in fact, a careful viewing of his face at the end of the film reveals a scar, as if he has directly participated in the Battle of Agincourt.[22] He literally changes face and this conversion from cynical observer to enthusiastic recruit mirrors the *volte face* of the film as a whole.

Harold Innocent's Burgundy suggests a bald-headed, conservative politician, a cross between Churchill and the then soon to be British Arts Minister, David Mellor. Visually and verbally he ties all the loose ends together; the flashbacks accompanying his lament for the wastes of war while concentrating on the victims of Henry's reign, provide the audience with a filmic curtain call, inviting us to savour the glorious moments of the film. In Olivier's film, Burgundy, played by Valentine Dyall, mournfully looks out of a painted window and the fairy-tale landscape, based on Pol de Limbourg's illustrations, is exchanged for a contemporary picture of two children, reflecting Burgundy's images of ruin and devastation: 'Even so our houses and ourselves and children / Have lost, or do not learn for want of time, / The sciences that should become our country, / But grow like savages'.[23] Surprisingly, we find ourselves in 1945 rather than 1420. Unlike Valentine Dyall's Burgundy, Harold Innocent's Burgundy is ultimately determined to look on the bright side; there is a sense of satisfaction in what has been achieved rather than lost in war. Rather than looking *forward*, this Burgundy looks *backward* – not to the ravages of war (as in the Olivier version) but back to images of merry England. The audience is invited first to mourn and then applaud the jolly faces paraded before them. Similarly, Branagh's film looks backward – while appearing to oppose Olivier's patriotic glorification of war and nationalisation of Shakespeare, it ultimately applauds it, reaffirming the myth of 'authentic Shakespeare'.

Initially, Branagh's film seems to call attention to the play's ironies, seemingly interrogating Henry's dubious political premises. But, if anything, Branagh's film is more a product of right-wing ideology than is Olivier's. While Olivier daringly pierces the illusion of stability in Burgundy's elegiac speech bringing the film audience into their own time, Branagh takes us back in time, cunningly consolidating Shakespeare as an ideological force, reaffirming the views of critics like E.M.W. Tillyard, Wilson Knight, and those responsible for teaching within the National Curriculum. The fighting spirit of the British combined with the eternal words of the Bard provide an ideal British export, a force to be reckoned with (or marketed) abroad.

The British National Curriculum Council consultation reports continue to put Shakespeare top of the list of reading for tests for 14-year-olds. The unimaginative and tedious nature of the exam questions was the focus of a series of conferences in 1993[24] aimed to combat the testing of Shakespeare as spokesman of Tory ideology (Nigel Lawson, for instance, claimed that Shakespeare is a Conservative through and through). In vehemently opposing the Shakespeare tests, a leading poet and dramatist was moved to say that Shakespeare is the only religion left to us. She objected to the government institutionalising and claiming authority over the Shakespeare Faith. She was backed by the majority of teachers present who agreed that Shakespeare should, in effect, be privatised: he must not be confined to a single correct reading, endorsed by the government, but Shakespeare – like God – is for everyone. Even the less able (or the less impressed) should be allowed contact with him. The teacher's role is an evangelical one, and in this respect not far removed from the preachers of English in the 1920s and 1930s who believed that everyone could 'gentle their condition' through exposure to the uplifting language of great literature, epitomised by the works of Shakespeare.[25]

To return to Branagh's film, it could be said that it is designed with an eye to providing a marketable teaching resource, a teaching resource which inspires appreciation (rather than 'understanding') of Shakespeare. Branagh's mission is to convert us firstly to Henry and then to Shakespeare. The religious atmosphere of the end of the film, reinforced by the City of Birmingham Symphony Orchestra's *Non nobis*, is a point which is hard to miss. The music, which begins with the mournful tones of a single singer and ends with a rousing chorus and orchestra (similar in effect to *Land of Hope and Glory*) combines the forces of spiritual celebration and national anthem, paying tribute to Shakespeare's (and Branagh's) achievement. Wilson Knight's words are worth requoting here as they are, surprisingly, more akin to the ultimate message of Kenneth Branagh in 1989 than of Laurence Olivier in 1945: 'we need expect no Messiah, but we might, at this hour, turn to Shakespeare ...'.[26]

Notes

1. *The Times*, 5 October 1989.

2. Graham Holderness, *Shakespeare Recycled: The Making of Historical Drama* (Brighton: Harvester Press, 1992).
3. *The Olive and the Sword*, (Oxford: Oxford University Press, 1944) p. 3.
4. Branagh, *Beginning* (1989; reprinted New York: Norton), p. 236.
5. It is, nonetheless, worth noting that when comparing Branagh's *Henry V* to Olivier's, our first impression is to note the inclusions, but compared to the play text, as Robert Lane outlines in '"When blood is their argument": class, character, and historymaking in Shakespeare's and Branagh's *Henry V*', *English Literary History*, 61 (1994), pp. 27–52, Branagh, like Olivier before him, evades a number of chinks in Henry's ideological armour, among them:

   i. Pistol's comments that the 'world is "Pitch and pay". / Trust note, faiths are water-cakes' (II, iii, 44–5) is left out.
   ii. Fluellen's historical analogy of Alexander and Henry in that they both killed their best friend (IV, vii, 20–37) is missing from Branagh's text.
   iii. Much of Henry's disclaimer of his responsibility for war to Williams is cut (IV, i).
   iv. Pistol's ransom scene with the French soldier is eliminated (IV, iv).
   v. Branagh removes the boy's complaint that Pistol lives while Bardolf and Nym are dead (IV, iv).
   vi. The scene in which Henry refers to Williams's challenge and offers him payment is cut (IV, viii).

6. See Maureen Turim, *Flashbacks in Film: Memory & History* (New York and London: Routledge, 1989).
7. 'Invisible bullets', *Shakespearean Negotiations* (Berkeley and Los Angeles: University of California Press, 1988), p. 56.
8. Jonathan Dollimore and Alan Sinfield, 'History and ideology: the instance of *Henry V*', in John Drakakis (ed.), *Alternative Shakespeares* (London: Methuen, 1985), pp. 206–27.

9. The message is 'but since men are a contemptible lot, and would not keep their promises to you, you too need not keep yours to them', trans. Machiavelli, *The Prince*, Mark Musa (New York: St Martin's Press, 1964) Chapter XVII, p. 145.

10. All references to *Henry V* are taken from the Oxford edition, ed. Gary Taylor (Oxford: Oxford University Press, 1995).

11. II, ii, 94; II, i, 116.

12. *The Times*, 5 October 1989.

13. Critics have often referred to the dead boy as 'anonymous', yet it is Christian Bale, the actor who plays the boy of the tavern company. The mistake is easily made as it is, strangely, hard to identify Bale in the long tracking shot of Branagh carrying the dead boy across the battlefield (see K. Branagh, *Beginning*, p. 236).

14. Holderness, *Shakespeare Recycled*, pp. 191–2.

15. There are, nonetheless, a few unintentional seams in the film's realism, such as Branagh's 1980s hairstyle (which in no way resembles the famous crop of Henry V); Branagh's hair seems to have been washed and blow dried in between cuts of the Harfleur sequence. At one point it is muddied and flattened, while a few moments later it has been restored to its earlier glory.

16. See Holderness, *Shakespeare Recycled*, p. 200.

17. 'A tale of two Branaghs: *Henry V*, ideology, and the Mekong Agincourt' in Ivo Kamps (ed.), *Shakespeare Left and Right* (London: Routledge, 1991), p. 270.

18. Lisa Buckingham, *Guardian*, 30 January 1990, p. 9.

19. Branagh, *Beginning*, p. 141.

20. Ibid., p. 228.

21. Ibid., p. 236. Reviews of the film, similarly, make such an identification. For example, Stanley Kauffmann, in 'Claiming the throne' (*New Republic*, 4 December 1989), writes: 'Possibly he sees an analogy between that army [i.e. Henry's] and Britain today and possibly thinks that, through this film, he – a young man – can help quicken morale in a country that is self-confessedly dispirited' (p. 30).

22. This is also noted by Peter Donaldson, 'Taking on Shakespeare: Kenneth Branagh's *Henry V*', *Shakespeare Quarterly*, 42, 1 (1991) pp. 60–70, at p. 63.
23. V, ii, 56–9.
24. Theatres', Universities' and Schools' Conference on Shakespeare, Birmingham, London and Durham, March 1993.
25. See, for example, George Sampson, *English for the English*, first published 1925.
26 Knight, *Olive and the Sword*, p. 3.

6

Consuming *Middlemarch*: the Construction and Consumption of Nostalgia in Stamford

Jenny Rice and Carol Saunders

When the BBC decided to film *Middlemarch* at Stamford in the summer of 1993 they were creating opportunities for the re-packaging of culture as nostalgia which could be consumed in a variety of ways. Stamford, as a location, rather than the 'real' setting of Coventry,[1] reflected a sanitised, nostalgic perception of nineteenth-century town life, focusing on grand Georgian villas, wide crescents and narrow lanes with quaint bow-fronted shops. Recontextualising a nineteenth-century novel as a television programme transforms traditional relationships between production and consumption. In its place we find an intertextuality of elements all available to be consumed. From conventional souvenirs to 'expert seminars', from behind-the-scenes videos to weekend breaks run by national hotel chains, there is an eclectic range of consumer activities. Our analysis will consider how this Stamford-as-Middlemarch experience is symptomatic of postmodern culture. The quest for nostalgia is Janus-faced: at once backward-looking, a search for self-identity in a more certain past, and forward-looking, providing an opportunity for the emergent service class to access the dominant culture.

George Eliot's *Middlemarch*, subtitled *A Study of Provincial Life*, was shown on BBC TV during the first two months of 1994. It marked the BBC's return to costume drama, a genre neglected for nearly five years. Andrew Davies transformed nearly eight hundred pages into six episodes, each of which had an audience averaging five million.[2] These ratings ensured the genre's revival, with *Persuasion* and *Pride and Prejudice* continuing the trend.

The choice of Stamford rather than Coventry enabled the production team to represent *Middlemarch* in a 'real' setting that resonates with our nostalgic images of Georgian Britain. It was selected for two reasons: first, the number of intact streets with 1830 and pre-1830 buildings; and second, these areas could be blocked off and insulated from outside traffic noise.[3] The BBC had expected to select many locations all over the country. As producer Louis Marks indicates, they assumed they would film:

> a street here, a square there, a house somewhere else. But then our researchers came back and told us they had found this marvellous town that had everything ... and ... they were right. Stamford is beautiful. Extraordinary.[4]

Stamford is now as identified with Middlemarch as Castle Howard is with *Brideshead Revisited* and Holmfirth is with *The Last of the Summer Wine*. This association mobilises consumer demand for nostalgia as spectacle, a feature of postmodern culture.

Nostalgia has been defined as a 'sentimental yearning *for* (some period of) the past'.[5] As Robert Hewison reminds us, 'nostalgic memory should not be confused with total recall', for unpleasant events are filtered out.[6] Many writers (notably Wood, Hewison, Strong) have sought to explain the preoccupation with nostalgia as a retreat from an uncertain present.[7] In part this uncertainty can be linked to the structural and cultural changes of postmodernism which can explain the current preoccupation with nostalgia and its consumption. Three key transformations have influenced the development of postmodern nostalgia: a dissolution of common cultural heritage, de-differentiation, and consumerism.

The age of postmodernity, while freeing individuals from past ideological constraints, has resulted in uncertainty about social and cultural identity, characterised by 'a loss of the social roots and the dissolution of a common cultural heritage that has normally shaped identity and self-concept'.[8] The nostalgic representation of Middlemarch created in Stamford can become that lost cultural heritage. Therefore to 'consume'

Middlemarch in Stamford as a commodity is one way of actively promoting self-identity.

Postmodernism not only involves a dissolving of boundaries between cultural forms such as tourism, television, shopping and architecture; but also within cultural spheres there is a merger described by Urry as de-differentiation. This involves the merging of high and low culture and the 'breakdown of some ... of the differences between the cultural object and the audience'.[9]

Televising classic novels for mass-audience consumption is an example of this merging of high and low culture. Writing in the *Guardian* (12 April 1995), Fay Weldon claimed that while sales of the book *Middlemarch* rocketed when it was televised in 1994, this did not imply an increase in George Eliot readers: 'most people, it is now said, opened the first page, read, and put it promptly down'.[10] Whilst there may be a reluctance to engage with the 'high culture' of the written text, the TV series is seen as having mass appeal. In the past (and for some today) reading was seen as a more worthy activity. Weldon nails her colours to the postmodern mast when she says:

> But times have moved on and now I see the matter differently. I no longer regard reading as necessarily superior to viewing. 'Viewing' has developed its own resource, its own history.[11]

Urry's recognition of the narrowing of the distance between cultural object and audience can be seen in the consumer orientation to Stamford-Middlemarch. This, together with the merging of high and low culture, raises the issue of the constituencies of such consumers. The process of consuming Stamford-Middlemarch is an example of the third key postmodernist transformation – consumerism, understood in this chapter, as a response to the transformations of cultural heritage and de-differentiation. It addresses the first issue of self-identity by filling the gaps left by the dissolution of cultural identity. As Rob Shields suggests there is a need:

> to treat consumption as an active, committed production of self and of society which rather than assimilating

individuals to styles, appropriates codes and fashions, which are made one's own.[12]

Furthermore, an implication of the de-differentiation between cultural object and audience is that there is more audience participation.[13] This is shown at Stamford in the range of experiences which are available for consumption. Illustrated talks, weekend breaks, Blue Badge guided tours and town trails continue to engage tourists. With sales worldwide to 24 countries, more international visitors are experiencing Stamford-Middlemarch.[14]

We suggest that these three key postmodern transformations are all implicated in both the production and consumption of the nostalgic Stamford-Middlemarch experience. In the process of filming the TV drama, Stamford was reconstructed as Middlemarch through a range of production and consumption relationships, some persisting long after the filming and first public showing took place.

Stamford became the location for the creation of a lost cultural heritage. This was initially achieved through the set designs of the production designer, Gerry Scott, who recreated an 1830s Middlemarch from 1993 Stamford. Whilst recognising the importance of historical accuracy, Scott's aim to convey the essence of the period rather than to focus on small details underlines an attempt to create a nostalgic rather than a faithful reconstruction. With the emphasis on creating an identifiable cultural heritage, there was, nevertheless, a selection process that, in this case, privileged the characters over the visual authenticity and this necessarily produces a tension of legitimation. Thus in her desire to foreground the characters, she preferred to decorate buildings and interiors with colours from the less obtrusive Georgian palette rather than the stronger Regency tones.[15]

Cultural heritage was further promoted when after the production of the drama a variety of consumable souvenirs were marketed as cultural heritage artefacts. These include typical examples such as postcards of the filming in the town (over 30,000 have been sold), notebooks, coasters and bookmarks and two videos of the making of the TV drama: an official BBC video for media studies students and an unofficial video of a bystander's view.[16] These are perhaps examples of the direct 'spin-offs' from the drama produced for the tourist industry. However, the production of consumables has also been exploited by traders less immediately connected to the heritage business. Middlemarch biscuits have been made by a local man tailoring his production to suit tour events. It is even possible to taste a 'Middlemarch Curry' ('offer extended for Middlemarch visitors'), an international dimension which has been popular with local residents rather than tourists.[17]

The crucial difference between the 'official' souvenirs and the commodities such as the biscuits and curries is that the latter reveal the more postmodern distinction of blurring of boundaries. Official souvenirs signify their status through identifiable signs; commodities such as the curry do not operate within this signifying system. Yet the two forms of commodities can be said to function within the same cultural sphere: a characteristic of de-differentiation, referred to earlier. It is not only commodities that show this key transformation. Other examples include the privileging of discourses, such as character to visual authenticity; and the unofficial video which captures the process of filming in a 'real' location: a jumble of 1830s streets with characters in period costume, and 1990s cars, women pushing baby buggies and actors smoking, perfectly demonstrates the blurring of distinctions between production and consumption and between cultural object and audience. These examples could be described as 'jumbling', identified by David Harvey as one of the 'more pervasive characteristics' of postmodernism.[18] The significance here is the way that such images contribute to shaping the past for contemporary viewers: a past in which Middlemarch and Stamford have themselves become 'jumbled'. The production of the TV drama and artefacts may contribute to creating a nostalgic common cultural heritage that could offer consumers a focus for developing a shared sense of identity.

The filming of *Middlemarch* was not responsible for bringing tourism to Stamford, already a hub of cultural interests with its arts centre, tourist office, museum, local stately homes and an annual Shakespeare festival. However, *Middlemarch* shifted the focus to a more participatory activity. As the owner of a dress shop indicates, 'The only difference is the people come to see Middlemarch rather than Stamford'.[19] Moreover, tourists' visits have become more experiential; in post-Fordist terms this is an example of the commodification of experience. Commodities are used up as they are consumed or involve the purchase of time and, as such, are potentially renewable.[20] At Stamford they are offered activities to participate in which blur the distinction between the two towns and encourage tourists to experience Stamford as Middlemarch. The museum town trail, entitled 'Stamford as Middlemarch', traces a route between all the main sites of buildings used for filming. A 'replica' map of Middlemarch superimposed on the actual town plan of Stamford is also available. This is drawn in nostalgic terms with Georgian buildings throughout the town (there is no sign of the new shopping centre) and decorated with horse-drawn coaches and Coats of Arms. The name 'Middlemarch' dominates the map in calligraphic lettering while the name 'Stamford' is drawn in less impressive lettering at the bottom. This map is being sold in aid of the Macmillan nurses' appeal, an example of how charities are widening their promotional activities.

Many other souvenirs and experiences articulate the link between the towns. Parallels are drawn in the booklets on sale at the *Stamford Mercury* offices. A pamphlet entitled, 'Middlemarch Revisited – Election Fever', includes a facsimile of the *Lincoln, Rutland and Stamford Mercury* for 13 August 1830, charting Election Reform fever. Even an educational activity such as the Museum Curator John Smith's lecture, 'Stamford and Middlemarch: two towns in 1830', focuses on politics and medicine, themes relevant to both Stamford and *Middlemarch*. Smith describes a realistic account of 1830s society in contrast to the many commercial ventures which give a sanitised vision of life in an early nineteenth-century town.[21]

The growth in tourists in search of Middlemarch is contributing to the production of Stamford as a heritage spectacle where the divisions between the 'real' and the 'fake' become confused. The visitors are not only audience but in some sense actors too; as they follow the town trail or guided tours they can experience going around 'Middlemarch', itself a fake. In some cases the visitors even seem confused as to which is the real town, as those who tried to book in at the 'White Hart Hotel' (in reality the Stamford Arts Centre) discovered.[22] Enquiries from visitors as to when Middlemarch changed its name to Stamford may be in the minority, but perhaps reflect the playful way in which the history of the two towns has been juxtaposed.

However, central to the balance between the fake and the real is the issue of authenticity; yet this does not seem of great importance to the visitor. This lack of concern is recognised by Umberto Eco, who suggests in *Travels in Hyperreality* that there is a more casual attitude towards the problem of authenticity in present society: 'Everything looks real, and therefore it is real; in any case the fact that it seems real is real, and the thing is real even if, like Alice in Wonderland, it never existed.'[23] For the tourist, the Georgian buildings themselves are the object of the 'tourist's gaze' because of their authenticity.[24] Overall the contrivance of Stamford as Middlemarch problematises the distinction between authenticity and fake: a postmodern experience which is fundamental in creating nostalgia. Furthermore it sets an agenda for a range of production and consumption relationships which are central in the intertextual consumption of nostalgia.

The recent growth in the popularity of museums and heritage spectacles has been well documented by Lowenthal, Hewison, Urry and Merriman.[25] Whilst more leisure time and a growth in disposable incomes have contributed to the increase in demand for tourist experiences, changes in media consumption raise expectations of those experiences. As John Urry argues, the impact of wider and more visual media consumption is likely to encourage consumers to widen their gaze away from the more ordinary tourist activities towards the more extra-ordinary.[26] This has resulted in increased consumption of special interest activities such as customised weekend breaks. There is an intertextuality of consumption as listeners and viewers are encouraged to read *Doris Archer's Diary*, visit Ambridge or take specialist George Eliot and *Middlemarch* weekend breaks at the Hilton National East Midlands.[27] In each of these cases consumers are likely to be drawn from a population of fans or enthusiasts. Our analysis now focuses on the consumers of the Stamford-Middlemarch experiences.

Both official and unofficial sources indicate evidence of a clear, if fragmented, 'Middlemarch effect' on the tourist industry at Stamford. Official museum records show that the numbers of visitors and associated contacts more than doubled between 1992/3 (12,345) and 1994/5 (25,650) with a small but perceptible increase in international tourists, mainly from the US and Australia.[28] An increase in demand for Blue Badge guided tours is reported, especially in 1994, although no formal records exist.[29] In addition, reports from traders suggest that there has been an increase in visitors to the town because of the *Middlemarch* connection. The duty manager at the George Hotel, a major hotel in Stamford, told us that as a direct result of *Middlemarch* the hotel caters for an increase in guests from Britain and the US.[30]

Research on the heritage industry, of which Stamford-Middlemarch is one example, has tended to concentrate on the producers rather than the consumers. Where consumers have been surveyed some researchers, for example Greene, Griggs and Hays-Jackson, are more concerned with consumer perceptions than social class constituencies.[31] Those who have investigated the backgrounds of consumers (Heady, Moore, Merriman) conclude that higher status groups and those with tertiary education predominate.[32] Merriman's research, drawing on the work of Bourdieu and Goldthorpe *et al.*, is a variation on the embourgeoisement thesis, this time applied to leisure.[33] Merriman argues that the relatively affluent may be using their leisure to increase their cultural capital as a way of promoting their chances of upward social mobility.[34] Our observation of a tour of Stamford indicated a predominance of women over men, in a generally middle-class and middle-aged sample. This has been confirmed as typical of such tours and provides some indication that the constituencies of visitors to Stamford resemble other heritage users.[35]

The significance of cultural or intellectual capital, as an alternative to economic capital, has been identified by Bourdieu as an important factor in terms of educational advancement.[36] Knowing how to engage with the dominant codes in literature, art or philosophy enhances cultural competences and facilitates access to a privileged status not dependent on economic status.

Postwar Britain has been characterised by changes in the class structure which include a growth in the service class. Although this is not an undifferentiated, homogeneous group in economic terms, many of the economic indices (for example, job security, home and share ownership) which would have provided measures of difference in the past have been eroded. As a consequence, cultural capital becomes an important differentiating factor. Lee puts this clearly when he says:

> since the second world war [as there has been] a genuine effacement of many of the economic differences by which class distinctions have traditionally been signalled, then questions of culture and cultural difference become paramount to our understanding of the manner in which hegemony and social order are both maintained and reproduced.[37]

The openness and accessibility of museums and heritage sites are identified by Merriman as providing opportunities for the service class to enhance their cultural capital.[38] Unlike other institutions such as societies and clubs, they are relatively cheap and do not rely on sponsorship. At Stamford it is possible to purchase the town trail and postcards of the filming for less than £3, tour Stamford with a Blue Badge Guide or enjoy a museum talk for around £2. Further, as Kevin Walsh argues, one way that the growing service class acquires cultural capital is through the 'traditionally English' method of 'integration through participation'.[39] The TV representation of *Middlemarch* and the opportunities to 'gaze upon the historical set for real' can facilitate the development of such capital.[40] Access to cultural capital and acquisition of cultural competence by the service class can be seen as one way in which cultural difference can be maintained and reproduced.

Middlemarch on TV is just one example of the way in which high culture is being transformed for a wider, mass audience. The distinctive feature of the transformation of *Middlemarch* is the Stamford connection, which goes beyond the TV series and draws on our nostalgic images of Britain's past. To visit Stamford is not to visit Middlemarch, although some consumables playfully challenge this divide. It is one way in which our cultural heritage is presented for consumers who are looking for more security in an insecure present. Post-Fordist commodification of experience is potentially renewable, although there may be limits as to how often tourists would be willing to do the town trail at Stamford. The Stamford experience is typical of postmodern culture in that it engages the audience with the cultural object. The representation of that object and the relationship with the audience are key features of the nostalgic debate.

Visitors to Stamford are presented with a sanitised representation of our cultural heritage insofar as they do not gaze on the impoverished and the politically weak. A similar point is made by Bob West in a penetrating critique of the heritagisation of Blists Hill at the Ironbridge Gorge Museum.[41] There is a particular irony in this heritagisation of Stamford, given that one of the main characters of the book, Dorothea, cultivates a role as a public benefactor. Are such visitors aware of the selective representations? Clearly there is more work to be done here but our case study suggests that there is a critical and sometimes challenging dimension to the presentation of history. Tourists are not merely passive consumers unaware of the divisions between the authentic and the fake, the rich and the poor and the gender divide. They are, however, likely to be encouraged to challenge these ideas further by a more politically sensitive portrayal by the nostalgia industry.

Nostalgia: is it what it used to be? Nicholas Zurbrugg categorises the final phase of postmodernism into 'Prophetic Pessimism' and 'Prophetic Optimism'.[42] He suggests that there is an optimism to be found in the creativity of such post-modernist multimedia artists as Laurie Anderson who, nevertheless, in her recent album *Bright Red* asks the question, 'And what I really want to know is: are things getting better or are they getting worse?'.[43] Theorists of the consumption of nostalgia are divided on the answer. Whilst some see the consumption of nostalgia as a feature of an economy in decline,[44] Hewison, in fact, goes further and argues that nostalgia neuters history and separates it from the present so that 'The true product of the heritage industry is not identity and security, but entropy. If history is over, then there is nothing to be done.'[45] Hewison, then, in some ways sees things getting worse, with nostalgia contributing to this decline. The construction and consumption of nostalgia serves to divert attention from the present, thereby preventing any critical appraisal.

There are some tensions here when compared with the view postulated by Walsh who points to the ways that the emergent service class may use the consumption of nostalgia to acquire cultural capital.[46] An active, engaged audience of the type we have observed consuming Middlemarch contributes to this process. This can be seen as part of a democratising hegemonic struggle to gain cultural competence and cultural capital. It suggests at least a dynamic which challenges the stasis of earlier theorists. Things may not be better but they have the potential to be so.

Notes

1. Kathleen Adams, *George Eliot: A Brief Biography* (Coventry: The George Eliot Fellowship, 1994) p. 19.
2. Broadcasters' Audience Research Board (BARB) 1994.
3. John Smith, Curator Stamford Museum, interview with authors, 5 June 1995.
4. Louis Marks in Stamford Museum Leaflet, Lincolnshire County Council.
5. J.B. Sykes, *The Concise Oxford Dictionary*, 6th edn (Oxford: Oxford University Press, 1976), p. 744.
6. Robert Hewison, *The Heritage Industry: Britain in a Climate of Decline* (London: Methuen, 1987), p. 46.
7. Michael Wood, 'Nostalgia or never: you can't go home again', *New Society*, 30, 631 (November 1974), pp. 343–6; Hewison, *The Heritage Industry*, p. 46, and Sir Roy Strong quoted in Hewison, p. 46.
8. Martyn J. Lee, *Consumer Culture Reborn* (London, New York, Canada: Routledge, 1993), p. 165.
9. John Urry, *The Tourist Gaze* (London, California, New Delhi: Sage, 1990), pp. 84–5, who notes his indebtedness to Scott Lash, *Sociology of Postmodernism* (London: Routledge, 1990).
10. *Guardian*, 12 April 1995.
11. Ibid.

12. Rob Shields (ed.), *Lifestyle Shopping, The Subject of Consumption* (London: Routledge, 1992), p. 2, who acknowledges M. de Certeau, *The Practice of Everyday Life* (Berkeley: University of California Press, 1984).
13. Urry, *The Tourist Gaze*, p. 85.
14. BBC Marketing Dept., June 1995.
15. Gerry Scott's interview is recorded by C. Bazalgette and C. James (eds), *Screening Middlemarch: C19th Novel to 90's Television* (BBC Education Pack in association with BFI, 1994).
16. A video for media studies has been produced by Bazalgette and James, *Screening Middlemarch* and the unofficial video *Middlemarch and Stamford* was shown at the Stamford Museum's exhibition of the filming of Middlemarch, 18 April–19 June 1994.
17. Advertisement in *Stamford & Middlemarch, A Rutland and Stamford Mercury Souvenir*, p. 24, and interview with the owners of Bombay Brasserie by the authors, 25 May 1995.
18. David Harvey, *The Condition of Postmodernity* (Oxford: Blackwell, 1989), p. 85.
19. Owner of Black Orchid dress shop, interview with authors, 25 May 1995.
20. Lee, *Consumer Culture*, p. 135.
21. John Smith, Curator Stamford Museum, interview with authors, 5 June 1995.
22. Jill Collinge, Blue Badge Guide, 22 June 1995.
23. Umberto Eco, *Travels in Hyperreality* (London: Picador, 1987), p. 16.
24. Urry, *Tourist Gaze*, p. 120.
25. David Lowenthal, *The Past is a Foreign Country* (Cambridge: Cambridge University Press, 1985), p. 4; Hewison, *Heritage Industry*, p. 9; Robert Hewison, 'The heritage industry revisited', *Museums Journal*, 91, 4 (April 1991), pp. 23–6; Urry, *Tourist Gaze*, p. 104; Nicholas Merriman, *Beyond the Glass Case* (Leicester: Leicester University Press, 1991), p. 92.
26. Urry, *Tourist Gaze*, pp. 101–2.
27. Jock Gallagher, *Doris Archer's Diary* (London: BBC, 1971); George Eliot and *Middlemarch* breaks are part of the Hilton National Hotel Chain's Special Interest Weekends.

28. Information supplied by John Smith, Curator Stamford Museum, May/June 1995 interviewed by the authors. Whilst no official records exist, museum staff and the tourist office note an increase in international visitors linked to the worldwide distribution of the TV series.

29. Jill Collinge, Blue Badge Guide, interview with authors, 22 June 1995.

30. Olf Ortmann, Duty Manager, The George Hotel, Stamford, 25 May 1995.

31. J.P. Greene, 'A visitor survey at Norton Priory Museum', *Museums Journal* 78, 1 (June 1978), pp. 7–9; S.A. Griggs and K. Hays-Jackson, 'Visitors' perceptions of cultural institutions', *Museums Journal* 83, 2/3 (Sept./Dec. 1983), pp. 121–5.

32. P. Heady, *Visiting Museums* (London: HMSO, 1984), pp. 12–20; R. Moore, 'Research Surveys', *Museums Journal* 88, 3 (December 1988), pp. 119–23; Merriman, *Glass Case*, p. 171.

33. Merriman, *Glass Case*, p. 93; P. Bourdieu, *Distinction* (London: Routledge and Kegan Paul, 1984); J. Goldthorpe *et al.*, *The Affluent Worker in the Class Structure* (Cambridge: Cambridge University Press, 1969).

34. Merriman, *Glass Case*, p. 93.

35. Authors' case study based on Blue Badge guided tour, 22 June 1995.

36. Pierre Bourdieu, *Distinction*, trans. Richard Nice (London: Routledge, 1992), p. 2; R. Bocock and K. Thompson, *Social and Cultural Forms of Modernity* (Oxford: Polity Press, 1992) pp. 146–8.

37. Lee, *Consumer Culture*, p. 34.

38. Merriman, *Glass Case*, p. 131.

39. Kevin Walsh, *The Representation of the Past: Museums and Heritage in the Post-Modern World* (London: Routledge, 1992), p. 126.

40. Ibid., p. 118.

41. Bob West, 'The making of the English working past: a critical view of the Ironbridge Gorge Museum', in Robert Lumley (ed.), *The Museum-Time Machine* (New York: Routledge, 1988), pp. 36–62.

42. Nicholas Zurbrugg, *The Parameters of Postmodernism* (London: Routledge, 1993), pp. 163–5.
43. Laurie Anderson, *Bright Red* (New York: Warner Brothers, 1994).
44. Hewison, 'Heritage Industry Revisited', p. 23.
45. Hewison, *Heritage Industry*, p. 187.
46. Walsh, *Representation of Past*, Ch. 7.

7

Pleasure and Interpretation: Film Adaptations of Angela Carter's Fiction

Catherine Neale

The starting-point of this chapter is the reception of Angela Carter's work in literary and cultural criticism, much of which has been feminist in approach. In both respects – that of criticism on Carter and that of feminist analysis – there are gaps and silences. It is widely known that a considerable amount of research on Carter is in progress, and the amount of published criticism is growing. But Carter has so far been the subject of a limited range of articles and chapters, and it is fairly easy to gain a sense of their general drift. An understandable element of hagiography has crept in since her death in 1992. More generally, probably because of her impressive range of reference, her sheer intelligence and humour, and her characteristic stance as 'demythologiser' providing her with the role of critic as well as creator, Carter receives sympathetic explication, commentary and contextualisation. What her work does not receive, it seems, is that element of critique that might examine the implications and potential contradictions of her projects, or place her work within a framework that is not dictated by Carter herself. This raises a very broad question of the nature of critique, particularly in respect of contemporary writing. More specifically, however, the absence of an explicit theoretical stance on the part of many of Carter's critics indicates the struggle that feminist criticism in particular has to identify a methodology.

One area of Carter's work is an exception: her depiction and treatment of sexuality. Patricia Duncker's article on *The Bloody Chamber* remains a significant point of dialogue with Carter's assumptions, and takes a clear line in stating a particular feminist point of view that cannot agree with Carter's resolutions.[1]

This chapter in fact takes a generally traditional line in drawing on Carter's work to identify an area where there appear to be tensions. The exercise is exacerbated, however, by another aspect challenging to the critic: the power and ubiquitousness of Carter's own commentary on her work, in interviews, occasional essays and television programmes. These prove virtually impossible to sidestep, providing as they do a number of suggestive ways of approaching her texts, and never conveying a sense of coy or mischievous misdirection. Carter refuses any distinction between the critical and the creative, and with her, commentary and fiction exist on a continuum ('narrative is an argument stated in fictional terms'[2]), so that the critic can, quite reasonably, accord authority to her statements. If one has lingering doubts about trusting the teller, Lorna Sage takes some trouble to define Carter's evolving construction of her role as writer and performer, culminating in what Sage calls 'the proliferation, rather than the death, of the author'.[3] Indeed, Sage's monograph clarifies another apparent contradiction: Carter's celebration of the anonymity and collective ownership of folk tales and her increasingly public profile through which she capitalised on the individualist opportunities available to the writer in the marketplace in contemporary times, even after her death.[4] Nevertheless, for the student of Carter there remains a methodological challenge in Carter's authorship and authority, especially in relation to her collaborative work on the film adaptations of her work, and the issue of intention.

With the theme of this collection in mind, it seems that there are a number of fruitful boundaries being questioned that are apposite to Carter. False distinctions between literature and film, and between high culture and popular culture, are the topic of much of her work:

> I think I must have started very early on to regard the whole of western European culture as a kind of folklore. I had a perfectly regular education, and indeed I'm a rather booksy person, but I do tend to regard all aspects of culture as coming in on the same level.[5]

The ironies of this point of view when considered alongside her own published work – the loss of collective storytelling, the intellectual self-consciousness that replaces a common culture – are recognised by Carter in *Nights at the Circus* in particular. For all of Carter's work is suffused with the self-consciousness of twentieth-century knowledge. It is not possible, as her fiction makes clear, to dream and to enjoy without interpretation. Her novels combine storytelling, argument and analysis in a way that places great demands on the reader, and that has several results in criticism of her work. There is an attempt to categorise her work, and thereby defuse it, by explaining it to be 'postmodernist' or 'magic realist' or 'surreal'. There are attempts to respond to her ideas by relating them to other paradigms, which I have suggested is Duncker's approach. There are excited and even flattered understandings of her books, in which an educated enjoyment is implicit. Carter seems to have succeeded in combining the illusion and magic of storytelling with self-consciousness for many of her readers.

Yet the case of the two films associated with her, adaptations of parts of *The Bloody Chamber* and of the novel *The Magic Toyshop*, raises questions about the shift from writing to image, from literature to film. Given Carter's engagement with cinema, and her identification of it as the predominant twentieth-century mode of collective pleasure (with all its inherent equivocations), her own films emerge as curiously downbeat hybrids. The important storytelling voices in Carter's fiction work to create a sense of a listening audience despite the privacy of the printed word, but the cinema remains a public and shared experience. The representation and reception of visual images are controversial for many engaged in cultural studies precisely because of their public identity, independent of an author. In addition, the technology of film allows for a range of effects and interpretations that pass beyond an essentially literary attention to narrative or argument within film.

'A critique of the Hollywood movie is a critique of the imagination of the twentieth century in the West', writes Carter in a review of Robert Coover's *A Night at the Movies*, and she identifies 'the magnificent gesticulations of giant forms, the bewildering transformations, the orgiastic violence that hurts nobody because it is not real' as 'all the devices of dream, or film, or fiction'.[6] In a subsequent review she stresses the marketplace of Hollywood, but concludes: 'The hell of it was, they made wonderful movies, then, when nothing in Hollywood was real except hard work, mass production, the conveyor belt, the tyrants, and madmen running the studios.'[7] In *Wise Children*, Carter conducts a simultaneous deconstruction and celebration of Hollywood in her depiction of a film version of *A Midsummer Night's Dream*: the film is the culmination of all Carter's ideas which favour the illegitimacies of popular culture; and the cultural icon of Shakespeare, of course, is both reduced and reinstated. In this, her final novel, Carter sets forth a determinedly optimistic view of the unofficial and its inevitable collusion with capitalism. She was less forgiving in 1977, in *The Passion of New Eve*. In that novel, the toils of ideology and of gender construction are attributed to Hollywood, and the alternatives offered are an equally problematic mythological past and a utopian notion of a new future.

For Carter, then, film, like dream or fiction, contains the possibilities for images to move through narrative in endless transformations. The 'movie' is the space of this illusion – which is also real – and the term itself evokes the glamour of Hollywood. In turn, Hollywood comes to represent the twentieth-century admixture of commercialism, exploitation and magic, and cinema signifies not only the film but the place of communal pleasure.

We should place these notions within a larger concern, in Carter's work, with the nineteenth and twentieth-century arenas of communal pleasure. After the storytelling circle, there remain the circus, the fairground, the music hall, and the cinema, all bearing strong associations with late nineteenth-century culture. Frequently these are contrasted with the high culture of opera (*The Bloody Chamber*) and with literature, by means of pervasive allusion.

Despite her wry acknowledgement that entertainment must now always be paid for (Uncle Philip in *The Magic Toyshop* abruptly reminds his niece of the economics of toymaking and business), Carter retains a utopian streak. This is often represented by her through reflections on the 1960s, and centres on her most controversial explorations into the nature of (hetero)sexuality. While she states in *The Sadeian Woman* that sexuality is possibly the least natural and most constructed of human activities, she nevertheless proposes that it offers a significant possibility for freedoms. Similarly, pleasure can be snatched from the jaws of exploitation and control.

Laura Mulvey begins an essay on Carter's cinema by stressing the possibilities for transformation and metamorphosis in the moving picture. Carter's writing, she says, features transformation so often that 'her books seem to be pervaded by this magic cinematic attribute even when the cinema itself is not present on the page'.[8] She notes that Freud was working on *The Interpretation of Dreams* during the same decade that cinema was developed. Mulvey emphasises Freud's habit of interpretation, but equally significant is Freud's description of the ability of dream-images to transform themselves: this, along with Freud's rational faith in interpretation, is the basis of Carter's equation of dream, narrative, film and fiction.

Both films, when viewed critically, are characteristic of Carter's approach. *The Company of Wolves*, which was released in 1984 and distributed beyond the art-house circuit, was co-scripted by Carter and Neil Jordan, and based on Carter's written work. Its concentric narrative structure, lurid colours and general lack of realist devices announce it as a defamiliarising film, and it combines storytelling with an exploration of the stories' implicit meanings. Carter scripted the 1988 film adaptation of *The Magic Toyshop*; the film bears manifest indications of Carter's desire for defamiliarisation. Here, it is achieved through abrupt cutting, and through the stilted performances of the actors, who thereby underline the equation of the puppets with the humans. There is consequently little developed characterisation, and Tom Bell's performance as Uncle Philip provides a semi-demented and alienating focus for the evident commentary on power and ideology. In both films there is congruence between Carter's themes, her commentary on those themes, and the translation of images on the screen. For example, the published book of *The Bloody Chamber* (from which the film *The Company of Wolves* is drawn) proposes that the distinction that western culture makes between human beings and animals is a false one; indeed, the narratives imply that animals' instinctive behaviour is nobler than the self-interest and materialistic urges of humans, and that humans have lost their impulses. This enables the film to envision numerous transformations between wolves and humans. In the novel of *The Magic Toyshop* Carter constructs another site of pleasure, the toyshop, which depends on commercialism. Within that, the toymaker, Uncle Philip, constructs puppets to act out scenarios on his private stage with the human beings within his power: scenarios of power and exploitation. Carter's equation of humans' need for toys to play with and the wilful dehumanisation of oppressed people is uncomfortable. Once again the film provides a valuable visual dimension in its depiction of Uncle Philip's performances, which self-consciously also draw the viewer into the position of manipulator, player, and voyeur.

Both films also create vivid images which require the viewer to engage in interpretation. Discussing *The Company of Wolves*, John Collick makes a useful point when he observes:

> The film constructs an elaborate framework of these, and other symbols. The problem with this web of signification is that it actually signifies very little, other than a string of familiar metaphors. What is being offered appears to be a parody of the Freudian dream work in which the dream symbols, instead of being scrambled images or 'puzzles' that represent unconscious wishes, turn out to be familiar literary images.[9]

What Collick identifies here as deliberate parody in fact occurs frequently in Carter's work, where over-signification leads the reader or viewer into a self-conscious distancing from their acts of interpretation. The films, like Carter's writings, combine illusion, seduction, interpretation and reflexivity. Collick's description of the films' symbols as 'familiar literary images', however, betrays the provenance of the films in the printed word.

There are two points in *The Company of Wolves* where the projects of seduction and defamiliarisation collide. A young girl gatecrashes an aristocratic wedding feast and her denunciation precipitates the transformation of the diners into wolves; in the ending to the film, the dreaming girl awakens to the wolves which burst through the window. These instances, dealt with in quite different technical ways, pose questions about the relationship between literature and film, in terms of their possible reception, and the possibilities and constraints that film specifically offers.

When the decadent aristos are metamorphosed into wolves, the echoes of Spencer Tracy's transformation in the 1941 film adaptation of *Dr Jekyll and Mr Hyde*, overlaid with a subsequent materialist analysis, are clear. What is less straightforward is how far the layers of historical reference can coexist with a viewing position that will respond to illusion. How can we simultaneously enjoy the illusion and register the references, without also registering laughable special effects, so deliberately out-of-date that they fail to convince? Mulvey describes *The Company of Wolves* as

> moving through a young girl's contemporary appropriation of the story for her own interior psychic needs to the social setting of oral culture, and then to the exteriorisation of the irrational in the ancient belief in monsters. In the cinema, worlds can open up and shift from one to another without verbal explanation. The cinema creates links and cross-references that share the imprecision manifested by the workings of the mind or the tangled displacements of collective fantasy.[10]

We are dealing here with a description of the possibilities of cinema, and an understanding of Carter's project, that are not tested against the celluloid artifact. The artifact remains crucial because it remains for Carter a locus of pleasure, visual and communal. Carter's emphasis on the material and physical constraints on film-making only accentuate the power of cinema to overcome them through fantasy and illusion. In the decision to sacrifice the illusion of transformation at this point in the film, presumably in order to force the viewer to appraise what they are seeing, elements of bathos and banality cannot be controlled.

In the case of the ending of the film, which is shot in a more transparently contemporary way, the benefits of such illusory realism paradoxically collide with the practical constraints of film. Carter's own commentary is a starting-point:

> The reason why the girl is pounced on by the wolves at the end is pure contingency, since the original ending that Neil wanted turned out to be impossible, literally not possible. He said that it must end on an 'extraordinary image' – an image of repression being liberated by libido – in which the girl would wake up and do the most beautiful dive into the floorboards ... there didn't seem to be any point in writing things he didn't want to film. In the final analysis any film is the director's movie. But the impossible remains impossible.[11]

Although Carter distances herself from authorship of the film here (while stating and reiterating her support for the film during the interview), the admission of the impossible places a constraint on the film that does not exist in the fiction. (Animation would have delivered the desired illusion, but would of course have undercut the aim of illusion within realism; this heretical reflection, however, serves to remind me of the essentially cerebral project within the film.)

In a discussion of the same sequence, John Collick describes three types of dreamfilms: those which present the viewer with dream imagery and cast the viewer as an analyst who will interpret the hidden meaning; those which replicate the experience of dreaming, unsettling the viewer's expectations of realism and narrative coherence; and those which interrogate Freudian frameworks and ultimately throw the viewer's own position into question. He argues that *The Company of Wolves* presents an apparent example of the first category, but that the conclusion promotes it to the third:

> the image makes explicit what has been implicit throughout the movie: that writing, filming and watching dreams (using the traditional Freudian methods of analysis to 'control' the unconscious) involve the adoption of inadequate and false positions of scientific objectivity ... A false, liberal and comforting conclusion is offered, and then effaced by the shot of the wolf bursting through the glass (which parallels

the destruction of the audience's position of authority as the incomprehensible meaning of the film 'bursts' through the screen).[12]

Any quibble that Collick makes a great deal out of a sequence that Carter implies was a concession to practical impossibility is only superficial: he has responded to the intention to present an 'extraordinary image'. Collick makes it clear that he is interested in dream films that are derived from texts, thus complying with Carter's implicitly literary approach to film. What is absent here is a consideration of how far the image (by its moving nature, both transient and irrecoverable for the viewer) can unite pleasure and defamiliarisation within the viewer.

Discussing the film of *The Magic Toyshop*, Laura Mulvey comments on the use of special effects:

> As Finn rehearses Melanie for her role as Leda, the cinema transforms his room into a wave-swept beach, where he can tell her his feelings and his determination to rebel. In Melanie's dream, the rose-coloured wallpaper of her room is turned into a rose garden, and the sad antlers nailed to the wall turn Finn into a faun.[13]

Here, film is effecting those transformations that for Carter both reflect the experience of dream and offer promises of liberation. Yet Mulvey herself goes on to betray that the film only assumes a role towards the end:

> [it] becomes freer in its use of cinema, with camera pans and tracks. It is as though the cinema's power to dream participates in the characters' assertion of their own desires and, at the same time, materialises them magically on the screen.[14]

This equivocal role of film, whereby it is made use of, but its distinctive possibilities only emerge, indicates again the literary angle from which both *The Company of Wolves* and *The Magic Toyshop* were made.

Angela Carter's strengths and interests lay in the sphere of the written word, and not in the extensive features of film.

The film adaptations of her writing seem particularly apposite because of her insistent fondness for the cinema. However, they remain adaptations, a part of the way in which many literary texts have been adopted for filmic representation. Carter herself may not have been disconcerted by this observation: after all, Hollywood's adaptation of *A Midsummer Night's Dream* is a central event in *Wise Children*, and comes to signify the translation of pleasure from one medium to another in the course of history. Nevertheless, the magical transformation of images, reflecting the workings of dream and the survival of illusion, when made possible by the technical advancement of film, undercuts the essentially literal and literate analysis of such illusion. There are differences of audience, of context and of technical circumstance that Carter may have wished to break down, but that also participate, ironically, in her version of twentieth-century culture.

Notes

1. Patricia Duncker, 'Re-imagining the fairy tales: Angela Carter's bloody chambers', *Literature and History* 10, 1 (1984), pp. 3–14.
2. Angela Carter, *Come unto these Yellow Sands: Four Radio Plays* (Newcastle upon Tyne: Bloodaxe Books, 1985), p. 7.
3. Lorna Sage, *Angela Carter* (Plymouth: Northcote House Publishers, 1994), p. 58.
4. Her literary executor writes that anything was to be done '"to make money for my boys" – her husband Mark and son Alexander. No vulgarity was to be spared; any one of her fifteen books could be set to music or acted on ice'; Susannah Clapp, Introduction to Angela Carter, *American Ghosts and Old World Wonders* (London: Chatto and Windus, 1993), p. ix.
5. John Haffenden, *Novelists in Interview* (London: Methuen, 1985), p. 85.
6. Angela Carter, *Expletives Deleted: Selected Writings* (London: Chatto and Windus, 1992), pp. 131, 132.
7. Carter, *Expletives Deleted*, p. 137.
8. Laura Mulvey, 'Cinema magic and the old monsters: Angela Carter's cinema', in Lorna Sage (ed.) *Flesh and the*

Mirror: Essays on the Art of Angela Carter (London: Virago, 1994), p. 230.

9. John Collick, 'Wolves through the window: writing dreams/dreaming films/filming dreams', *Critical Survey* 3, 3 (1991), p. 286.
10. Mulvey, 'Cinema magic and the old monsters', pp. 239–40.
11. Haffenden, *Novelists in Interview*, pp. 84–5.
12. Collick, 'Wolves through the window', p. 286.
13. Mulvey, 'Cinema magic and the old monsters', p. 237.
14. Ibid., p. 237.

8

Capitalism Most Triumphant: Bill & Ted's Excellent History Lesson

I.Q. Hunter

Since the late 1980s an important new mini-genre has emerged in American films: the Dumb White Guy movie. Owing a little, perhaps, to Jerry Lewis and the Three Stooges and rather more to anarchic gross-out comedies like *Porky's* and *National Lampoon's Animal House*, films such as *Wayne's World*, *Forrest Gump*, *Dumb and Dumber*, *Airheads* and the TV show *Beavis and Butthead* glorify the Dumb White Guy as an all-American cultural hero. Apparently endorsing the cliché that, driven remorselessly downward by TV, American popular culture is becoming ever more stupid, hedonistic and anti-social, these movies celebrate the virtues of dumbness, slacking and trash culture, either as cynical escapes from responsibility or as styles of incoherent revenge against respectability, intellectualism and the horrors of political correctness.

At least that is one popular interpretation, vigorously expressed by pundits in the quality press. Another reading is possible, however. In my view, the films are neither lurid symptoms of anomie and cultural degeneration, nor, as squeamish liberals might insist, boorish manifestations of a white male backlash. Instead I see them as working through the cultural contradictions of what Francis Fukuyama notoriously called 'the end of history': the simultaneous triumphs of consumer capitalism and American popular culture. Fukuyama's 1989 essay 'The end of history?' and his subsequent book *The End of History and the Last Man*, argued, somewhat prematurely as it turned out, that with the collapse of communism, a certain kind of utopia had arrived, in the sense that no further ideological development was possible.[1]

111

Drawing on a curious amalgam of ideas, from Plato to Hegel to Kojève, and reworking the 'end of ideology' thesis of the 1950s, Fukuyama claimed that consumer capitalism would from now on be the model for human aspiration. There were several reasons for this: the most important for our purposes is that capitalism offered dreams that money can buy, its triumph representing what Fukuyama called 'the victory of the VCR' – the utopian appeal of consumerist plenty.[2]

Fukuyama's historicist triumphalism was, however, sharply modified by a sense of the banality, triviality and boredom to which consumerism seemed thereby to condemn the future. Fukuyama was concerned that consumers 'risk becoming secure and self-absorbed' with no interest in 'striving for higher goals in our pursuit of private comforts', with subsequent damage both to a sense of community and to the puritan ethic necessary for capitalism to flourish.[3] By a fine paradox, the capitalist utopia achieved in the US and dreamt about everywhere else was turning out to be unbearably banal, trashy, relativistic and – more predictable, perhaps – selfishly materialist. Not only, as Krishan Kumar remarks, might it undermine 'the sense of solidarity and community' but it 'might bore us to death, in its lack of challenge to our more active faculties'.[4] Still, as Kumar goes on to say, 'If only this were all! For if so, most of us might settle for a quiet private life of comfort and consumption, and let those who want to worry about the higher things of the mind.'[5]

This well-appointed utopia nurtures what Fukuyama calls, following Nietzsche, 'Last Men', who, lacking religious or philosophical props, crave nothing else than leisure, material pleasures and a nice, easy-going 'lifestyle'. Laid-back and unheroic, snugly cocooned from romantic yearnings and existential shocks, these Last Men represent 'the victory of "sloth", the nihilistic sense that there can be nothing worth seriously affirming or negating'.[6] As Dennis Cooper notes, commentators have 'variously identified [the Last Man] with the self-satisfied, convention-bound bourgeois salaud; the faceless product of what Mill called "rational socialist" society; the zombies of Orwell's and Huxley's allegories; or the dully contented hedonist, the "pig satisfied"'.[7] Cooper, perturbed that capitalism has itself become the main engine of individualistic pluralism, argues – I think disingenuously – that the morality of the Last Man is really

> manifested in the 'laid back' attitude of young people, including those students upon whose relativism, according to Allan Bloom, professors can today rely, [for whom] seeking one's pleasures and indulging one's preferences – now dignified as 'choice of lifestyle' or 'conception of the good life' – are elevated into 'human rights'.[8]

Dumb White Guys are the shock troops of the end of history, who benevolently further the spread of consumerism by trashing morality, high culture and taste. Culturally, they are in the avant-garde, their postmodern affectlessness promoting the pluralistic values of the Last Man. For if, as Fukuyama argued, the US is the economic model for any future society, its success appears necessarily to have come at the price of an amnesiac, hedonistic 'dumb' culture corrosive of hierarchies of taste and value. And it is this culture, the Dumb White culture of TV, Hollywood movies and rock music, which is becoming truly universal, having proved the most effective advertisement for the American utopia. As James Twitchell remarks, commenting on Fukuyama:

> What legitimizes [his] claim ['the eluctable spread of consumerist Western culture'] is that it is demonstrably true. For better or worse, American culture is already world culture. Certainly one of the unadvertised aspects of the New World Order is the dominance of world-wide conglomerated media and the effacement of culture-specific aesthetic categories like high art ... [It is] likely that the globalization of show business will result in the heroic materialism of an ever-increasing worldwide consumerist culture.[9]

This brings us back to the unfortunate contradiction between the high ideals of capitalism and marketplace realities. As it responds to the desires of the masses, consumerism is as amoral as it is democratic. Relativism, the upshot of all this, is very often identified with (and, for some reason, blamed on) the scary catch-all, 'postmodernism'. Relativism has inspired considerable anxiety among the likes of Allan Bloom, E.D. Hirsch and Gertrude Himmelfarb (echoed, though, by many on the Left), who are distressed by the uncoupling of consumer capitalism from traditional moral and cultural values. But such alarm at 'the vulgarisation of culture in postmodern America' (Twitchell's phrase) is merely the rage of Caliban seeing his own face – or rather the faces, to switch the cliché, of countless dumb white Frankenstein's monsters.[10] For – an obvious point – capitalism's triumph, splendid as it was, owed a great deal to the seductive vulgarity of consumerist popular culture, as well as to the irresistible appeal of becoming Last Men.

Bill & Ted's Excellent Adventure, directed in 1988 by Stephen Herek and one of the first of these 'dumb' films, is a witty account of these ambiguous implications of consumerist tri- umphalism. The setting is contemporary San Dimas, California where two 15 year olds, Bill S. Preston Esquire (Alex Winter) and Ted 'Theodore' Logan (Keanu Reeves), noted for their gormlessness and command of valley-speak idiolect, are threatened with failing a history exam. Rufus (George Carlin), from 700 years into the future, intervenes to prevent this by lending them his time-machine. Bill and Ted kidnap various historical figures, including Napoleon, Freud and Socrates, and put them in a rock-show-like presentation that enables them to pass the course. Bill and Ted are then free to form their rock band, Wyld Stallyns, and so bring about world peace and the survival of the planet. In the future, it seems, Bill and Ted are regarded as the 'great ones', whose music and ideas have become the basis for civilisation.

Despite generally poor or condescending critical reaction, *Bill & Ted's Excellent Adventure* did well enough at the box-office to ensure a sequel, *Bill & Ted's Bogus Journey* (1991), and franchised spin-offs such as a comic book and a cartoon TV series, *Bill & Ted's Excellent Adventures*, voiced by Reeves and Winter. The original film is now a cult item, not least because of its heroes' ritualised and creatively hyperbolic dialogue, a pastiche of surfer jargon and the valley girl-speak parodied in Frank Zappa's song 'Valley Girl'. In fact *Bill & Ted* is among an increasing number of ready-made cult movies, whose numerous references and in-jokes are specifically designed to encourage audience loyalty and lucrative repeat viewings.

Though a teen comedy, *Bill & Ted* is a droll satire of contemporary worries about the 'dumbing down' of popular culture and of American teen culture in particular. Bill and Ted are ignorant, steeped in mass culture, and lack all sense of historical tradition. Julius Caesar, according to Bill, was a 'solid-dressing dude'; Napoleon a 'short, dead dude'; Joan of Arc was probably Noah's wife. What little they do know consists of clichés, quotations from pop culture and fragments gleaned from unlikely sources: George Washington is the 'father of the country', 'the dollar bill guy ... born on President's day' and – a significant reference – the dude in Disneyland's Hall of Presidents. The film does well to focus on historical ignorance, which is often regarded as one of the defining qualities of our alleged postmodern malaise. From Bloomians fearing the loss of the sustaining traditions of Western civilisation, to Marxists like Fredric Jameson who gloomily diagnose the waning of historical sense, the charge is that, as Jim Collins puts it, 'evil postmodern culture has "reduced" the world to images that it then cannibalizes'.[11] In many ways *Bill & Ted* underwrites these contemporary fears, not least by representing youth culture as terminally inane, trivialising and self-absorbed. Yet the film's address to the audience is very far from dumb. Though each of the main characters is a Dumb White Guy, the implied addressees are surely not, if they are to make sense of the film at all. *Bill & Ted* requires not only skills of cine-literacy and ironic detachment (as indeed do all postmodern films) but, more important, an assured, cynical familiarity with current moral panics about consumerism, teenagers and pop culture. (After all, doesn't *everyone* know that American kids nowadays are stupid, badly educated and obsessed by rock music and TV?) The film's postmodern address short-circuits patronising accounts of popular culture, accounts it gleefully incorporates in the forms of parody and exaggeration.

Bill & Ted is a curiously hybridized teen-movie. It combines elements of campus comedy (*Back to School, Fast Times at Ridgemont High*) and science fiction (*Back to the Future I–III, Time Bandits*) and even the old Bob Hope/Bing Crosby road movies, but this gives little sense of the generic complexity afforded by its time-travel conceit. (Most Hollywood films are 'hyphenates' these days, opportunistic fusions of successful formulae. Thus *Under Siege* is *Die Hard*-on-a-boat, *Waterworld* is *Mad Max*-on-water, and so on. *Bill & Ted* might be pitched along the lines of *Back to the Future*-meets-*Revenge of the Nerds*.) Individual scenes parody specific genres – the western, medieval movies, futuristic science fiction – but more often genericity is signified by glancing allusions to famous movies instead of by sustained pastiche. (The medieval sequence, for example, turns on a rescue scene imitating the Errol Flynn *Adventures of Robin Hood*.) This quickfire allusionism is taken even further in the sequel, whose channel-surfing approach to genre is virtually freeform, taking in the horror film (possession scenes inspired by *The Exorcist*), religious imagery (visits to Heaven and Hell) and the art film (Death appears, complete with Swedish accent, as in Bergman's *The Seventh Seal*; this is an all-purpose reference to European movies – he also turns up in *Last Action Hero*). The allusions are complicated by being not only movie-specific but also cross-referenced with heavy metal imagery. In *Bogus Journey*, for instance, God is found at the top of the stairway from *A Matter of Life and Death*. But this unlikely filmic quotation (like Death, it introduces 'art-house' allusions possibly unfamiliar to the intended audience) is also an unforced comic homage to Led Zeppelin: in the US Powell and Pressburger's film was retitled *Stairway to Heaven*. Hell, too, while owing something to Dante, owes rather more to representations on heavy metal album covers (though Bill is disconcerted that it does not precisely concur with them: 'We've been totally lied to by our album covers, man').

Reflexivity is usual in postmodern films. What is telling here is that Bill and Ted, as connoisseurs of the impertinent allusion, are entirely at home regardless of the location and historical period. Popular culture has conveniently recycled history into a series of theme-park locations and pleasurable restagings of old movies. Bill and Ted are delighted when a bar fight breaks out in the Old West simply because the past is acting in character ('This is just like Frontierland!'). When they kidnap Napoleon in 1805, they look across at his armies and see stock footage of *War and Peace*: the past is literally textualised. Popular culture offers a lingua franca by which Bill and Ted can negotiate any situation. Their mass cultural capital is surprisingly useful, offering a bathetic parallel for the most outlandish occasion. Socrates is compared with Ozzy Osbourne because both were 'accused of corrupting youth'; Bill and Ted woo the 'medieval babes' and philosophise with Socrates by quoting rock lyrics ('All we are is dust in the wind,' Ted declares, to Socrates' delight); in *Bogus Journey*, they already have the measure of Death – 'Don't fear the reaper', Bill says, taking his cue from Blue Oyster Cult.

The key metaphor for this absurd promiscuity of reference is the time-machine lent by Rufus, a telephone booth (presumably a nod to Dr Who's Tardis), which enables them to call up and 'bag' history. Bill and Ted, unthinking cultural imperialists, literalise postmodern culture's instant access to and eclectic appropriation of the past. They encounter only what Eco called anticipated quotations of simulated histories, reprocessed in their culture's own image. The result is a sophisticated and multi-levelled game with perceptions of the past, reflecting, in Jim Collins's words, 'not just the increasing sophistication of the cinematic literacy of ... audiences (and the profoundly intertextual nature of that literacy), but also the entertainment value that the ironic manipulation of that stored information now provides'.[12]

By calling the film 'postmodern', I don't mean that Herek necessarily intended it that way. Intention is certainly undervalued in current writing about film, but the knowing playfulness of texts like *Bill & Ted* is not really evidence of traffic between high and low culture, of Godardian tricks percolating downwards by the efforts of frustrated art-movie *auteurs*. To a large extent, popular culture simply *is* postmodernism: wilfully ironic, tricksily referential and permanently within quotation marks. For example, given that effects of ironic distanciation are often regarded as signs of avant-garde intent, it is worth noting how frequently they turn up even in so-called exploitation films. *Scumbusters*, a little-known but representative exploitation movie from 1988, 'warns' audiences of impending scenes of nudity and violence with, respectively, a 'hooter horn' and a 'gore gong'. Similarly, Fred Olen Ray's *Bad Girls from Mars* indulges in numerous comic asides to the audience, quirky metanarrational devices that serve to underline the genre's ridiculous conventions. In one scene, while characters decry the gratuitous nudity in 'this kind of film', a woman performs a striptease in the foreground. It is a perfectly judged 'deconstructive' moment.

This kind of knowing self-reference throws up problems for critical analyses, especially for determinedly symptomatic ones. A good example is that postmodern films tend to confuse text and subtext, to the point where critical disinterment of hidden or symptomatic meanings seems rather a wasted effort. *Scumbusters* and *Bad Girls from Mars* are not unusual in anticipating critical moves. *Bill & Ted*, for instance, is very knowing (or sardonic) about its Oedipal subtexts (signalled by the inclusion of Freud as a key historical figure). The viewer, drawing on some cultural capital, can easily work up a pop psychoanalytical reading of the film; indeed, we are actively encouraged to. Bill's stepmother is Missy, his contemporary and the source of much Oedipal confusion – Ted had once taken her out; Bill's father makes love to her in his son's bedroom; Bill needs frequently to be reminded that 'She's your stepmom, dude!' At the same time the film offers a series of oppressive, castrating fathers: Bill's, who possesses Missy; Ted's, who wants to send his son to Oates Military Academy; and the medieval babes', who threatens to encase Bill and Ted in an 'iron maiden' (a *vagina dentata*) and afterwards behead them. The plot is quite clearly about Bill and Ted's resolution of the Oedipal complex (Ted, at a key moment, *steals his father's keys*) and their induction into patriarchy by various 'good' father figures (Rufus, Lincoln, the other 'forefathers'). At the end, Bill and Ted become forefathers themselves, of a world based narcissistically around their creative efforts. I labour this obvious point not to suggest that crude psychoanalytic readings of the film are out of bounds to critics with nothing better to do – unfortunately they never are – but that, on the contrary, their possibility is teasingly foregrounded. The film's dollar-book Freudism is made explicit at the presentation, when Freud explains that Ted's father takes out his insecurities on his son. Bill shies away from analysis, explaining, to Missy's bafflement, that he's just got a minor Oedipal problem. The point, of course, is that postmodern popular culture recycles symptomatic interpretations along with everything else. The critic, in seeming to read deeply into a postmodern text, more often finds that it will always keep one step ahead.

The roll-call of historical figures kidnapped by Bill and Ted is a parodic reduction of Western Civ. Each stands for a period in history, visually represented by a clutch of movie references. Socrates embodies the ancient world, in other words sword-and-sandal movies; Billy the Kid, 'the western movement in America in the nineteenth century', in other words cowboy films. Each of the figures is reduced to an appropriately cartoonish compulsion: far from offering a cynical alternative view of San Dimas (as the Savage in *Brave New World* provides of modern civilisation), these great figures discover in its shopping mall, bowling alley and waterpark, a 'most unprecedented' leisure outlet for their special talents. They throw themselves overenthusiastically into the pleasures of postmodern culture, often misreading its simplest rules and conventions. Set loose in a shopping mall, Joan of Arc directs her energies into aerobics. Genghis Khan wrecks a sports store, dressed up in American football gear and wielding a baseball bat. Socrates, Freud and Billy the Kid cruise the local talent. Beethoven, who finds a synthesiser in a music shop, is so carried away with his new toy that he must be restrained by the police. Rufus introduces the 'medieval babes' to the delights of the mall and credit cards; they are instantly transformed into stereotypical Californian girls, as if that were indeed their true, natural state. Napoleon's all-devouring will to power is sublimated into mere greed for junk food: he wins a Ziggy-Piggy badge, having consumed a monstrous 'Ziggy Pig' ice-cream. His megalomaniac drives are further expended at the bowling alley and Waterloo, the local waterpark (the park's name is itself a brilliant metaphor not only of the culture's 'affectless' and levelling appropriation of great historical events but of violence transformed into harmless communal play). When each of these figures performs at Bill and Ted's presentation and passes judgement on San Dimas, the past is transformed into spectacle. The presentation is staged as a rock concert, but comes across, appropriately enough, as a theme-park reconstruction of history. The visitors wholly approve of San Dimas, having been inadvertently postmodernized by the experience. Beethoven's favourite music now includes both Mozart's Requiem and

Bon Jovi's *Slippery When Wet*, making comically irrelevant all distinctions between high and low culture. 'Socrates loves San Dimas' because it lives by his philosophy that 'true wisdom is to know that you know nothing'. (Postmodern relativism thus finds itself an ancient pedigree.) Joan of Arc decides to institute an aerobics regime for her soldiers on her return to France. Genghis Khan – 'that very excellent barbarian' – favours Twinkies for their high energy rush. And Napoleon, bagged in 1805 before his own Waterloo, is moved to include waterslides in his future battle-plans. The presentation builds to an address by Lincoln, who confirms the general enthusiasm for the state of modern consumerism. Reworking the Gettysburg Address, he offers a minimalist postmodern ethic 'as true today as it was in my time': 'Be excellent to each other – and party on, dudes!'

And so the past underwrites consumerism. *Bill & Ted* is equal to *Blade Runner* as a visualisation of the postmodern condition, its highly intertextual treatment of genres and allusions meshing with a vivid and coherent image of leisure culture. While *Blade Runner* is the canonical dystopian vision of postmodernity, Bill and Ted is its comically utopian counterpart, drawing on and parodying both the complacent ethnocentric boosterism of the Reagan years and its fears of cultural disintegration. Postmodernism (itself an apocalyptic subgenre of science fiction) has fewer utopias than dystopias, visualised – or rather allegorised by critics – in texts like *Blade Runner*, *RoboCop* and *Virtual Light*, where the future has collapsed into incomprehensible chaos. It is often said that postmodernism lends itself to spatial metaphors, usually urban or architectural: specific places which either represent the lived experience of postmodernism at its most acute or can be seen as futuristic incubators of globalising trends. The usual suspects are shopping malls and Disneyland; others include Las Vegas, the Pompidou Centre, the Bonaventure Hotel, the desert and the virtual realities of cyberspace. These, contrasting with the dystopian city (postmodern utopias tend to be suburban, nostalgic recreations of the past, or sealed off from urban reality), are zones of pleasure and consumption. Although descriptions of them are often more sarcastic than celebratory – one thinks of Eco on the 'degenerate utopia' of Disneyland

– they do invoke concrete postmodern utopias, founded on a recognition of contingency, diversity and desire.[13] As George Steiner put it, they embody the '"California promise" that the USA has offered to the common man on this tired earth. American standards of dress, nourishment, locomotion, entertainment, housing are today the concrete utopias in revolution.'[14] San Dimas is just such a place. The historical visitors become tourists (Bill acts as a tour guide in the mall, 'where people in today's world hang out'). They consume, windowshop and encounter spaces, such as Waterloo, entirely given over to mindless frivolity. The visitors fit in quite easily (no one, in this individualistic, easy-going paradise, blinks an eye at their historical fashions) and, naturally, they are won over. Yet, in the film's ironic perspective, it is uncertain whether San Dimas 1988 represents an easy, more or less frictionless life (for it is not entirely without problems: Napoleon gets thrown out of a bowling arcade for lack of money; exams are still to be passed, Military Academies to be avoided) or mindless submission to an infantilised and homogenised brave new world. For all its utopianism, the film does throw in fragments of other, more critical perspectives. We catch a glimpse, for example, of another student's presentation (interestingly, she is black), which refers to continuing class differences: the masses were once told to eat cake, she says, now they must watch TV.

The film therefore has an optimistic but distinctly ironic vision of historical progress. San Dimas 1988 is, strictly speaking, pre-utopian but contains all the elements of future perfection: leisure, an easy-going sense of community, and an unproblematic devotion to rock music and waterslides. Utopia itself, however, will only ever come about if Bill and Ted spread San Dimas's laid-back values globally through the music of Wyld Stallyns, 'putting an end to war and poverty, aligning the planets ... and leading to communication with aliens'. This ridiculous premise is more subtle than it appears; for all its unabashed Americanism, the film doesn't simply recycle Reaganite propaganda. As Stjepan Mestrovic has noticed, it shares the nervously apocalyptic tone of much *fin de siècle* popular culture. Its theme, albeit 'camouflaged in "fun" images', is, after all, the survival of civilisation itself.[15] *Bill & Ted* presents a comic but thoroughly contingent view of history, at once a parody of 'great man' theories (the 'great ones' here are two amiable idiots) and, more to the point, a cynical postmodern satire of historical metanarratives. Civilisation is very fragile in this film. The utopian society does not emerge because of historical necessity; its triumph is merely accidental and must be endlessly ensured by intervention from the future. History is always at risk of being set off course, rewritten and started up again.[16] The film admirably illustrates the postmodern view of history, disabused of Just So stories about inevitability and progress. As Stephen Jay Gould explains in *Wonderful Life*, the central principle of all history is indeed contingency.[17] From human evolution to the smallest occurrence, events might easily have been otherwise; the only rule is the cliché that the unexpected will usually happen. Long a mainstay of fiction, this principle has found unexpectedly powerful expression in recent popular films. Time-travel films such as *Back to the Future* (discussed by Gould) and *The Terminator* movies turn on the enormous consequences of the most trivial events – one mistake and history is, as it were, history. There is no underlying pattern, only the unintended consequences of ambiguously intended acts. *Bill & Ted*, no less 'chaotically', offers an apocalyptic vision of historical progress as contingent upon two idiots passing an examination.

The film's satirical utopianism is most apparent in the flash-forward to San Dimas 2700. Naturally, given the film's compulsive refererentiality, San Dimas 2700 is parodic of familiar modernist science fiction future states – all white domes, advanced but unobtrusive technology, and cleanliness (Rufus makes a point of this at the start of the film) – as well as conforming to more contemporary desires, being peaceful, multicultural, well-supplied with waterslides and founded on a universal popular culture. (*Bogus Journey*, in the visit to Heaven, offers an equivalent utopia, underlining this interpretation. Heaven, initially resembling a Holiday Inn, seems remarkably like San Dimas in 2700 – St Peter is black, God is benevolent and cool.) Thanks to Bill and Ted's peace-inducing music, the future is entirely rock-orientated. Its three elders are rock musicians, among them Clarence Clemons (Bruce Springsteen's saxophonist; he is black) and Fee Waybill of

The Tubes. This is a take-off (relevant in the wake of Live Aid) of popular music's imperialistic pretensions to cultural salvation. Rock magically resolves the problem of community: henceforth everyone will like the same music. But, ironically, this undermines the subversive appeal of rock music. It is no longer individualistic in the future but soulless, no longer diverse but an homogenised MOR, piped into the atmosphere like Muzak. In fact, although Rufus describes the future as 'great', the audience, cued by nagging allusions to other such science fiction futures (as in *Logan's Run* and *The Time Machine*), is likely to interpret it cynically as benevolent fascism. Everyone performs the same actions (the universal greeting is to play an air guitar), and dresses identically. The film's Dumb White Male fantasy – from which the audience, unlike Bill and Ted, is assumed to keep an ironic distance – ends with the elimination of all signs of difference. *Bill & Ted*'s key joke is that the supposed salvational music is white heavy metal, the most despised and unhip (and monocultural) of genres. The future is indeed a long revenge of the nerds.

Notes

1. Francis Fukuyama, 'The end of history?', *The National Interest* 16, pp. 3–18; Francis Fukuyama, *The End of History and the Last Man* (Harmondsworth: Penguin, 1992).
2. Fukuyama, *The End of History*, p. 98.
3. Ibid., p. 328.
4. Krishan Kumar and Stephan Bann, *Utopias and the Millenium* (London: Reaktion, 1993), p. 79.
5. Ibid., p. 79.
6. Dennis E. Cooper, 'Doing it my way – or your way', *Times Literary Supplement*, 27 April–3 May 1990, p. 444.
7. Ibid., p. 444.
8. Ibid., p. 444.
9. James B. Twitchell, *Carnival Culture: The Trashing of Taste in America* (New York: Columbia University Press, 1992), pp. 272–3.
10. Ibid., p. 253. See also Allan Bloom, *The Closing of the American Mind: How Higher Education Has Failed Democracy and Impoverished the Souls of Today's Students* (New York:

Simon & Schuster, 1987); E.D. Hirsch, Jr., *Cultural Literacy: What Every American Needs to Know* (Boston: Houghton Mifflin, 1987); Neil Postman, *Amusing Ourselves to Death: Public Discourse in the Age of Show Business* (New York: Viking, 1985).

11. Jim Collins, *Architectures of Excess: Cultural Life in the Information Age* (New York: Routledge, 1995), p. 138.
12. Ibid., p. 139.
13. Umberto Eco, 'The city of robots', in Thomas Docherty (ed.), *Postmodernism: A Reader* (Brighton: Harvester Press, 1993), p. 202.
14. Kumar, *Utopias*, p. 73.
15. Stjepan G. Mestrovic, *The Coming Fin de Siècle: An Application of Durkheim's Sociology to Modernity and Post-modernism* (London: Routledge, 1991), p. 3.
16. See Karen B. Mann, 'Narrative entanglements: The Terminator', *Film Quarterly* 43, 2 (Winter 1989–90) pp. 17–27.
17. Stephen Jay Gould, *Wonderful Life: The Burgess Shale and the Nature of History* (London: Hutchinson Radius, 1989), pp. 283–91.

I want to thank Cerys Evans for sharing with me her insights into *Bill & Ted's Excellent Adventure*.

9

Robin Hood: Men in Tights: Fitting the Tradition Snugly

Stephen Knight

Written and produced by Mel Brooks in 1993, one more in his series of pantsdown pastiches, *Men in Tights* was hated by most reviewers. To the sensitive newspaper types, this travesty of outlaw nobility (whether fraternally British or just Warner Brothers) was so crass it made them cross. More surprisingly, the postmodernist pontificators of the marginal journals found it worse yet, the jokes being too broad for their narrow understanding of parodic transgression.

Perhaps there was also a famine of Robin Hood scholarship. Well it's time to tuck in; or to Friar Tuck in. Or to Rabbi Tuchman in, to refer to one of Brooks's characteristic moments of irreverence.[1] Actually, having just written a paper on the outlaw in Scotland called 'Rabbie Hood' I thought of calling this one 'Rabbi Hood', but let it pass.

My purpose here is to respond to the trashing that Brooks's film received by arguing that it is in fact in the mainstream of the Robin Hood tradition, or one of them. When you excavate the Robin Hood materials as I have recently done[2] you find that comedy, parody, transgression and farce are intimate and dynamic parts of the whole from the beginning to the present. This is a popular myth in many ways, including in its vulgar forms.

There are many strands running through the Robin Hood tradition which are *not* woven into *Men in Tights* – social conflict, gentrification, heritage, nationalism, romantic individualism and many another ism and schism. Three strands which are relevant to this film, and which recur through the whole five hundred and more years of the recorded myth, are: borrowing with change, local reference, and comic transgression. In *Men in Tights* the third of these, comic transgression,

125

is clearly the master code and pervades the other two, but there is nothing unusual in one theme dominating and directing the others – as in the stodgy liberalism of the Kevin Costner film (1991) and in the not unrelated tub-thumping nationalism of Scott's *Ivanhoe*: in both cases local reference dominates and directs the structure of borrowing with change. To give some instances of these three strands through the tradition, before looking at the film in these terms, it might be helpful to fix just what they can encompass and also to show how the first two, more obviously theme-oriented, can in earlier formations also be imbued with transgressive comedy.

A typical strand of borrowing with change can be traced by focusing, for once, on Marian, and this also often illustrates the burlesque features of the tradition. Marian, Robin Hood's partner, doesn't appear in the earliest ballads. Basically she emerges when the rough-handed social bandit of those texts is transmuted into a displaced gentleman; being a lord, he needs a lady, so he can leave his land to someone. The name Marion appears to come in part from the morris dance tradition, and may originally in this genre mean the 'Maurean' or the black one, but it is condensed with the Marion figure from medieval French romantic songs featuring Robin et Marion.

Yet the woman appears first in the Robin Hood legend in a decidedly unladylike form when, in a short play version of the conflict between Robin and the Friar,[3] it is the holy man who gets the girl. And what a girl:

> She is a trull of trust
> To serve a friar at his lust,
> A prycker, a prauncer, a tearer of sheetes,
> A wagger of ballockes when other men slepes.

It is not clear if the active party in the last two lines is this proto-Marion or the friar; one text turns 'A wagger of ballockes' into 'A wagger of buttockes', but is this a euphemism or simply a masculinisation of the action?

Perhaps it is just as well that Mel Brooks's research didn't go this far. His Marian is more closely related to the ladylike heroine brought forward in Anthony Munday's two plays, the *Downfall* and *Death* of Robin Hood, which appeared in

1598–99. Here she is really Lady Matilda Fitzwater (a solidly Norman name) who becomes Marian in her forest exile, just as the Earl of Huntingdon became Robin Hood. Even here though she experienced transgression: in the ballad where her story is told, she flees to the forest in disguise, meets a fierce outlaw who insists on fighting with this personable young gentleman until: 'The blood ran apace from Bold Robin's face / And Marian was wounded sore'.[4] They make friends of course, as Robin does with his other sparring partners. They are identified as a couple, but as lord and lady, not like Friar and girlfriend. Location conditions reference: this is a gentrified context, a pastoral world where passion does not run. That absence of overt emotive discourse was, as historians of the family and affect have argued, an acculturated form of local reference, and it changes as the locale ideologically alters.

A higher level of affect gathers around Robin and Marian in later versions, and these romanticising changes occur within a framework of borrowing both from the tradition and other sources. Diane Elam has argued in *Romancing the Postmodern*[5] that it is on the basis of the open structure of romance, to her inherently a non-realistic and so postmodern form, that myths of history, in all their factitious certainty can be constructed. This is a vertiginous argument, and this is not the place to try the handholds, but Elam has a clear place and time in mind. However, it is certainly intriguing to note that it is just as Scott and then Peacock locate the Robin Hood story in the domain of history and nationalism that romantic notions such as passion, jealousy and pro-active love enter the tradition. Ivanhoe has to choose between the socially (genetically?) important Saxon princess Rowena and the personally magnetic Jewess Rebecca. As the Robin Hood tradition develops along these emotively conflicted lines of identity and romance, it is the diabolically handsome sheriff who entraps, and threatens to entrance, Robin's female other. The triangle structure has played an especially strong role in American popular culture, from Reginald de Koven's musical version in the late nineteenth century on, and it is vigorously alive today, including, in comic mode, *Men in Tights*.

Brooks's version of Marian is basically a bedroom Barbie, and this has its own filmic sources as I will shortly suggest. But the modern period has also constructed, in radically changeful borrowing, the outlaw woman as an exact opposite to the triangular receptor, in the fiercely sleeves-rolled-up hero (for so she is) of BBC television's series *Maid Marian*, best described as feminist farce. Here Robin is a less than macho costume-designer and his one-time frail beloved, vividly and vigorously played by Kate Lonergan, has to train the burlesque guerrillas.

Ideological relocation works in those ways to renovate the tradition transgressively. It can have large forms, as above, or lower and more specific versions. An 1846 pantomime identified the sheriff as a spec builder who was, as was indeed then the case, covering Sherwood with little brick houses. Location can also be ideological: Martin Parker in 1632 placed the narrative firmly in the discourse of protestantism, making Robin's true heroism his resistance against a corrupt church; and it can be historical as with the anti-Nazi nuances of Michael Curtiz's 1938 film starring Errol Flynn.

As for burlesque transgression through the tradition, a couple of ripe instances should give the flavour and make the film seem quite traditional. After the success of Munday's Robin Hood plays, his company, the Admiral's Men, seem to have set out on a voyage of intoxicated discovery in the myth, and produced the highly intricate disguise comedy *Looke Aboute You* in 1600.[6] This seems to have been the product of all the company's writers working together, and drinking together too to judge by the zany plot, and especially by my favourite stage direction: '*Enter Robin Hood in the Lady Faukenbridge's gowne, night attire on his hed*'. Little John was too big for that sort of cross-dressing, but not for his own form of burlesque. In one of the eighteenth-century Robin Hood musicals John becomes entangled with the wife of the Pindar of Wakefield. But the Pindar comes home, so John hides under the bed disguised as Towzer the dog, and is then given scraps to eat by the cuckolded but pet-loving husband – it's a piece of classic comic business. The Pindar leaves, and John is back at it, but then hubbie of course returns again, and this time John is hidden in the cradle, to be well kissed by the affectionate father. The sequence ultimately comes from the ancient Wakefield Second Shepherd's Play's parody of the birth of Jesus and both are in the fine tradition of transgressive farce that, like borrowing with change and local reference, are all part of the traditional quality of *Men in Tights*.

Analysis of the film itself finds a substantial amount of borrowing with change, with references to most of the recent film versions of the tradition and also less elaborate but still significant elements of local reference, and pure transgressive burlesque. Let's look at the details.

Especially in its opening sequences, *Robin Hood: Men in Tights* refers frequently to recent films in the outlaw tradition. The precredit sequence has fire arrows flying in improbable numbers across the screen, so burlesquing the 'mourning the dead' sequence at the end of 'The Sorcerer' episode of Harlech TV's *Robin of Sherwood* (1984), crossed with the trick shots of arrows used in Morgan Creek's *Robin Hood: Prince of Thieves* (1991). In this opening sequence the villagers complain about the regularity with which film companies burn their village, and so a mocking finger is pointed at the first episode of *Robin of Sherwood*, a Vietnam-inspired piece of Norman brutality. When a black rapper and supporting group talk us into the story, Brooks refers to the droll opening to the BBC's *Maid Marian* (1988) given by Danny John Jules as Barrington, a Rastafarian Allan a Dale; and then the escape from an Arab prison with a powerful African-American called Asneeze makes legitimate fun of the opening of *Prince of Thieves* where Costner's Robin is supported by a real black Moslem.

Minor references abound: in the opening the hands-through-the-grill shot mocks a similar but melodramatically sombre sequence in *Robin of Sherwood*. More pervasively, Cary Elwes, in his diminutive fashion, has an accent, costume and habit of beard-stroking very like that borne more grandly by Errol Flynn in *The Adventures of Robin Hood*, directed by Michael Curtiz in 1938. Another link to that landmark production comes when the Normans, after Robin arrives in England, beat his new friend, Achoo, son of Asneeze, much as they attacked Much in Curtiz's version.

The sightless servant who sits in the lavatory of Robin's ancestral hall reading a braille *Playboy* is a grotesque version of the highly sentimentalised ancient blind retainer in Costner's film, while Roger Rees continues that connection with his replay of Alan Rickman's barnstorming villain as the Sheriff of

Rottingham. Geraldine McEwen's somewhat threatening witch from the 1991 film is here transmogrified for laughs by Tracy Ullman as the lust-crazed loathly lady Latrine – she has changed her name from Shithouse, no doubt a nod to the old Jewish gag about the man who changed his name from Levy to Cohen because it was more respectable.

The 1938 film is obviously referred to when Brooks's tiny Robin staggers into the hall carrying a pig, of all things (Flynn swaggered in bearing a stag). Then there is a ludicrous version of the fight on the bridge where Robin and John keep breaking their staffs and end up at a catscradle level of conflict. The famous fencing encounter between Flynn and Sheriff Rathbone is replayed by Elwes and Rees, introduced with the mode-transgressive announcement, 'prepare for the fight scene', and featuring a version of the original fighting shadows on the wall, which they turn to a farcical game of shadow play with finger-modelled rabbit and duck.

Flynn and friends are not the only celluloid nobility to be invoked. The appearance of the grandly Scottish Patrick Stewart (from the later versions of *Star Trek*) as King Richard naturally refers to Sean Connery's sudden unveiling as the returning king in Costner's version (which itself had links with Jason Connery's appearance as Robert, Earl of Huntington, in the second sequence of *Robin of Sherwood*, not to mention Sean's starring role as the outlaw in *Robin and Marion*, 1976, in a sort of filial filiation).

This all indicates that Brooks and his advisers had looked carefully at the recent Robin Hood movies and television – but not, it would seem, at the other 1991 film starring Patrick Bergin and Uma Thurman – though in its rather politicised account of the myth, it might have been judged less burlesquable. However a much less well known Robin Hood film is clearly a partial source for *Men in Tights*. In 1984 there appeared *The Zany Adventures of Robin Hood* (from the team who made *Love at First Bite*) starring George Segal in distinctly baggy green tights as an earnest, timid and often puzzled version of the outlaw hero. Most spectacularly it starred Morgan Fairchild as a distinctly randy Marian – 'I'll soon be Old Maid Marian' she cried with feeling – and the chastity belt equipped cutie of *Men in Tights*, played by Amy Yasbeck, is clearly a low voltage version of this formidable figure. In the same way, the final joke of hero and heroine being married by one Rabbi Tuchman – whom Brooks fully equipped with dreadlocks and circumcising gear – links with the 1984 film's wonderfully bizarre sequence in which, Marian being imprisoned as usual, Robin goes to a friend to borrow money for bribery. It is no one but Isaac of York, from Scott's *Ivanhoe*, who (in the excitable person of Kenneth Griffith acting his head off) regrets his poverty but recommends some friends: Robin enters the castle with a team of Israeli commandoes, who perform the rescue, mutter 'Shalom' and steal off into the dark. By comparison with this farrago of Jewish referentiality, Brooks's appearance as Tuchman, like the sweet frustrations of Yasbeck's Marian, is simply modest fun.

If the film is in these ways deeply indebted to aspects of the recent Robin Hood tradition, strongly exemplifying the mainstream function of borrowing with change, it also exhibits richly a form of localisation.

Several of the changes already described point in a Hollywood direction – the Jewish humour and the Morgan Fairchild material, for instance. Then there's the naming of Will Scarlett O'Hara, as well as the guying of other Robin Hood films as in the tiny imitation of Flynn, the shadow-play scene and the assertion that this Robin at least can (unlike Costner) speak with an English accent. Stronger reference to the frenetic Californian world is found in the representation of Prince John by Richard Lewis as a flamboyant but cowardly type, a producer to the life, in the Hollywood musical assemblage of the villagers and outlaws on several occasions, and the especially farcical scene where Robin sings to, or rather at, Marian with all the heavy-handedness of a Mario Lanza tonsil opera: her hair-do is desperately windblown by his powerful top notes.

Other stray localisations are the imitation of *Home Alone* when the small (and not uncostneresque) boy at the beginning is pursued by the Normans,[7] and the sideswipe at those who managed to join the National Guard rather than go on Crusade. But finally this sort of Hollywood localisation verges over into the third of the mainstream strands in this film, when at the archery contest Robin loses – or appears to, when his opponent splits Robin's arrow. Stung by this surprising event, Robin, and then all the other major players, pull out the script and discover he really wins. The hero brings together referentiality, localisation and transgression by firing from his bow a Patriot Arrow straight from the Gulf War which does the generically rectifying trick.

Self-conscious burlesque is the essence of comic transgressiveness and it runs right through the film. Robin's early entry to the Arab dungeon is supervised by a Brown Derby style Maitre de Dungeon called Felafel; Robin is tortured with a grotesquely elastic piece of tongue pulling; as they escape the camels bear racetrack numbers; Achoo has the latest pump shoes; Locksley Hall is being trundled off on home-moving rollers as a result of a repossession; there is a parking lock on a horse; Robin's speech to the people (very much a la Flynn) ends up promising to protect the forests and ensure affordable health care. Towards the end this level of transgressive comedy and even brainless fun becomes more and more a matter of good old theatrical reliables: they send a 'fax' strapped to the side of (in a broad American accent) a fox. Simpler yet, there is much laughter, a good few minutes of mugging, when the Sheriff's first name is revealed at his wished-for marriage to Marian, as 'Mervyn'; the hangman, after the foiled execution, receives back the arrow-cut hangman's noose with the execrable joke 'No noose is good noose.' The final moment of this grotesque level of childish fun is when Robin, feeling he has defeated his victim in a final fight scene obviously lifted from the Costner film, smartly slaps his sword under his arm and in so doing effortlessly spits the sheriff, creeping up behind with a typically treacherous dagger.

All ends in farce, reference, harmless and tasteless fun, and so the film resolves itself fully in one of the many mainstream modes of the Robin Hood tradition, a tradition so powerful that it encloses, as in any trickster-based genre, its own empowering element of trash and self-trashing.

The theatricality and referentiality, the ultimately banal, familiar, pre and postmodern vitality of the whole performance is well conveyed in the sequence when Robin sings to Marian. By accident they are behind a white sheet. On the other side gather the outlaws, quite a large audience in this greenwood picture show, like any body of easily entertained and excitable folk, ourselves to the life. However, they think they see a very different story in shadow, as Robin's sword, while he leans back for the high notes, erects itself from the level of his groin to an angle well above horizontal.

The moment is potent. Like Brooks's whole version of the Robin Hood tradition, it is only teasing, and yet there is a promise and an avowal in the shadow play of an exciting form of jouissance. In this cinematic foreplay we sense the thrust of a myth whose traditional vitality is in part embodied in its power to be trashed, that is referentially, relocationally, transgressively mocked. And so re-created.

Notes

1. Acknowledgements to Seymour Chatman for confirming that Robin Hood was a topic of one of Brooks's parody scripts for the Sid Caesar show; he also offered the tail-note that 'Tuch' in Yiddish means 'ass' or, in Britain, 'arse'.

2. See *Robin Hood: A Complete Study of the English Outlaw* (Oxford: Blackwell, 1994).

3. Printed at the end of the *Gest of Robin Hood* in William Copland's edition, *c.*1560; for a text see R.B. Dobson and Taylor, *Rymes of Robin Hood* (London: Heinemann, 1976), pp. 208–14.

4. See 'Robin Hood and Maid Marian', in F.J. Child, *The English and Scottish Popular Ballads*, reprint ed. (New York: Dover), vol. III, pp. 218–19.

5. Diane Elam, *Romancing the Postmodern* (London: Routledge, 1993); this discussion is conducted through the Introduction, pp. 1–19 and Ch. 2, 'Walter Scott and the progress of romance', pp. 51–79.

6. Anthony Munday, *Looke Aboute You* (London: Ferbrand, 1600; reprinted London: Malone Society, 1913).

7. An acknowledgement to David Knight, youthful researcher, for this reference.

10

Pulpmodernism: Tarantino's Affirmative Action

Peter and Will Brooker

No one can doubt that Tarantino and his works are a cult. Over two thousand disappointed British Film Institute members applied in advance for the 616 tickets (including overspill) available for his personal appearance and a showing of his favourite film *Rio Bravo* at the National Film Theatre at the end of January 1995. The box office reported up to four hundred calls a day up to the Saturday of his visit; hundreds queued for stand-bys, and touts were selling tickets at four times their original price.[1]

The Tarantino phenomenon is of course inspired, somewhat uniquely, by more than his own two directed films. Other films with which he is associated include *True Romance* (screenplay), *Natural Born Killers* (screenplay) and *Killing Zoe* (associate producer). The published screenplays and soundtracks of *Reservoir Dogs* and *Pulp Fiction* have reached unprecedented sales for this kind of publication. The *Pulp Fiction* screenplay topped the 1994 pre-Christmas lists in the UK and at the time of writing the soundtrack is at no. 4 in the albums chart. As Mark Kermode points out, thanks to the soundtrack album, many fans 'would have known whole speeches *before* they even saw the film'.[2] This kind of exponential popularity is only further spiced by the fact that Oliver Stone managed to temporarily block the publication of the screenplay of *Natural Born Killers* and that *Reservoir Dogs* was refused video certification for a year. *Pulp Fiction* renewed interest in *Reservoir Dogs* and in the other spin-offs, boosting Tarantino's reputation as writer, producer, sometime actor and populist man about cinema for our fractured, non-hierarchical times ('To be elitist about the film industry is a cancer', he has said).[3] His picture is

135

everywhere, a portrait of the artist as young fan, the defender of popular American cinema (who cites *Rio Bravo* and Sylvester Stallone rather than *High Noon* or Anthony Hopkins), the smart kid and one-time videoshop salesman who's made it, the slacker as *auteur*.

Much of this is reported with no more than the amused eye of the bystander used to the passing fame and spectacle expected of the postmodern. Tarantino's films themselves meanwhile have been both much praised and a cause of concern and controversy. James Wood, for example, has seen his 'brilliant' films as symptoms of our *fin de siècle* 'hectic postmodern', a period of 'trivial' and 'vacant' mass media and of a 'vaguely prurient' interest in increasing violence. Tarantino captures all this, says Wood, but is its trapped victim.[4]

Wood's comments are themselves symptomatic of a reaction to the postmodern and postmodernism whose 'final triumph', as represented by Tarantino, he says, 'is to empty the artwork of all content, thus voiding its capacity to do anything except helplessly *represent* our agonies (rather than to contain or comprehend)'.[5] In the same vein Fintan O'Toole would place Tarantino's films as 'Exhibit A in the museum of postmodern moral vacuity'. His brilliance, O'Toole thinks, shines less in his film-making than in his clever exploitation of the jaded appetites of the mass culture market. What he has 'done with violence' is pornographic since it appears on screen without even the rudimentary trappings of sequential plot or any pretence 'that his characters are more than stock borrowings from old movies'. He ' has disavowed all moral or social intent and gone straight for the sadism'.[6] Both critics speak out against postmodernism in the name of a beleaguered humanism and organicist aesthetic (Wood's notion in particular of art's function being to contain or comprehend our agonies echoes down a long tradition, most famously associated with Matthew Arnold). Not surprisingly this perspective requires its bad twin to sustain it. This these critics find in Tarantino and postmodernism, or what we have to say is a version of postmodernism (Wood invokes a second expression of the postmodern, though he recruits this to his own view, in comparing Tarantino to Don DeLillo). This same perspective is adopted by, amongst others, Mark Kermode, though for an apparently opposite purpose. Tarantino's work is referenced to other films, Kermode has said; it is film about film, 'the entertainment value of watching it is entirely cinematic'.[7] Kermode offers this as a defence of the film's merits. We might think that this view therefore refutes Wood and O'Toole's arguments but it does not, for it is fundamentally to see the film in the same way: as empty of social and moral content. In a fuller and more explicit reading which reveals how compatible these views in fact are, Amanda Lipman detects a series of warped repeats of several actors' earlier roles in what she terms 'this rag bag of film references'.[8] Thus Bruce Willis is seen to play a version of his *Die Hard* persona, Rosanna Arquette might be her character in *After Hours*, Harvey Keitel stages a domesticated reprise of his role 'in the *Nikita* remake *The Assassin*' and John Travolta is the street boy dancer Tony Manero of *Saturday Night Fever* a few years on and a few pounds heavier. If Tarantino has anything to say in all this, Lipman concludes, it is that 'there is no morality or justice in the patterns of life or death. Instead, the nihilist argument continues, there is trivia.'[9]

If we seek neither to celebrate nor judge the film in these terms but to understand it in relation to contemporary artistic and social trends, the issue that current discussion puts before us is that of 'violence', or the rights and wrongs of a supposed new 'aesthetic of violence' (stretching from Sarah Kane's *Blasted* to Eric Cantona's temper). Manhola Dargis pigeonholed *Pulp Fiction* six months before its release as another 'bone-shattering, skin-splitting, blood spurting' contribution to Tarantino's 'cinema of viscera ... written on the flesh of outlaw men and women.'[10] Violence is Tarantino's 'watchword', Amanda Lipman agrees, but what he says with it is that 'Life in the 90s ... is speedy and worthless'.[11] In Kermode's view, Tarantino's work is 'so postmodern' that the portrayal of violence 'doesn't mean anything'.[12]

What, in this light, can be said if we ask less about this art's forms (which are of concern to both Wood and Kermode) than its function: who is it for and what does it do? One reply is that Tarantino's fans are young males bereft of role models needing some guidance in how to get by in a violent world. Yet some significant social facts, as well as the aesthetic experience of the film, contradict or at least qualify this, contextualising its moments of violence in a different way. The *Guardian*, for example, reported that the London National Film Theatre audience was 'a cross section of age and gender'.[13] Beyond this metropolitan audience it's a fair guess (if only a guess) that the bulk of fans – who tend to miss events in the capital – are students, both male and female. (In courses taught by the authors two women and one man have volunteered class presentations on Tarantino.) Arguably, violence is an issue for these fans because it has been made one by the media. And if we say, rightly, that violence is nonetheless a real contemporary social issue we should note that, aside from the issues of class and social division it entails, this concern has brought a new critical attention to violence by women and to its cultural representation as well as to violent acts by men.[14]

If we are going to understand the relevance to this issue of Tarantino's work, it is unhelpful, not to say crass, to associate his films and postmodernism in an undifferentiated way with the amoral, superficial and self-referential portrayal of violence. We are concerned mainly here with *Pulp Fiction* but it is clear that the tone and nature of violence in this film is different from the previous *Reservoir Dogs* (both of which ought in turn to be distinguished from *Killing Zoe* and *Natural Born Killers*). The torture scene in *Reservoir Dogs* presents a different mode of violence to the careless shooting of Marvin, to cite the most obviously violent scene in the second film. It would be surprising if these scenes did not provoke a different reaction or serve a different possible 'social function', just as they function differently in the film's internal worlds. More to the point, however, what viewers respond to most immediately in *Pulp Fiction* are the dialogue and the monologues these often harbour, and above all scenes like the opening car ride, Vincent's dance at Jackrabbit Slim's 50s retro restaurant and the Wolf's clean-up campaign at Jimmie's house. These scenes are not about violence but about relationships and about style. In their dress, speech and manner, the characters display an attitude, in its fullest sense, of cool eccentricity. And again although the male characters are attractive and comic in this way to both male and female audiences, so too are Mia Wallace (Uma Thurman) and a minor character such as Jody (played by Rosanna Arquette).

We have to think beyond a traditional humanist aesthetic and more broadly than an 'aesthetic of violence' if we are to account for these features and for this kind of pleasure. We have, that is to say, to think with more discrimination and subtlety about the aesthetic forms and accents of postmodernism – so famously 'all about style' but not by that token always only about 'merely' style. *Pulp Fiction's* postmodernism does not produce a *hermetic* self-mirroring intertextualism nor administer *only* to male narcissism and a subordinated female gaze (which are less constraining than film theory sometimes likes to believe). Nor do we have to deny the film's self-knowingness (and the audience's pleasure in this and their own) to argue that it relates to moral issues and how to live rather than kill and die. We want to show that *Pulp Fiction* in particular, though importantly not in isolation, is more affirmative, less vacuous and nihilistic than critics like Wood and O'Toole believe and less self-enclosed than Kermode accepts; that in keeping with its own revaluative inflection of a postmodern aesthetic it offers a 'life-style' – otherwise so cheap a phrase of the end of century – which redeems and recasts the pulp of the postmodern in the very style and structure of its fictional narrative. To appreciate this we need to return firstly to the question of the film's cult status and secondly to consider its relation to the more familiar features of postmodernism.

Umberto Eco presents Michael Curtiz's *Casablanca* (1942) as an exemplary case of the cult film.[15] 'A cult movie is proof', he says, 'that, as literature comes from literature, cinema comes from the cinema' (p. 447). The cult film is characterised by an improvised, intertextual collage of stereotypical situations, or 'intertextual archetypes', already logged in the encyclopedia of cinema narrative, which when once again recycled, provoke an 'intense emotion' of recognition and the desire for repetition. But this repetition and the expression of affection for the film takes a particular form. 'A perfect movie', says Eco, 'remains in our memory as a whole' (p. 447). The cult movie, on the other hand, is imperfect, dislocated and 'unhinged ... It must live on, and because of, its glorious ricketiness' (p. 447). The fan will therefore recall discontinuous, selected images, or characters or snatches of dialogue, quoting 'characters and episodes as if they were aspects of the fan's private sectarian world, a world about which one can make up quizzes and play trivia games so that the adepts of the sect recognise through each other a shared expertise' (p. 446). This experience, Eco suggests, is culturally specific: the archetypes are 'particularly appealing to a given cultural area or a historical period' (p. 448). Rather than pursue the kind of social or cultural semiotics this would argue is appropriate to the film, however, Eco proceeds to offer a formalist and abbreviated thematic analysis, shot by shot, of the first twenty minutes of *Casablanca*. His entire discussion, moreover, is very clearly shadowed by a traditional aesthetic. Thus the cult is ramshackle and imperfect, it has no 'central idea or emotion' or 'coherent philosophy of composition' (p. 449). The cult movie, indeed works 'in defiance of any aesthetic theory'; it is primitive archetype, anonymous live textuality, 'outside the conscious control of its creators' (p. 447). 'Nature', he concludes, 'has spoken in place of men' (p. 454). Though he sees a sublimity in this self-perpetuating creation, it is clear that in the scale of aesthetic values Eco assumes the truly venerated terms are all on the other side of the cult film – and are much the same as those invoked by Wood and O'Toole. On this reckoning, the cult film can only be identified as the opposite of the authentic work of art understood as the conscious, coherent creation of the individual artist who 'tames' the raw matter of cultural cliché in the name of beauty and civilisation. In the postmodern film (Eco cites *Bananas*, *Raiders of the Lost Ark* and *ET*) the intertextuality which characterises the cult movie becomes predictably more self-conscious, for now both film-maker and viewer are 'instinctive semioticians' (p. 454): a development that Eco presents with a nostalgia for what perversely appears as the innocence of the original cult film, or cult of cult films which is *Casablanca*.

Certainly *Pulp Fiction* conforms to much in Eco's description. The film's status is confirmed and re-confirmed by the mere citation of a favourite cameo role or sequence, the imitation of a look or action (the dance, the costume of black suit, white shirt, straight tie carried over from *Reservoir Dogs*), by a quoted passage of dialogue and above all by the repetition, the echoing back to the film, of individual lines and phrases ('Royale with cheese' matching Bogart's 'Here's looking at you kid' or 'Play it again Sam'). Tarantino's admirers might not all be fans, of course, and not all fans will be cult fans. It is likely, however, that all viewers will be aware to some degree of the text or intertexts of its world of internal and ongoing reference. The rituals of repetition or mirroring, a saying back to the film and other fans, can be a way of expressing common or popular knowledge, or of displaying exceptionally detailed or new knowledge (culled, say, from a bootleg video or out-of-the-way interview). A fan's response will be affirming and self-affirming rather than questioning or analytical, more reflexive than reflective, but if this self-generating world (producing fan upon fan, cinema from cinema) can be trivial, pedantic and exclusive, it is not thereby finally confining nor isolating. Rather the reverse. Eco points to this double life of fandom in referring to the fan's 'private sectarian world' and 'shared expertise' above. There can be no solitary fan of the cult film. A cult enthusiasm is at once exclusive and shared, a socially expressed aesthetic built upon a fundamentally social emotion and experience.

The social form engendered by Tarantino's work, which helps counter the emphasis on the film's portrayal of violence as its main social content, is that of the group. According to Tarantino, before signing up for *Pulp Fiction*, Bruce Willis and his brothers would spend afternoons at home 'riffing on scenes from *Dogs*' – 'like old buddies', Mark Kermode adds, 'enjoying a communal singalong'.[16] Kermode talks, without further comment, of the suitability of the speeches on the *Pulp Fiction* soundtrack for 'drunken rendition'.[17] If this is indeed the social form fandom takes, we have some reason for thinking of its pleasures as predominantly and stereotypically 'male'. Even so, however adolescent and boorish we might find this front-room camaraderie, it is not of itself violent – any more than pub or football terrace culture are – nor amoral.

The cult world of the films also has a quite different potential, however, once again both paradoxically internalised and expanding. For the hard-core fan Tarantino as *auteur* has created an entire world of cross-references across not two but in the first instance at least four films. Thus Vince Vega is traceable as cousin, or brother, to Vic 'Mr Blonde' Vega in *Reservoir Dogs*, while Vic's parole officer, Scagnetti, is a central character in

Natural Born Killers. Mr White's reference to his old flame
Alabama leads us back to *True Romance*, while a scene cut from
the completed film reveals that the nurse who Nice Guy Eddie
was going to fetch for the mortally-wounded Orange is Bonnie,
Jimmie's wife from *Pulp Fiction*. The path of this cross-referencing
leads us to identify Mr Brown/Tarantino and Jimmie/Tarantino
as one and the same man. This is the boys-own stuff of the
Internet possibly, but it is only a film's width away from the
erudition of literary scholarship, from learned revelations on
the modernist classics or poststructuralist readings of a story
by Edgar Allan Poe. That this is an active, producerly reading
of the Tarantino texts would be hard to deny. It is in the nature
of intertextuality also that it extends itself, across film texts and
popular media in this case, to the music of the 1950s and
1960s on the film soundtracks, to the stories of *Black Mask*
magazine, the crime writer Charles Willeford who Tarantino
alludes to, to Ralph Meeker in *Kiss Me Deadly*, to Aldo Ray in
Jacques Tourneur's *Nightfall* (a role he and Willis agreed on as
a model for Butch in *Pulp Fiction*), to the films of Roger Corman
and Howard Hawkes, and to the selections from American
and European cinema he has introduced in a programme of
films at the National Film Theatre.

If this appears to threaten a relation of pied-piping movie
sage to cloned disciples, winding their way down the endless
by-ways of pulp (would a true fan pause to check out all the
Roger Corman films pictured on the posters in Jackrabbit
Slim's?), we might remember the nature of the dispute, as
Tarantino sees it, between himself and Oliver Stone. 'He wants
every single one of you to walk out thinking like he does. I
don't. I made *Pulp Fiction* to be entertaining. I always hope that
if one million people see my movie, they saw a million different
movies.'[18] This unfettered libertarianism goes hand in hand
with an expanding intertextuality and contrasts not only with
the closed world the term 'cult' at first suggests but with the
aesthetic ideal of containment and the comprehension of our
agonies assumed by Wood above. Both ideas of art's function
are didactic and both, contrary again to Wood's belief, have
a moral aspect.

The romantic humanist aesthetic that Wood, O'Toole and
Eco espouse has long been questioned within modernism and

contemporary theory alert to the key significance of the fragment, the internally contradictory, and the marginal. The deconstructive effect of an intertextual postmodernism is precisely to challenge distinctions between the original and authentic and true, the unified, high and centred on the one hand and the copy, the false, the low, the supplementary and marginal on the other. The problem with a traditional aesthetic lies not so much in the position itself, however, as the nostalgia and presumption with which it is held, leading these and other writers to simplify and so patronise or dismiss the challenge of postmodernism. To see this tendency in contemporary culture as no more than a nihilistic indulgence in clever-clever bricolage, a provocative but unfeeling cultivation of excess, is to take a commentator like Jean Baudrillard and declarations on the contemporary loss of the real and any ethical perpective at their word. There are more testing questions to ask about postmodernism's oppositional, critical and liberating aspect and its relation to a social and cultural past and future, and there are quite obvious distinctions also between kinds of postmodernism, or accents within the range of cultural expression the term encompasses. If some examples of postmodern art are at once scandalous and vacant, or 'merely' playful, others are innovative and deeply problematising. If some are symptomatic, others are exploratory. Like postmodern society, cultural postmodernism is various and contradictory: fatalistic, introverted, open, inventive, and enlivening. *Pulp Fiction* visits these contradictions and requires a fuller, dialectical reading if we are to appreciate its own double aspect.

Much that has been said above of the film's intertextuality might be glossed by reference to what now pass as the leading features of postmodernism: its pastiche, self-imitation, loss of affect, loss of historical sense, loss of social reference and hence critical or affirmative influence. This is the stuff of the charges brought against the film above. Unquestionably, *Pulp Fiction* echoes and alludes to other films (most conspicuously to Godard's *Bande A Part* for the dance scene in Jackrabbit Slim's). It has no specific location nor setting in time. If the reference to McDonald's and Burger King in Europe, Jody's body-piercing or Jules's cellular phone indicates a present time in the late 1980s or early 1990s, Vince's car is a '74 Chevy

Nova, the music belongs to the 1960s and 1970s, the TV references (to *Kung Fu*, *Happy Days*, and Mia's pilot *Fox Force Five* – both the latter already party to *le mode retro*) suggest the late 1970s, the dialogue on occasion ('daddy-o' and 'kooties') belongs to the 1950s or the 1950s recycled, and the movie-star look-alike waiters and waitresses of Jackrabbit Slim's itself to the no time/any time of echt postmodern period pastiche.

On this evidence we might indeed read the film as an amusing but pathological symptom of postmodern superficiality, unwitting proof of the randomised indifference of a thoroughly commercialised, magpie aesthetic, which blithely apes the supposed free flow of goods across the global markets of late capitalism. Yet at the same time *Pulp Fiction* displays some important contrary features. Those associated with its cult following and open, enlightening intertextuality we have already pointed to. Here we want to comment particularly on the film's episodic, circling narrative structure. This is once more a conspicuous, popularly noticed feature of the film (distinguishing it in composition and structure of feeling from *Reservoir Dogs* and other films associated with Tarantino, while suggesting a resemblance with, say, *Short Cuts* and a number of postmodern prose narratives) whose effects also have a significant bearing on the issue of violence.

The attitude towards narrative in postmodern theory is well-known, and conveniently summarised by Edward Said. Both Lyotard and Foucault, he says, have turned their attention away from the forces of radical opposition and insurgency to problem-solving games, local issues, and the 'microphysics of power' surrounding the individual:

> The self was therefore to be studied, cultivated, and, if necessary, refashioned and constituted. In both Lyotard and Foucault we find precisely the same trope employed to explain the disappointment in the politics of liberation: narrative which posits an enabling beginning point and a vindicating goal, is no longer adequate for plotting the human trajectory in society. There is nothing to look forward to: we are stuck within our circle.[19]

Circling mini-narratives do not have this necessary set of implications, however. In *Pulp Fiction*, two characters, first of all, Jules and Butch undergo or contrive a transformation in which they gain new purpose and a sense of 'long-term' direction. Jules believes he has been saved from death by divine intervention and sets to reinterpret the text of Ezekiel 25:17 (a fake quotation) which he customarily recites before a killing to new ends. If he has been the 'evil man' rather than the 'righteous man' of this text, striking down those 'who attempt to poison and destroy my brothers' in a parody of the vengeful agent of the Lord, he believes he can become the blessed man who 'shepherds the weak through the valley of darkness'. He forsakes a life of violent crime for the ancient grand narrative of 'charity and good will' ('I'm tryin', I'm tryin' real hard to be a shepherd' he says, and soon after in closing his criminal life does spare Pumpkin – 'Wanna know what I'm buyin', Ringo? Your life. I'm giving you that money so I don't hafta kill your ass'). For his part Butch backtracks on a narrative of pure self-preservation to save Marsellus from the humiliation of rape, and is able, with the 'blessing' of his enemy, to embark on the mythic narrative of a newly invented self, free of the 'violent' and crooked world of boxing.

Clearly these stories, and Butch's in particular, posit an ethical view of the world. Though it might require a trans-formative epiphany to realise its 'righteous' side, this ethical view is all the same consistent, on its 'bad' side, with the emphasis on partnership and group loyalty (a textual inspiration and reinforcement to some degree surely of fan loyalty) in both *Reservoir Dogs* and *Pulp Fiction*. This in turn is grounded in the disadvantaged circumstances of the male characters as working-class professional hoodlums (this shared class identity is strongly suggested in the opening scene of *Reservoir Dogs*, where Mr White argues the importance of tipping waitresses on a minimum wage). Lives of routine danger, the films tell us, require mutual support and a code of professional conduct if they are not to flare out of routine control. Jules insists in the first scene of *Pulp Fiction* that he and Vince 'get into character' before they make the hit. The hoods in *Reservoir Dogs* are bonded at the level of their abstract common identity. But the coded roles that marshall their actions are evidently narrow and brittle, tested by the undertow of quotidian dialogue they can barely squeeze out of the hitman's prescribed rhetoric, and broken by the crises the films' narratives unfold. Thus in *Reservoir Dogs* the blank, professional code deemed necessary to survival is transgressed by the pathological Mr Blonde and impersonated by Mr Orange. Real identities, bringing real friction and extreme violence, but also signs of a deeper comradeship, seep through their allotted anonymity and apparent sameness – as in the rapport that emerges between Mr White and Mr Orange. Both films explore the need for and fragility of fixed identities and relationships and do this ana-logically, through the use of stock generic characters such as 'the undercover cop', 'the hitman' and 'the boxer' and stereo-typical scenarios such as 'the heist gone wrong', 'the hit', 'the crooked fight'. The films' characters are contained by or revert to these roles (Mr White, who has revealed himself as 'Larry', reverts to the relationship of cop and criminal once Mr Orange's duplicity is exposed). Or, on occasion, as in the examples of Jules and Butch, characters can redefine these roles and redirect their lives. Jules is finally neither 'the hitman', nor 'the bum' Vince says he will become: 'I'll just be Jules Vincent', he says, 'no more, no less.' Tarantino does not merely repeat nor pastiche the conventions of pulp cinema, therefore; he reinvents and extends these conventions, exposing their abstract 'cartoon' like rudiments, adding unexpected dialogue, a concentrated intensity or relaxed attenuation of plot or hyperbole of character. He gives them new life, we might say, just as Jules and Butch and Marsellus and Mia are granted new life and, at another level, the dipping, repetitive careers of actors such as Willis and Travolta are also revived.

One remarkable instance of this inventive and affirmative mode is perhaps worth particular comment and is of interest once more in relation to the topic of violence. Escorted home from the dance at Jackrabbit Slim's, Mia Wallace overdoses while Vince is in the bathroom. He races her to his dealers and plunges a syringe into her chest, guided by a handbook for such emergencies. His efforts save her life. Like the accidental killing of the black youth in Vince's car, this is a key scene in terms of the film's treatment of violence. Vince and Jules's reaction in this second case is callous in the extreme, but their combined indifference and heated bickering over the state of their clothes and of the car provoke a common audience reaction of dismay and disbelief, at their actions and the playing of the scene itself, rather than outrage. The moment edges scandalously towards slapstick and if we half suspect that their cold 'professionalism' is being parodied in this incident we know for sure that this is the intent of the following scene in which the Wolf cleans up the mess with military impersonality ('A please would be nice', Vince says huffily, as if to emphasise that common decency is not part of the Wolf's professional repertoire). Mia's 'resurrection', on the other hand, provokes a reaction of near hysterical relief. What is indeed disturbing rather than conformist about these scenes and helps re-channel stock reactions to the stock 'violence' underlying them is their mixed tone. Just as cinematic conventions are opened out, set in the fluctuating rhythms and distracting debris and dialogue of real life, so the conventions of viewing response are angled away from expectations. Scenes from the gangster genre, that is to say, are touched with unexpected comedy. Dan Glaister sees the image of 'a hypodermic needle plunged into the chest of an actress' as further evidence of Tarantino's graphic portrayal of violence,[20] when in fact this is the most graphic illustration of the film's theme of re-invention and rebirth. In plain terms, Mia is brought back from the dead. What is more, Vincent's life-saving stab decisively changes the tone of the film, to the point of unsettling its assumed generic base.

Tarantino's postmodernism therefore moves off from and against a fixed base, but not so as to become aimlessly decentred. No more is the narrative of *Pulp Fiction* pointlessly circling or enclosing. One thinks of Vincent Vega's dance at Jackrabbit Slim's – a controlled improvisation upon the standard form of the twist. And indeed the creative flexibility or accent which shapes the film's aesthetic and informs its ethical view is most strikingly developed in relation to this character. The 'long narratives' of hope and renewal associated with Jules and Butch strike off at a tangent from the film's main narrative movement. Vincent's fictional story, however, is entirely encompassed by it. Yet its effect, returning us to a scene before his death, is not to encircle or eliminate this character but to foreground and literally enliven him.

By implication the violence of Vince's death, and other acts of violence, are perceived as matters of fiction and not 'real' at all. This is what critics of postmodernism complain of, of course, seeking some effective relation of moral commentary between the two. But to be aware of fictionality does not entail a substitution of the unreal for the real so much as a realisation that the real is always constructed, its chronological plot always narrativised, our judgements upon it a matter of tone and perspective. In manipulating chronology, moreover, fiction can return us to better moments, as it does here in returning us to Vincent Vega in beach shirt and Bermudas with his buddy Jules, edgy but on top of his game, rather than the Vincent Vega who lies dead in a toilet, his white shirt blood-spattered because he was caught alone and off-guard. This episode also gives us our last glimpse of Marsellus Wallace, once more the untouchable gangster king and ordering in the Wolf on his poolside phone as if his rape had never happened; which of course, at this time, it has not. Creative memory (in an era that has lost a sense of the past) defies the deadly fate of conventional linear progression. Our perspective is once again angled away from the scene and sight of violence.

Vince is the only one of the four main characters to die rather than begin a new life. It is important, however, to see that this death is in a sense reasoned rather than arbitrary. In three significant moments Vincent retires to the bathroom (to talk himself into controlling the immediate future, to read the pulp novel *Modesty Blaise*). If these scenes function self-reflexively as an interlude to consult the narrative of *this* pulp fiction and its subsequent course, they gives Vince no effective guidance, since he returns to an utterly changed world where death is threatened (Mia's, as above; Jules and the others' in the cafe held up by Pumpkin and Honey Bunny) and where in the third instance he meets his own, shot by Butch with his own gun. Through Vince in particular we see the contemporary world as utterly contingent, transformed, disastrously, in the instant you are not looking. There is as they say a 'moral' here. Like Jules and Butch, Vince is given brief moments of reflection, when his story is effectively held on freeze-frame. When his narrative returns to speed, however, the world is changed around him and he adapts to it, but not in the gesture of radical self-revision that Jules and Butch bring to their equivalent moments of decision. The world of radical contingency requires a ready adjustment to the present composition and re-composition of events, a dialectical responsiveness (most decisively at a critical, life-threatening moment) that makes it possible to switch from the path of evil to the path of righteousness, to convert the fixed and routine into the original.

Perhaps after all Vince's dancing is too controlled, a set-piece without sufficient improvisation. The tension between stereotypes, from *Black Mask* and B movies, and the eccentric, transgressive variations upon them with which Tarantino invests plot and character determines the tragic outcome of *Reservoir Dogs* where Mr White must revert to type. Vince too dies as he lives, a hitman, and it is his personal tragedy that he does not exploit the moment of betweenness when in sidling out of the diner having saved the cafe, and granted Pumpkin his life, he is that hitman still but out of uniform, his gun stuck down his Bermuda shorts. Here in this moment too, he is significantly with his partner still. In a contingent world where anything might happen, including being blown away, the loner, slow to change, is surprised and lost.

But where Vince fails personally, the film's narrative does not fail him. If a fixed mode or code of conduct is ill-fitted to this world, so too is a linear narrative with beginning point, middle and end. The film's circling mini-narratives enable it to question the finality of this fated end, returning us to Vince's most potentially self-transformative moment in the diner (in which comedy serves again to unsettle the fixed type). In *this* end, the mosaic narrative movement of the film works miraculously to bring the dead Vincent Vega back to life, revived by Tarantino; not as in a sentimental reprise, but as if to start again, to consider from a new angle what might have been. (In the scene of the Hit we see from Marvin's point of view in the bathroom; in the diner Honey Bunny's dialogue re-commences after the earlier freeze-frame, and is heard differently by Jules.)

We should think then finally of an 'aesthetic of contingency' rather than of an 'aesthetic of violence'. While this describes a postmodern condition where 'anything can happen', including acts of extreme violence, it is not to endorse the undifferentiated 'anything goes' of a Baudrillardian postmodernism, or an indifference – with which the film is charged – to matters of life and death.

Tarantino's world is evidently saturated with enthusiasms, discriminations and declared preferences. It is full and affirmative rather than empty and nihilistic. His films have not sought to master, shape and control the contingent (the Wolf is the film's example of this traditional and high modernist ambition; now become, appropriately enough, mythological). Instead, both films and scripts select broadly and fluently from amongst cinematic motifs and cultural styles to assemble newly woven, open narratives which bring life to the dead, the has-been, the jaded, the banal. The past is recycled, its 'waste' products put to new creative advantage. The fixed and conventional are opened to new artistic and human connections. In this way *Pulp Fiction*, in particular, offers a *modus vivendi*: a way of telling, of living a postmodern narrative deeply embedded in world of narratives, which in giving new life to the familiar and conventional can spin out of the hermetic enclosure both of a narrowly defined genre fiction and a traditional fiction seeking a correspondence to 'reality'. The intertextual bricolage which makes avant-garde technique a popular pleasure is joined by an underlying, if frustrated, ethic of companionship; a surviving will to do another some good. This is the best that the best of modernism ever aimed for and the best perhaps that the humanism which takes such high-minded offence at the films can aspire to.

Yet Tarantino takes on more than either of these modes. For in making it new in the days of the postmodern, an affirmative popular art must reach lower, digging its way, eyes open, through the cultural strata to sample the mass and mess of pulp, the brutality of low and criminal life, and root it back up to the spreading generic surface of popular cinema entertainment.

Notes

1. *Independent on Sunday*, 27 January 1995, p. 2; *Guardian*, 30 January 1995, p. 22.
2. 'Endnotes', *Sight and Sound*, February 1995, p. 62.

3. *Guardian*, 30 January 1995.
4. *Guardian*, 19 November 1994, p. 31.
5. Ibid.
6. 'Bloody minded', *Guardian*, 3 February 1995, p. 16.
7. *The Late Show*, BBC2, 24 January 1995.
8. *Sight and Sound*, November 1994, p. 51.
9. Ibid.
10. *Sight and Sound*, May 1994, p. 6.
11. *Sight and Sound*, November 1994.
12. *The Late Show*, 24 January 1995. The panellists in this discussion, including Ros Coward and Stephen Daldry, were asked by Fintan O'Toole to address the question of an 'aesthetic of violence'.
13. *Guardian*, 30 January 1995, p. 22.
14. See, for example, Helen Birch (ed.), *Moving Targets: Women, Murder and Representation* (London: Virago, 1993) which includes discussion of the cases of Myra Hindley, the 'dingo baby murder', and Tracey Wigginton, and the films *Black Widow*, *Thelma and Louise* and *Fatal Attraction*. We might add the cases of Beverley Allitt and Rosemary West and the recent film *Heavenly Creatures*.
15. 'Casablanca: cult movies and intertextual collage', in *Travels in Hyperreality*, reprinted in David Lodge (ed.), *Modern Criticism and Theory* (London: Longman, 1988), pp. 446–55. Further page references are given in the text.
16. *Sight and Sound*, February 1995, p. 62.
17. Ibid.
18. *Guardian*, 30 January 1995, p. 22.
19. Edward Said, *Culture and Imperialism* (London: Chatto and Windus, 1993), p. 29.
20. *Sight and Sound*, May 1994, p. 6.

Index

Index by Auriol Griffith-Jones